MYSTIC LONDON:

OR, PHASES OF OCCULT LIFE IN

THE METROPOLIS.

BY

REV. CHARLES MAURICE DAVIES, D.D.

AUTHOR OF "ORTHODOX" AND "UNORTHODOX
LONDON," ETC.

"There are more things in heaven and earth, Horatio,

Than are dreamt of in your philosophy."

Hamlet.

Originally published in 1875.

CONTENTS

INTRODUCTION.

It is perhaps scarcely necessary to say that I use the term Mystic, as applied to the larger portion of this volume, in its technical sense to signify my own initiation into some of the more occult phases of metropolitan existence. It is only to the Spiritualistic, or concluding portion of my work, that the word applies in its ordinary signification.

C. M. D.

CHAPTER I.

LONDON ARABS.

Of all the protean forms of misery that meet us in the bosom of that "stony-hearted stepmother, London," there is none that appeals so directly to our sympathies as the spectacle of a destitute child. In the case of the grown man or woman, sorrow and suffering are often traceable to the faults, or at best to the misfortunes of the sufferers themselves; but in the case of the child they are mostly, if not always, vicarious. The fault, or desertion, or death of the natural protectors, turns loose upon the desert of our streets those nomade hordes of Bedouins, male and female, whose presence is being made especially palpable just now, and whose reclamation is a perplexing, yet still a hopeful problem. In the case of the adult Arab, there is a life's work to undo, and the facing of that fact it is which makes some of our bravest workers drop their hands in despair. With these young Arabs, on the contrary, it is only the wrong bias of a few early years to correct, leaving carte blanche for any amount of hope in youth, maturity, and old age. Being desirous of forming, for my own edification, some notion of the amount of the evil existing, and the efforts made to counteract it, I planned a pilgrimage into this Arabia Infelix—this Petræa of the London flagstones; and purpose setting down here, in brief, a few of my experiences, for the information of stay-at-home travellers, and still more for the sake of pointing out to such as may be disposed to aid in the work of rescuing these little Arabs the proper channels for their beneficence. Selecting, then, the Seven Dials and Bethnal Green as the foci of my observation in West and East London respectively, I set out for the former one bleak March night, and by way of breaking ground, applied to the first police-constable I met on that undesirable beat for information as to my course. After one or two failures, I met with an officer literally "active and intelligent," who convoyed me through several of that network of streets surrounding the Seven Dials, leaving me to my own devices when he had given me the general bearings of the district it would be desirable to visit.

My first raid was on the Ragged School and Soup Kitchen in Charles Street, Drury Lane, an evil-looking and unfragrant locality; but the institution in question stands so close to the main thoroughfare that the most fastidious may visit it with ease. Here I found some twenty Arabs assembled for evening school. They were of all ages, from seven to fifteen, and their clothing was in an inverse ratio to their dirt—very little of the former, and a great deal of the latter. They moved about with their bare feet in the most feline way, like the veritable Bedouin himself. There they were, however, over greasy slates and grimy copy-books, in process of civilization. The master informed me that his special difficulties arose from the attractions of the theatre and the occasional intrusion of wild Arabs, who came only to kick up a row. At eight o'clock the boys were to be regaled with a brass band practice, so, finding from one of the assembled Arabs that there was a second institution of the kind in King Street, Long Acre, I passed on thereto. Here I was fortunate enough to find the presiding genius in the person of a young man engaged in business during the day, and devoting his extra time to the work of civilizing the barbarians of this district. Sunday and week-day services, night schools, day schools, Bands of Hope, temperance meetings, and last, not least, the soup kitchen, were the means at work here. Not a single officer is paid. The task is undertaken "all for love, and nothing for reward," and it has thriven so far that my presence interrupted a debate between the gentleman above-mentioned and one of his coadjutors on the subject of taking larger premises. The expenses were met by the weekly offerings, and I was surprised to see by a notice posted in the room where the Sunday services are held, that the sum total for the past week was only 19s. 4d. So there must be considerable sacrifice of something more than time to carry on this admirable work. Under the guidance of the second gentleman mentioned above, I proceeded to the St. George's and St. Giles's Refuge in Great Queen Street, where boys are admitted on their own application, the only qualification being destitution. Here they are housed, clothed, boarded, and taught such trades as they may be fitted for, and not lost sight of until they are provided with situations. A hundred and fifty-four was the number of this truly miraculous draught from the great ocean of London streets, whom I saw all comfortably bedded in one spacious dormitory. Downstairs were the implements and products of the day's work, dozens of miniature cobblers' appliances, machines for sawing and chopping firewood, &c., whilst, in a spacious refectory on the first floor, I was informed, the resident Arabs extended on a Friday their accustomed hospitality to other tribes, to such an extent, that the party numbered about 500. Besides the 154 who were fortunate enough to secure beds, there were twenty new arrivals, who had to be quartered on the floor for the night; but at all events they had a roof above them, and were out of the cruel east wind that made Arabia Petræa that evening an undesirable resting-place indeed. Lights were put out, and doors closed, when I left, as this is not a night refuge; but notices are posted, I am informed, in the various casual wards and temporary refuges, directing boys to this. There is a kindred institution for girls in

Broad Street. Such was my first experience of the western portion of Arabia Infelix.

The following Sunday I visited the Mission Hall belonging to Bloomsbury Chapel, in Moor Street, Soho, under the management of Mr. M'Cree, and the nature of the work is much the same as that pursued at King Street. The eleven o'clock service was on this particular day devoted to children, who were assembled in large numbers, singing their cheerful hymns, and listening to a brief, practical, and taking address. These children, however, were of a class above the Arab type, being generally well dressed. I passed on thence to what was then Mr. Brock's chapel, where I found my veritable Arabs, whom I had seen in bed the previous evening, arrayed in a decent suit of "sober livery," and perched up in a high gallery to gather what they could comprehend of Mr. Brock's discourse—not very much, I should guess; for that gentleman's long Latinized words would certainly fire a long way over their heads, high as was their position. I found the whole contingent of children provided for at the refuge was 400, including those on board the training ship Chichester and the farm at Bisley, near Woking, Surrey. This is certainly the most complete way of dealing with the Arabs par excellence, as it contemplates the case of utter destitution and homelessness. It need scarcely be said, however, that such a work must enlarge its boundaries very much, in order to make any appreciable impression on the vast amount of such destitution. Here, nevertheless, is the germ, and it is already fructifying most successfully. The other institutions, dealing with larger masses of children, aim at civilizing them at home, and so making each home a centre of influence.

Passing back again to the King Street Mission Hall, I found assembled there the band of fifty missionaries, male and female, who visit every Sunday afternoon the kitchens of the various lodging-houses around the Seven Dials. Six hundred kitchens are thus visited every week. After roll-call, and a brief address, we sallied forth, I myself accompanying Mr. Hatton—the young man to whom the establishment of the Mission is due—and another of his missionaries. I had heard much of the St. Giles's Kitchens, but failed to realize any idea of the human beings swarming by dozens and scores in those subterranean regions. Had it not been for the fact that nearly every man was smoking, the atmosphere would have been unbearable. In most of the kitchens they were beguiling the ennui of Sunday afternoon with cards; but the game was invariably suspended on our arrival. Some few removed their hats—for all wore them—and a smaller number still joined in a verse or two of a hymn, and listened to a portion of Scripture and a few words of exhortation. One or two seemed interested, others smiled sardonically; the majority kept a dogged silence. Some read their papers and refused the tracts and publications offered them. These, I found, were the Catholics. I was assured there were many men there who themselves, or whose friends, had occupied high positions. I was much struck with the language of one crop-headed young fellow of seventeen or eighteen, who, seeing me grope my way, said, "They're not very lavish with the gas here, sir, are they?" It may appear that this "experience" has little bearing on the Arab boys; but really some of the inmates of these kitchens were but boys. Those we visited were in the purlieus of the old "Rookery," and for these dens, I was informed, the men paid fourpence a night! Surely a little money invested in decent dwellings for such people would be well and even remuneratively spent. The kitchens, my informant—who has spent many years among them—added, are generally the turning point between honesty and crime. The discharged soldier or mechanic out of work is there herded with the professional thief or burglar, and learns his trade and gets to like his life.

The succeeding evening I devoted first of all to the Girls' Refuge, 19, Broad Street, St. Giles's. Here were sixty-two girls of the same class as the boys in Great Queen Street, who remain until provided with places as domestic servants. A similar number were in the Home at Ealing. The Institution itself is the picture of neatness and order. I dropped in quite unexpectedly; and any visitor who may be induced to follow my example, will not fail to be struck with the happy, "homely" look of everything, the clean, cheerful appearance of the female Arabs, and the courtesy and kindness of the matron. These girls are considered to belong to St. Giles's parish, as the boys to Bloomsbury Chapel. So far the good work has been done by the Dissenters and Evangelical party in the Established Church. The sphere of the High Church—as I was reminded by the Superintendent Sergeant—is the Newport Market Refuge and Industrial Schools. Here, besides the male and female refuges, is a Home for Destitute Boys, who are housed and taught on the same plan as at St. Giles's. Their domicile is even more cosy than the other, and might almost tempt a boy to act the part of an "amateur Arab." I can only say the game that was going on, previously to bed, in the large covered play room, with bare feet and in shirt sleeves, was enough to provoke the envy of any member of a Dr. Blimber's "Establishment." The Institution had just had a windfall in the shape of one of those agreeable 1000l. cheques that have been flying about lately, or their resources would have been cramped; but the managers are wisely sensible that such windfalls do not come every day, and so forbear enlarging their borders as they could wish.

Strangely enough, the Roman Catholics, who usually outdo us in their work among the poor, seemed a little behindhand in this special department of settling the Arabs. They have schools largely attended in Tudor Place, Tottenham Court Road, White Lion Street, Seven Dials, &c., but, as far as I could ascertain, nothing local in the shape of a Refuge. To propagate the faith may be all very well, and will be only the natural impulse of a man sincere in his own belief; but we must not forget that these Arabs have bodies as well as souls, and that those bodies have been so shamefully debased and neglected as to drag the higher energies down with them; and it is a great question whether it is not absolutely necessary to begin on the very lowest plane first, and so to work towards the higher. Through the body and the mind we may at last reach the highest sphere of all.

Without for one moment wishing to write down the "religious" element, it is, I repeat, a grave question whether the premature introduction of that element does not sometimes act as a deterrent, and frustrate the good that might otherwise be done. Still there is the great fact, good is being done. It would be idle to carp at any means when the end is so thoroughly good. I could not help, as I passed from squalid kitchen to kitchen that Sunday afternoon, feeling Lear's words ring through my mind:—

O, I have ta'en

Too little care of this. Take physic, pomp,

Expose thyself to feel what wretches feel,

That thou mayst shake the superflux to them,

And show the heavens more just.

And now "Eastward ho!" for "experiences" in Bethnal Green.

CHAPTER II.

EAST LONDON ARABS.

Notwithstanding my previous experiences among the Western tribes of Bedouins whose locale is the Desert of the Seven Dials, I must confess to considerable strangeness when first I penetrated the wilderness of Bethnal Green. Not only was it utterly terra incognita to me, but, with their manifold features in common, the want and squalor of the East have traits distinct from those of the West. I had but the name of one Bethnal Green parish and of one lady— Miss Macpherson—and with these slender data I proceeded to my work, the results of which I again chronicle seriatim.

Passing from the Moorgate Street Station I made for the Eastern Counties Terminus at Shoreditch, and soon after passing it struck off to my right in the Bethnal Green Road. Here, amid a pervading atmosphere of bird-fanciers and vendors of live pets in general, I found a Mission Hall, belonging to I know not what denomination, and, aided by a vigorous policeman, kicked—in the absence of knocker or bell—at all the doors, without result. Nobody was there. I went on to the Bethnal Green parish which had been named to me as the resort of nomade tribes, and found the incumbent absent in the country for a week or so, and the Scripture-reader afraid, in his absence, to give much information. He ventured, however, to show me the industrial school, where some forty children were employed in making match-boxes for Messrs. Bryant and May. However, as I was told that the incumbent in question objected very decidedly to refuges and ragged schools, and thought it much better for the poor to strain a point and send their little ones to school, I felt that was hardly the regimen to suit my Arabian friends, who were evidently teeming in that locality. I was even returning home with the view of getting further geographical particulars of this Eastern Arabia Petræa, when, as a last resource, I was directed to a refuge in Commercial Street. I rang here, and found myself in the presence of the veritable Miss Macpherson herself, with whom I passed two pleasant and instructive hours.

At starting, Miss Macpherson rather objected to being made the subject of an article—first of all, for the very comprehensible reason that such publicity would draw down upon her a host of visitors; and when I suggested that visitors probably meant funds, she added a second, and not quite so comprehensible an objection—that these funds themselves might alloy the element of Faith in which the work had been so far carried on. She had thoroughly imbibed the spirit of Müller, whose Home at Bristol was professedly the outcome of Faith and Prayer alone. However, on my promise to publish only such particulars—name, locality, &c.—as she might approve, this lady gave me the details of her truly wonderful work. The building in which I found her had been erected to serve as large warehouses, and here 110 of the most veritable Arabs were housed, fed, taught, and converted into Christians, when so convertible. Should they prove impressionable, Miss Macpherson then contemplates their emigration to Canada. Many had already been sent out; and her idea was to extend her operations in this respect: not, be it observed, to cast hundreds of the scum of the East End of London upon Canada—a proceeding to which the Canadians would very naturally object—but to form a Home on that side to be fed from the Homes on this, and so to remove from the old scenes of vice and temptation those who had been previously trained in the refuges here. She has it in contemplation to take a large hotel in Canada, and convert it into an institution of this kind; and I fancy it was the possibility that publicity might aid this larger scheme which eventually induced the good lady to let the world so far know what she is doing. At all events, she gave me carte blanche to publish the results of my observations.

In selecting and dealing with the inmates of her refuges, Miss Macpherson avails herself of the science of phrenology, in which she believes, and she advances good reason for so doing. I presume my phrenological development must have been satisfactory, since she not only laid aside her objection to publicity, but even allowed me to carry off with me her MS. "casebooks," from which I cull one or two of several hundred:—

"1. T. S., aged ten (March 5, 1869).—An orphan. Mother died in St. George's Workhouse. Father killed by coming in contact with a diseased sheep, being a slaughterman. A seller of boxes in the street. Slept last in a bed before Christmas. Slept in hay-carts, under a tarpaulin. Says the prayers his mother 'teached him.'"

"2. J. H., aged twelve (March 5).—No home but the streets. Father killed by an engine-strap, being an engineer. Mother died of a broken heart. Went into —— Workhouse; but ran away through ill-treatment last December. Slept in ruins near Eastern Counties Railway. Can't remember when he last lay in a bed."

"3. A. R., aged eleven (March 5).—Mother and father left him and two brothers in an empty room in H—— Street. Policeman, hearing them crying, broke open the door and took them to the workhouse. His two brothers died. Was moved from workhouse by grandmother, and she, unable to support him, turned him out on the streets. Slept in railway ruins; lived by begging. July 24, sent to Home No. 1 as a reward for good conduct."

Besides thus rescuing hundreds of homeless ones, Miss Macpherson has in many instances been the means of restoring runaway children of respectable parents. Here is an instance:—

"Feb. 25th.—S. W. T., aged fourteen, brought into Refuge by one of the night teachers, who noticed him in a lodging-house respectably dressed. Had walked up to London from N——, in company with two sailors (disreputable men, whom the lodging-house keeper declined to take in). Had been reading sensational books. Wrote to address at N——. Father telegraphed to keep him. Uncle came for him with fresh clothes and took him home. He had begun to pawn his clothes for his night's lodging. His father had been for a fortnight in communication with the police."

The constables in the neighbourhood all know Miss Macpherson's Refuge, and her readiness to take boys in at any time; so that many little vagrants are brought thither by them and reclaimed, instead of being locked up and sent to prison, to go from bad to worse. Besides this receptacle for boys, Miss Macpherson has also a Home at Hackney, where girls of the same class are housed. The plan she adopts is to get a friend to be responsible for one child. The cost she reckons at 6l. 10s. per annum for those under ten years, and 10l. for those above.

But this excellent lady's good works are by no means catalogued yet. Besides the children being fed and taught in these Homes, the parents and children are constantly gathered for sewing classes, tea meetings, &c. at the Refuge. Above 400 children are thus influenced; and Miss Macpherson, with her coadjutors, systematically visits the wretched dens and lodging-houses into which no well-dressed person, unless favourably known like her for her work among the children, would dare to set foot. I was also present when a hearty meal of excellent soup and a large lump of bread were given to between three and four hundred men, chiefly dock labourers out of employ. It was a touching sight to notice the stolid apathy depicted on most of the countenances, which looked unpleasantly like despair. One of the men assured me that for every package that had to be unladen from the docks there were ten pair of hands ready to do the work, where only one could be employed. Many of the men, he assured me, went for two, sometimes three, days without food; and with the large majority of those assembled the meal they were then taking would represent the whole of their subsistence for the twenty-four-hours. After supper a hymn was sung, and a few words spoken to them by Miss Macpherson on the allegory of the Birds and Flowers in the Sermon on the Mount; and so they sallied forth into the darkness of Arabia Petræa. I mounted to the little boys' bedroom, where the tiniest Arabs of all were enjoying the luxury of a game, with bare feet, before retiring. Miss Macpherson dragged a mattress off one of the beds and threw it down in the centre for them to tumble head-over-tail; and, as she truly said, it was difficult to recognise in those merry shouts and happy faces any remains of the veriest reprobates of the London streets.

Let us hear Miss Macpherson herself speak. In a published pamphlet, "Our Perishing Little Ones," she says: "As to the present state of the mission, we simply say 'Come and see.' It is impossible by words to give an idea of the mass of 120,000 precious souls who live on this one square mile.... My longing is to send forth, so soon as the ice breaks, 500 of our poor street boys, waifs and strays that have been gathered in, to the warm-hearted Canadian farmers. In the meantime, who will help us to make outfits, and collect 5l. for each little Arab, that there be no hindrance to the complement being made up when the spring time is come?... Ladies who are householders can aid us much in endeavours to educate these homeless wanderers to habits of industry by sending orders for their firewood—4s. per hundred bundles, sent free eight miles from the City." And, again, in Miss Macpherson's book called "The Little Matchmakers," she says: "In this work of faith and labour of love among the very lowest in our beloved country, let us press on, looking for great things. Preventing sin and crime is a much greater work than curing it. There are still many things on my heart requiring more pennies. As they come, we will go forward."

Miss Macpherson's motto is, "The Word first in all things; afterwards bread for this body." There are some of us who would be inclined to reverse this process—to feed the body and educate the mind—not altogether neglecting spiritual culture, even at the earliest stage, but leaving anything like definite religious schooling until the poor mind and body were, so to say, acclimatized. It is, of course, much easier to sit still and theorize and criticise than to do what these excellent people have done and are doing to diminish this gigantic evil. "By their fruits ye shall know them" is a criterion based on authority that we are none of us inclined to dispute. Miss Macpherson boasts—and a very proper subject for boasting it is—that she belongs to no ism. It is significant, however, that the Refuge bears, or bore, the name of the "Revival" Refuge, and the paper which contained the earliest accounts of its working was called the Revivalist, though now baptized with the broader title of the Christian. Amid such real work it would be a pity to have the semblance of unreality, and I dreaded to think of the possibility of its existing, when little grimy hands were held out by boys volunteering to say a text for my behoof. By far the most favourite one was "Jesus wept;" next came "God is love"—each most appropriate; but the sharp boy, a few years older, won approval by a longer and more doctrinal quotation, whilst several of these held out hands again when asked whether, in the course of the day, they had felt the efficacy of the text given on the previous evening, "Set a watch, O Lord, before my mouth; keep Thou the door of my lips." Such an experience would be a sign of advanced spirituality in an adult. Is it ungenerous to ask whether its manifestation in an Arab child must not be an anticipation of what might be the normal result of a few years' training? May not this kind of forcing explain the cases I saw quoted in the books—of one boy who "felt like a fish out of water, and left the same day of his own l;" another who "climbed out of a three-floor window caped?"

However, here is the good work being done. Let us not carp at the details, but help it on, unless we can do better ourselves. One thing has been preeminently forced in upon me during this brief examination of our London Arabs— namely, that individuals work better than communities amongst these people. The work done by the great establishments, whether of England, Rome, or Protestant Dissent, is insignificant compared with that carried out by persons labouring like Mr. Hutton in Seven Dials and Miss Macpherson in Whitechapel, untrammelled by any particular system. The want, and sorrow, and suffering are individual, and need individual care, just as the Master of old worked Himself, and sent His scripless missionaries singly forth to labour for Him, as—on however incommensurate a scale—they are still labouring, East and West, amongst our London Arabs.

CHAPTER III.

LONDON ARABS IN CANADA.

In the previous chapter an account was given of the Arabs inhabiting that wonderful "square mile" in East London, which has since grown to be so familiar in men's mouths. The labours of Miss Macpherson towards reclaiming these waifs and strays in her "Refuge and Home of Industry, Commercial Street, Spitalfields," were described at some length, and allusion was at the same time made to the views which that lady entertained with regard to the exportation of those Arabs to Canada after they should have undergone a previous probationary training in the "Home." A short time afterwards it was my pleasing duty to witness the departure of one hundred of these young boys from the St. Pancras Station, en route for Canada; and it now strikes me that some account of the voyage out, in the shape of excerpts from the letters of the devoted ladies who themselves accompanied our Arabs across the Atlantic, may prove interesting; while, at the same time, a calculation of their probable success in their new life and homes may not improbably stimulate those who cannot give their time, to give at least their countenance, and it may be, their material aid, to a scheme which recommends itself to all our sympathies—the permanent reclamation of the little homeless wanderers of our London streets.

The strange old rambling "Home" in Commercial Street, built originally for warehouses, then used as a cholera hospital, and now the Arab Refuge, presented a strange appearance during the week before the departure of the chosen hundred. On the ground-floor were the packages of the young passengers; on the first floor the "new clothes, shirts, and stockings, sent by kind lady friends from all parts of the kingdom, trousers and waistcoats made by the widows, and the boots and pilot jackets made by the boys themselves." The dormitory was the great store-closet for all the boys' bags filled with things needful on board ship; and on the top floor, we can well imagine, the last day was a peculiarly melancholy one. The work attendant upon the boys' last meal at the Refuge was over, and there, in the long narrow kitchen, stood the cook wiping away her tears with her apron, and the six little waiting maids around them, with the novel feeling of having nothing to do— there, where so much cutting, buttering, and washing-up had been the order of the day. When the summons came to start, the police had great difficulty in clearing a way for the boys to the vans through the surging mass of East London poverty. Some of the little match-box makers ran all the three miles from Commercial Street to St. Pancras Station to see the very last of their boy-friends.

Derby was the stopping-place on the journey to Liverpool, and the attention of passengers and guards was arrested by this strange company gathering on the platform at midnight and singing two of the favourite Refuge hymns. Liverpool was reached at 4 a.m., and the boys filed off in fours, with their canvas bags over their shoulders, to the river side, where their wondering eyes beheld the Peruvian, which was to bear them to their new homes.

At this point, Miss Macpherson's sister—who is carrying on the work of the Refuge during that lady's absence— wrote as follows:—"Could our Christian friends have seen the joy that beamed in the faces of those hundred lads from whom we have just parted—could they know the misery, the awful precipice of crime and sin from which they have been snatched—we are sure their hearts would be drawn out in love for those little ones. If still supported," she continues, "I hope to send out another party of fifty boys and fifty girls while my sister remains in Canada, and shall be happy to forward the name and history of a boy or girl to any kind friend wishing to provide for a special case. In the broad fields of that new country where the farmers are only too glad to adopt healthy young boys or girls into their families, hundreds of our perishing little ones may find a happy home."

On Thursday, the 12th of May, the Peruvian dropped down the river; and, as the last batch of friends left her when she passed out into the Channel, these one hundred boys, with Miss Macpherson, leaned over the bulwarks, singing the hymn, "Yes, we part, but not for ever."

From Derry Miss Macpherson wrote under date May 13th:—"With the exception of two, all are on deck now, as bright as larks; they have carried up poor Jack Frost and Franks the runner. It is most touching to see them wrap them up in their rugs. Michael Flinn, the Shoreditch shoeblack, was up all night, caring for the sick boys. Poor Mike! He and I have exchanged nods at the Eastern Counties Railway corner these five years. It is a great joy to give him such a chance for life."

The voyage out was prosperous enough, though there were some contrary winds, and a good deal of sea-sickness among the lads. The captain seems to have been quite won by the self-denying kindness of the ladies, and he lightened their hands by giving occupation to the boys. Then came out the result of training at the Refuge. Those who had been some time there showed themselves amenable to discipline; but the late arrivals were more fractious, and difficult to manage. These were the lads "upon whom," as Miss Macpherson says, "the street life had left sore marks." Even when only nearing the American coast, this indomitable lady's spirit is planning a second expedition. "As far as I dare make plans, I should like to return, starting from Montreal July 16th, reaching the Home July 27th; and then return with another lot the second week in August. This second lot must be lads who are now under influence, and who have been not less than six months in a refuge." The finale to this second letter, written from

Canada, adds: "The boys, to a man, behaved splendidly. The agent's heart is won. All have improved by the voyage, and many are brown hearty-looking chaps fit for any toil."

In the Montreal Herald, of May 27th, there is an account of these boys after their arrival, which says:—"Miss Macpherson is evidently a lady whose capacity for organization and command is of the very highest order; for boys, in most hands, are not too easily managed, but in hers they were as obedient as a company of soldiers.... These boys will speedily be placed in positions, where they will grow up respectable and respected members of society, with access to the highest positions in the country freely open to them.... We hope that Miss Macpherson will place all her boys advantageously, and will bring us many more. She is a benefactor to the Empire in both hemispheres."

The importance of this testimony can scarcely be overrated, since many persons hold themselves aloof from a work of this nature through a feeling that it is not fair to draft our Arab population on a colony. It will be seen, however, that it is not proposed to export these boys until they shall have been brought well under influence, and so have got rid of what Miss Macpherson so graphically terms the "sore marks of their street life."

Apropos of this subject, it may not be irrelevant to quote a communication which has been received from Sir John Young, the Governor-General of Canada, dated Ottawa, May 3rd, 1870:—"For emigrants able and willing to work, Canada offers at present a very good prospect. The demand for agricultural labourers in Ontario during the present year is estimated at from 30,000 to 40,000; and an industrious man may expect to make about one dollar a day throughout the year, if he is willing to turn his hand to clearing land, threshing, &c., during the winter. But it is of no use for emigrants to come here unless they make up their minds to take whatever employment offers itself most readily, without making difficulties because it is not that to which they have been accustomed, or which they prefer."

I visited the Refuge and Home of Industry a few nights afterwards, and, though Miss Macpherson was absent, found all in working order. Sixty-three boys were then its occupants. The superintendent was anxiously looking forward to be able to carry out the plan of despatching fifty boys and fifty girls during the ensuing summer. The sum required for an East End case is 5l.; for a special case, 10l. The following are specimens of about sixty cases of boys whom she would like to send out, knowing that in Canada they could readily obtain places:—

P. E., aged seventeen.—Mother died of fever, leaving seven children; father a dock labourer, but cannot get full employment.

L. J., aged thirteen.—Mother dead; does not know where her father is; has been getting her living by singing songs in the lodging-houses; is much improved by her stay in the Home, and will make a tidy little maid. This is just one of the many who might thus be rescued from a life of sin and misery.

Returning home through the squalid streets that night, where squatters were vending old shoes and boots that seemed scarcely worth picking out of the kennel, and garments that appeared beneath the notice of the rag merchant, I saw the little Bedouins still in full force, just as though no effort had been made for their reclamation and housing. As they crowded the doorsteps, huddled in the gutters, or vended boxes of lights and solicited the honour of shining "your boots, sir," I could not help picturing them crossing the sea, under kindly auspices, to the "better land" beyond, and anon, in the broad Canadian fields or busy Canadian towns, growing into respectable farmers and citizens; and straightway each little grimed, wan face seemed to bear a new interest for me, and to look wistfully up into mine with a sort of rightful demand on my charity, saying to me, and through me to my many readers, "Come and help us!"

After the foregoing was written, a further letter arrived from Miss Macpherson. All the boys were well placed. The agent at Quebec wished to take the whole hundred in a lump, but only eleven were conceded to him. At Montreal, too, all would have been taken, but twenty-one only were left. All found excellent situations, many as house servants at 10l. and 15l. a year. Eight were in like manner left at Belleville, half way between Montreal and Toronto. Sixty were taken on to Toronto; and here we are told "the platform was crowded with farmers anxious to engage them all at once. It was difficult to get them to the office." A gentleman arrived from Hamilton, saying that sixty applications had been sent in for boys, directly it was known that Miss Macpherson was coming out. So there is no need of anticipating anything like repugnance on the part of the Canadians to the reception of our superfluous Arabs.

CHAPTER IV.

WAIFS AND STRAYS.

Among the various qualifications for the festivities of
Christmastide and New Year, there is one which is,
perhaps, not so generally recognised as it might be. Some
of us are welcomed to the bright fireside or the groaning
table on the score of our social and conversational
qualities. At many and many a cheery board, poverty is the
only stipulation that is made. I mean not now that the
guests shall occupy the unenviable position of "poor
relations," but, in the large-hearted charity that so widely
prevails at that festive season, the need of a dinner is being
generally accepted as a title to that staple requirement of
existence. Neither of these, however, is the distinction
required in order to entitle those who bear it to the
hospitality of Mr. Edward Wright, better known under the
abbreviated title of "Ned," and without the prefatory "Mr."
That one social quality, without which a seat at Ned
Wright's festive board cannot be compassed, is Felony. A
little rakish-looking green ticket was circulated a few days
previously among the members of Mr. Wright's former
fraternity, bidding them to a "Great Supper" in St. John's
Chapel, Penrose Street (late West Street), Walworth, got
up under the auspices of the South-East London Mission.
The invitation ran as follows:—

"This ticket is only available for a male person who has
been convicted at least once for felony, and is not
transferable. We purpose providing a good supper of bread
and soup, after which an address will be given. At the close
of the meeting a parcel of provisions will be given to each

man. Supper will be provided in the lower part of the chapel. Boys not admitted this time.—Your friend, for Christ's sake,

"Ned Wright."

Why juvenile felons should be excluded "this time," and whether the fact of having been convicted more than once would confer any additional privileges, did not appear at first sight. So it was, however; adult felonious Walworth was bidden to the supper, and to the supper it came. Among the attractions held out to spectators of the proceedings was the announcement that a magistrate was to take part in them—a fact that possibly was not made generally known among the guests, in whose regard it is very questionable whether the presence of the dreaded "beak" might not have proved the reverse of a "draw." However, they came, possibly in happy ignorance of the potentate who was awaiting them, and than whom there is one only creation of civilized life considered by the London cadger his more natural enemy, that is the policeman.

Six o'clock was the hour appointed for the repast, and there was no need for the wanderer in Walworth Road to inquire which was Penrose Street. Little groups of shambling fellows hulked about the corner waiting for some one to lead the way to the unaccustomed chapel. Group after group, however, melted away into the dingy building where Ned was ready to welcome them. With him I found, not one magistrate, but two; one the expected magnate from the country, the other a well-known occupant of the London bench, with whom, I fancy, many of the guests could boast a previous acquaintance of a character the reverse of desirable. Penrose Street Chapel had been formerly occupied by the Unitarians, but was then taken permanently by Ned Wright at a rental of between 60l. and 70l. per annum, and formed the third of his "centres," the others being under a railway arch in the New Kent Road, and the Mission Hall, Deptford. As row by row filled with squalid occupants, I could but scan from my vantage-ground in the gallery the various physiognomies. I am bound to say the typical gaol-bird was but feebly represented. The visitors looked like hard-working men—a little pinched and hungry, perhaps, and in many cases obviously dejected and ashamed of the qualification which gave them their seat. One or two, mostly of the younger, came in with a swagger and a rough joke; but Ned and his guests knew one another, and he quickly removed the lively young gentleman to a quiet corner out of harm's way. A fringe of spectators, mostly female, occupied the front seat in the gallery when proceedings commenced, which they did with a hymn, composed by Ned Wright himself. The ladies' voices proved very useful in this respect; but most of the men took the printed copies of the hymns, which were handed round, and looked as if they could read them, not a few proving they could by singing full-voiced. After the hymn, Wright announced that he had ordered eighty gallons of soup—some facetious gentleman suggesting, "That's about a gallon apiece"—and he hoped all would get enough. Probably about 100 guests had by this time assembled, and each was provided with a white basin, which was filled by Ned and his assistants, with soup from a washing jug. A paper bag containing half a quartern loaf was also given to each, and the contents rapidly disappeared. As the fragrant steam mounted provokingly from the soup-basins up to the gallery, Mr. Wright took occasion to mention that at the last supper Mr. Clark, of the New Cut, furnished the soup gratuitously—a fact which he thought deserved to be placed on record.

In the intervals of the banquet, the host informed me that he had already witnessed forty genuine "conversions" as the results of these gatherings. He had, as usual, to contend with certain obtrusive gentlemen who "assumed the virtue" of felony, "though they had it not," and were summarily dismissed with the assurance that he "didn't want no tramps." One mysterious young man came in and sat down on a front row, but did not remain two minutes before a thought seemed to strike him, and he beat a hasty retreat. Whether he was possessed with the idea I had to combat on a previous occasion of the same kind, that I was a policeman, I cannot tell, but he never reappeared. I hope I was not the innocent cause of his losing his supper. The only "felonious" trait I observed was a furtive glance every now and then cast around, and especially up to the gallery. Beyond this there really was little to distinguish the gathering from a meeting of artisans a little bit "down on their luck," or out on strike, or under some cloud of that sort.

As supper progressed, the number of spectators in the gallery increased; and, with all due deference to Ned Wright's good intentions, it may be open to question whether this presence of spectators in the gallery is wise. It gives a sort of spurious dash and bravado to the calling of a felon to be supping in public, and have ladies looking on, just like the "swells" at a public dinner. I am sure some of the younger men felt this, and swaggered through their supper accordingly. There certainly was not a symptom of shame on the face of a single guest, or any evidences of dejection, when once the pea-soup had done its work. Some of the very lively gentlemen in the front row even devoted themselves to making critical remarks on the occupants of the gallery. As a rule, and considering the antecedents of the men, the assembly was an orderly one; and would, I think, have been more so, but for the presence of the fair sex in the upper regions, many of whom, it is but justice to say, were enjoying the small talk of certain oily-haired young missionaries, and quite unconscious of being the objects of admiring glances from below.

Supper took exactly an hour, and then came another hymn, Ned Wright telling his guests that the tune was somewhat difficult, but that the gallery would sing it for them first, and then they would be able to do it for themselves. Decidedly, Mr. Wright is getting "æsthetic." This hymn was, in fact, monopolized by the gallery, the men listening and evidently occupied in digesting their supper. One would rather have heard something in which they could join. However, it was a lively march-tune, and they evidently liked it, and kept time to it with their feet, after the custom of the gods on Boxing Night. At this point Ned and five others mounted the little railed platform, Bible in hand, and the host read what he termed "a portion out of the Good Old Book," choosing appropriately Luke xv., which tells of the joy among angels over one sinner that repenteth, and the exquisite allegory of the Prodigal Son, which Ned read with a good deal of genuine pathos. It reminded him, he said, of old times. He himself was one of the first prisoners at Wandsworth when "old Brixton" was shut up. He had "done" three calendar months, and when he came out he saw an old grey-headed man, with a bundle. "That," said Ned, "was my godly old father, and the bundle was new clothes in place of my old rags."

The country magistrate then came forward, and drew an ironical contrast between the "respectable" people in the gallery and the "thieves" down below. "God says we have all 'robbed Him.' All are equal in God's sight. But some of us are pardoned thieves." At this point the discourse became theological, and fired over the heads of the people down below. They listened much as they listen to a magisterial remark from the bench; but it was not their own language, such as Ned speaks. It was the "beak," not the old "pal." It was not their vernacular. It did for the gallery—interested the ladies and the missionaries vastly, but not the thieves. It was wonderful that they bore it as well as they did. The magisterial dignity evidently overawed them; but they soon got used to it, and yawned or sat listlessly. Some leant their heads on the rail in front and slept. The latest arrivals left earliest. They had come to supper, not to sermon.

Another of Ned Wright's hymns was then sung—Mr. Wright's muse having been apparently prolific in the past year, no less than six hymns on the list being written by himself during those twelve months. It is much to be hoped that these poetical and æsthetical proclivities will not deaden his practical energies. This hymn was pitched distressingly high, and above the powers of all but the "gallery" and a very few indeed of the guests; but most of them put in a final "Glory, Hallelujah," at the end of each stanza. Mr. Wright's tunes are bright and cheerful in the extreme, without being vulgar or offensively secular.

The host himself then spoke a few words on the moral of the Sermon on the Mount: "Seek ye first the kingdom of God and His righteousness." He claimed many of those before him as old pals who had "drunk out of the same pot and shuffled the same pack of cards," and contrasted his present state with theirs. Then they listened, open-mouthed and eager-eyed, though they had been sitting two full hours. He pictured the life of Christ, and His love for poor men. "Christ died for you," he said, "as well as for the 'big people.' Who is that on the cross beside the Son of God?" he asked in an eloquent apostrophe. "It is a thief. Come to Christ, and say, 'I've no character. I'm branded as a felon. I'm hunted about the streets of London. He will accept you.'" He drew a vivid picture of the number of friends he had when he rowed for Dogget's Coat and Badge. He met with an accident midway; "and when I got to the Swan at Chelsea," he said, "I had no friends left. I was a losing man. Christ will never treat you like that. He has never let me want in the nine years since I have been converted." After a prayer the assembly broke up, only those being requested to remain who required advice. The prayer was characteristic, being interspersed with groans from the gallery; and then a paper bag, containing bread and cakes, was given to each, Ned observing, "There, the devil don't give you that. He gives you toke and skilly." Being desired to go quietly, one gentleman expressed a hope that there was no policeman; another adding, "We don't want to get lagged." Ned had to reassure them on my score once more, and then nearly all disappeared—some ingenious guests managing to get two and three bags by going out and coming in again, until some one in the gallery meanly peached!

Only some half-dozen out of the hundred remained, and Ned Wright kneeling at one of the benches prayed fervently, and entered into conversation with them one by one. Two or three others dropped in, and there was much praying and groaning, but evidently much sincerity. And so with at least some new impressions for good, some cheering hopeful words to take them on in the New Year, those few waifs and strays passed out into the darkness, to retain, let it be hoped, some at least of the better influences which were brought to bear upon them in that brighter epoch in their darkened lives when Ned Wright's invitation gathered them to the Thieves' Supper.

CHAPTER V.

A LUNATIC BALL.

One half of the world believes the other half to be mad; and who shall decide which moiety is right, the reputed lunatics or the supposed sane, since neither party can be unprejudiced in the matter? At present the minority believe that it is a mere matter of numbers, and that if intellect carried the day, and right were not overborne by might, the position of parties would be exactly reversed. The dilemma forced itself strongly on my consciousness for a solution when I attended the annual ball at Hanwell Lunatic Asylum. The prevailing opinion inside the walls was that the majority of madmen lay outside, and that the most hopelessly insane people in all the world were the officers immediately concerned in the management of the establishment itself.

It was a damp, muggy January evening when I journeyed to this suburban retreat. It rained dismally, and the wind nearly blew the porter out of his lodge as he obeyed our summons at the Dantesque portal of the institution, in passing behind which so many had literally abandoned hope. I tried to fancy how it would feel if one were really being consigned to that receptacle by interested relatives, as we read in three-volume novels; but it was no use. I was one of a merry company on that occasion. The officials of Hanwell Asylum had been a little shy of being handed down to fame; so I adopted the ruse of getting into Herr Gustav Küster's corps of fiddlers for the occasion. However, I must in fairness add that the committee during the evening withdrew the taboo they had formerly placed on my writing. I was free to immortalize them; and my fiddling was thenceforth a work of supererogation.

High jinks commenced at the early hour of six; and long before that time we had deposited our instruments in the Bazaar, as the ball-room is somewhat incongruously called, and were threading the Dædalean mazes of the wards. Life in the wards struck me as being very like living in a passage; but when that preliminary objection was got over, the long corridors looked comfortable enough. They were painted in bright warm colours, and a correspondingly genial temperature was secured by hot-water pipes running the entire length. Comfortable rooms opened out from the wards at frequent intervals, and there was every form of amusement to beguile the otherwise irksome leisure of those temporary recluses. Most of my hermits were smoking—I mean on the male side—many were reading; one had a fiddle, and I scraped acquaintance immediately with him; whilst another was seated at the door of his snug little bedroom, getting up cadenzas on the flute. He was an old trombone-player in one of the household regiments, an inmate of Hanwell for thirty years, and a fellow-bandsman with myself for the evening. He looked, I thought, quite as sane as myself, and played magnificently; but I was informed by the possibly prejudiced officials that he had his occasional weaknesses.

A second member of Herr Küster's band whom I found in durance was a clarionet-player, formerly in the band of the Second Life Guards; and this poor fellow, who was an excellent musician too, felt his position acutely. He apologized sotto voce for sitting down with me in corduroys, as well as for being an "imbecile." He did not seem to question the justice of the verdict against him, and had not become acclimatized to the atmosphere like the old trombone-player.

That New Year's night—for January was very young—the wards, especially on the women's side, were gaily decorated with paper flowers, and all looked as cheerful and happy as though no shadow ever fell across the threshold; but, alas, there were every now and then padded rooms opening out of the passage; and as this was not a refractory ward, I asked the meaning of the arrangement, which I had fancied was an obsolete one. I was told they were for epileptic patients. In virtue of his official position as bandmaster, Herr Küster had a key; and, after walking serenely into a passage precisely like the rest, informed me, with the utmost coolness, that I was in the refractory ward. I looked around for the stalwart attendant, who is generally to be seen on duty, and to my dismay found he was quite at the other end of an exceedingly long corridor. I do not know that I am particularly nervous; but I candidly confess to an anxiety to get near that worthy official. We were only three outsiders, and the company looked mischievous. One gentleman was walking violently up and down, turning up his coat-sleeves, as though bent on our instant demolition. Another, an old grey-bearded man, came up, and fiercely demanded if I were a Freemason. I was afraid he might resent my saying I was not, when it happily occurred to me that the third in our party, an amateur contra-bassist, was of the craft. I told our old friend so. He demanded the sign, was satisfied, and, in the twinkling of an eye, our double-bass friend was struggling in his fraternal embrace. The warder, mistaking the character of the hug, hastened to the rescue, and I was at ease.

We then passed to the ball-room, where my musical friends were beginning to "tune up," and waiting for their conductor. The large room was gaily decorated, and filled with some three or four hundred patients, arranged Spurgeon-wise: the ladies on one side, and the gentlemen on the other. There was a somewhat rakish air about the gathering, due to the fact of the male portion not being in full dress, but arrayed in free-and-easy costume of corduroys and felt boots. The frequent warders in their dark blue uniforms lent quite a military air to the scene; and on the ladies' side the costumes were more picturesque; some little latitude was given to feminine taste, and the result was that a large portion of the patients were gorgeous in pink gowns. One old lady, who claimed to be a scion of royalty, had a resplendent mob-cap; but the belles of the ball-room were decidedly to be found among the female attendants, who were bright, fresh-looking young women, in a neat, black uniform, with perky little caps, and bunches of keys hanging at their side like the rosary of a sœur de charité, or the chatelaines with which young ladies love to adorn themselves at present. Files of patients kept streaming into the already crowded room, and one gentleman, reversing the order assigned to him by nature, walked gravely in on the palms of his hands, with his legs elevated in air. He had been a clown at a theatre, and still retained some of the proclivities of the boards. A wizen-faced man, who seemed to have no name beyond the conventional one of "Billy," strutted in with huge paper collars, like the corner man in a nigger troupe, and a tin decoration on his breast the size of a cheeseplate. He was insensible to the charms of Terpsichore, except in the shape of an occasional pas seul, and laboured under the idea that his mission was to conduct the band, which he occasionally did, to the discomfiture of Herr Küster, and the total destruction of gravity on the part of the executants, so that Billy had to be displaced. It was quite curious to notice the effect of the music on some of the quieter patients. One or two, whose countenances really seemed to justify their incarceration, absolutely hugged the foot of my music-stand, and would not allow me to hold my instrument for a moment when I was not playing on it, so anxious were they to express their admiration of me as an artist. "I used to play that instrument afore I come here," said a patient, with a squeaky voice, who for eleven years has laboured under the idea that his mother is coming to see him on the morrow; indeed, most of the little group around the platform looked upon their temporary sojourn at Hanwell as the only impediment to a bright career in the musical world.

Proceedings commenced with the Caledonians, and it was marvellous to notice the order, not to say grace and refinement with which these pauper lunatics went through their parts in the "mazy." The rosy-faced attendants formed partners for the men, and I saw a herculean warder gallantly leading along the stout old lady in the mob-cap. The larger number of the patients of course were paired with their fellow-prisoners, and at the top of the room the officials danced with some of the swells. Yes, there were swells here, ball-room coxcombs in fustian and felt. One in particular was pointed out to me as an University graduate of high family, and on my inquiring how such a man became an inmate of a pauper asylum the official said, "You see, sir, when the mind goes the income often goes too, and the people become virtually paupers." Insanity is a great leveller, true; but I could not help picturing that man's lucid intervals, and wondering whether his friends might not do better for him. But there he is, pirouetting away with the pretty female organist, the chaplain standing by and smiling approval, and the young doctors doing the polite to a few invited guests, but not disdaining, every now and then, to take a turn with a patient. Quadrilles and Lancers follow, but no "round dances." A popular prejudice on the part of the majority sets down such dances as too exciting for the sensitive dancers. The graduate is excessively irate at this, and rates the band soundly for not playing a valse. Galops are played, but not danced; a complicated movement termed a "Circassian circle" being substituted in their place. "Three hours of square dances are really too absurd," said the graduate to an innocent second fiddle.

In the centre of the room all was gravity and decorum, but the merriest dances went on in corners. An Irish quadrille was played, and an unmistakable Paddy regaled himself with a most beautiful jig. He got on by himself for a figure or two, when, remembering, no doubt, that "happiness was born a twin," he dived into the throng, selected a white-headed old friend of some sixty years, and impressed him with the idea of a pas de deux. There they kept it up in a corner for the whole of the quadrille, twirling imaginary shillelaghs, and encouraging one another with that expressive Irish interjection which it is so impossible to put down on paper. For an hour all went merry as the proverbial marriage bell, and then there was an adjournment of the male portion of the company to supper. The ladies remained in the Bazaar and discussed oranges, with an occasional dance to the pianoforte, as the band retired for refreshment too, in one of the attendants' rooms.

I followed the company to their supper room, as I had come to see, not to eat. About four hundred sat down in a large apartment, and there were, besides, sundry snug supper-parties in smaller rooms. Each guest partook of an excellent repast of meat and vegetables, with a sufficiency of beer and pipes to follow. The chaplain said a short grace before supper, and a patient, who must have been a retired Methodist preacher, improved upon the brief benediction by a long rambling "asking of a blessing," to which nobody paid any attention. Then I passed up and down the long rows with a courteous official, who gave me little snatches of the history of some of the patients. Here was an actor of some note in his day; there a barrister; here again a clergyman; here a tradesman recently "gone," "all through the strikes, sir," he added. The shadow—that most mysterious shadow of all—had chequered life's sunshine in every one of these cases. Being as they are they could not be in a better place. They have the best advice they could get even were they—as some of them claim to be—princes. If they can be cured, here is the best chance. If not—well, there were the little dead-house and the quiet cemetery lying out in the moonlight, and waiting for them when, as poor maddened Edgar Allen Poe wrote, the "fever called living," should be "over at last." But who talks of dying on this one night in all the year when even that old freemason in the refractory ward was forgetting, after his own peculiar fashion, the cruel injustice that kept him out of his twelve thousand a year and title? Universal merriment is the rule to-night. Six or seven gentlemen are on their legs at once making speeches, which are listened to about as respectfully as the "toast of the evening" at a public dinner. As many more are singing inharmoniously different songs; the fun is getting fast and furious, perhaps a little too fast and furious, when a readjournment to the ball-room is proposed, and readily acceded to, one hoary-headed old flirt remarking to me as he went by, that he was going to look for his sweetheart.

A long series of square dances followed, the graduate waxing more and more fierce at each disappointment in his anticipated valse, and Billy giving out every change in the programme like a parish clerk, which functionary he resembled in many respects. It was universally agreed that this was the best party that had ever been held in the asylum, just as the last baby is always the finest in the family. Certainly the guests all enjoyed themselves. The stalwart attendants danced more than ever with a will, the rosy attendants were rosier and nattier than before, if possible. The mob-cap went whizzing about on the regal head of its owner down the middle of tremendous country dances, hands across, set to partners, and then down again as though it had never tasted the anxieties of a throne, or learnt by bitter experience the sorrows of exile. Even the academical gentleman relaxed to the fair organist, though he stuck up his hair stiffer than ever, and stamped his felt boots again as he passed the unoffending double-bass with curses both loud and deep on the subject of square dances. At length came the inevitable "God Save the Queen," which was played in one key by the orchestra, and sung in a great many different ones by the guests. It is no disrespect to Her Majesty to say that the National Anthem was received with anything but satisfaction. It was the signal that the "jinks" were over, and that was quite enough to make it unpopular. However, they sang lustily and with a good courage, all except the old woman in the mob-cap, who sat with a complacent smile as much as to say, "This is as it should be, I appreciate the honour done to my royal brothers and sisters."

This is the bright side of the picture; but it had its sombre tints also. There were those in all the wards who stood aloof from the merriment, and would have none of the jinks. Lean-visaged men walked moodily up and down the passages like caged wild beasts. Their lucid interval was upon them, and they fretted at the irksome restraint and degrading companionship. It was a strange thought; but I fancied they must have longed for their mad fit as the drunkard longs for the intoxicating draught, or the opium-eater for his delicious narcotic to drown the idea of the present. There were those in the ball-room itself who, if you approached them with the proffered pinch of snuff, drove you from them with curses. One fine, intellectual man, sat by the window all the evening, writing rhapsodies of the most extraordinary character, and fancying himself a poet. Another wrapped round a thin piece of lath with paper, and superscribed it with some strange hieroglyphics, begging me to deliver it. All made arrangements for their speedy departure from Hanwell, though many in that heart-sick tone which spoke of long-deferred hope—hope never perhaps to be realized. Most painful sight of all, there was one little girl there, a child of eleven or twelve years—a child in a lunatic asylum! Think of that, parents, when you listen to the engaging nonsense of your little ones—think of the child in Hanwell wards! Remember how narrow a line separates innocence from idiocy; so narrow a line that the words were once synonymous!

Then there was the infirmary full of occupants on that merry New Year's night. Yonder poor patient being wheeled in a chair to bed will not trouble his attendant long. There is another being lifted on his pallet-bed, and having a cup of cooling drink applied to his parched lips by the great loving hands of a warder who tends him as gently as a woman. It seemed almost a cruel kindness to be trying to keep that poor body and soul together.

Another hour, rapidly passed in the liberal hospitality of this great institution, and silence had fallen on its congregated thousands. It is a small town in itself, and to a large extent self-dependent and self-governed. It bakes and brews, and makes its gas; and there is no need of a Licensing Bill to keep its inhabitants sober and steady. The method of doing that has been discovered in nature's own law of kindness. Instead of being chained and treated as wild beasts, the lunatics are treated as unfortunate men and women, and every effort is made to ameliorate, both physically and morally, their sad condition. Hence the bright wards, the buxom attendants, the frequent jinks. Even the chapel-service has been brightened up for their behoof.

This was what I saw by entering as an amateur fiddler Herr Küster's band at Hanwell Asylum; and as I ran to catch the last up-train—which I did as the saying is by the skin of my teeth—I felt that I was a wiser, though it may be a sadder man, for my evening's experiences at the Lunatic Ball.

One question would keep recurring to my mind. It has been said that if you stop your ears in a ball-room, and then look at the people—reputed sane—skipping about in the new valse or the last galop, you will imagine they must be all lunatics. I did not stop my ears that night, but I opened my eyes and saw hundreds of my fellow-creatures, all with some strange delusions, many with ferocious and vicious propensities, yet all kept in order by a few warders, a handful of girls, and all behaving as decorously as in a real ball-room. And the question which would haunt me all the way home was, which are the sane people, and which the lunatics?

CHAPTER VI.

A BABY SHOW.

There is no doubt that at the present moment the British baby is assuming a position amongst us of unusual prominence and importance. That he should be an institution is inevitable. That he grows upon us Londoners at the rate of some steady five hundred a week, the Registrar-General's statistics of the excess of births over deaths prove beyond question. His domestic importance and powers of revolutionizing a household are facts of which every Paterfamilias is made, from time to time, unpleasantly aware. But the British baby is doing more than this just at present. He is assuming a public position. Perhaps it is only the faint index of the extension of women's rights to the infantile condition of the sexes. Possibly our age is destined to hear of Baby Suffrage, Baby's Property Protection, Baby's Rights and Wrongs in general. It is beyond question that the British baby is putting itself forward, and demanding to be heard—as, in fact, it always had a habit of doing. Its name has been unpleasantly mixed up with certain revelations at Brixton, Camberwell, and Greenwich. Babies have come to be farmed like taxes or turnpike gates. The arable infants seem to gravitate towards the transpontine districts south of the Thames. It will be an interesting task for our Legislature to ascertain whether there is any actual law to account for the transfer, as it inevitably will have to do when the delicate choice is forced upon it between justifiable infanticide, wholesale Hospices des Enfants Trouvés, and possibly some kind of Japanese "happy despatch" for high-minded infants who are superior to the slow poison administered by injudicious "farmers." At all events, one fact is certain, and we can scarcely reiterate it too often—the British baby is becoming emphatic beyond anything we can recollect as appertaining to the infantile days of the present generation. It is as though a ray of juvenile "swellishness," a scintillation of hobbledehoyhood, were refracted upon the long clothes or three-quarter clothes of immaturity.

For, if it is true—as we may tax our infantile experiences to assure us—that "farmed" infants were an article unknown to husbandry in our golden age, it is equally certain that the idea of the modern Baby Show was one which, in that remote era, would not have been tolerated. Our mothers and grandmothers would as soon have thought of sacrificing an innocent to Moloch as to Mammon. What meant it then—to what can it be due—to precocity on the part of the British baby, or degeneracy on the part of the British parent—that two Baby Shows were "on" nearly at the same moment—one at Mr. Giovannelli's at Highbury Barn, the other at Mr. Holland's Gardens, North Woolwich?

Anxious to keep au courant with the times, even when those times are chronicled by the rapid career of the British baby—anxious also to blot out the idea of the poor emaciated infants of Brixton, Camberwell, and Greenwich, by bringing home to my experience the opposite pole of

infantile development—I paid a visit, and sixpence, at
Highbury Barn when the Baby Show opened. On entering
Mr. Giovannelli's spacious hall, consecrated on ordinary
occasions to the Terpsichorean art, I found it a veritable
shrine of the "Diva triformis." Immediately on entering I
was solicited to invest extra coppers in a correct card,
containing the names, weights, and—not colours; they
were all of one colour, that of the ordinary human
lobster—but weights, of the various forms of Wackford
Squeers under twelve months, who were then and there
assembled, like a lot of little fat porkers. It was, in truth, a
sight to whet the appetite of an "annexed" Fiji Islander, or
any other carnivorous animal. My correct card specified
eighty "entries;" but, although the exhibition only opened
at two o'clock, and I was there within an hour after, I found
the numbers up to 100 quite full. The interesting juveniles
were arranged within rails, draped with pink calico, all
arrayed in "gorgeous attire," and most of them partaking of
maternal sustenance. The mammas—all respectable
married women of the working class—seemed to consider
the exhibition of their offspring by no means infra dig., and
were rather pleased than otherwise to show you the legs
and other points of their adipose encumbrances. Several
proposed that I should test the weight, which I did
tremulously, and felt relieved when the infant Hercules
was restored to its natural protector. The prizes, which
amounted in the gross to between two and three hundred
pounds, were to be awarded in sums of 10l. and 5l., and
sometimes in the shape of silver cups, on what principle I
am not quite clear; but the decision was to rest with a jury
of three medical men and two "matrons." If simple
adiposity, or the approximation of the human form divine
to that of the hippopotamus, be the standard of excellence,
there could be no doubt that a young gentleman named
Thomas Chaloner, numbered 48 in the correct card, aged

eight months, and weighing 33lbs., would be facile princeps, a prognostication of mine subsequently justified by the event. I must confess to looking with awe, and returning every now and then to look again, on this colossal child. At my last visit some one asked on what it had been fed. Shall I own that the demon of mischief prompted me to supplement the inquiry by adding, "Oil cake, or Thorley's Food for Cattle?"

On the score, I suppose, of mere peculiarity, my own attention—I frankly confess I am not a connoisseur—was considerably engrossed by "two little Niggers." No doubt the number afterwards swelled to the orthodox "ten little Niggers." One was a jovial young "cuss" of eleven months—weighted at 29lbs., and numbered 62 on the card. He was a clean-limbed young fellow, with a head of hair like a furze-bush, and his mother was quite untinted. I presume Paterfamilias was a fine coloured gentleman. The other representative of the sons of Ham—John Charles Abdula, aged three months, weight 21lbs., and numbered 76—was too immature to draw upon my sympathies; since I freely acknowledge such specimens are utterly devoid of interest for me until their bones are of sufficient consistency to enable them to sit upright and look about as a British baby should. This particular infant had not an idea above culinary considerations. He was a very Alderman in embryo, if there are such things as coloured Aldermen. Then there were twins—that inscrutable visitation of Providence—three brace of gemini. Triplets, in mercy to our paternal feelings, Mr. Giovannelli spared us.

There was one noteworthy point about this particular exhibition. The mothers, at all events, got a good four days' feed whilst their infantile furniture was "on view." I heard, sotto voce, encomiums on the dinner of the day confidingly exchanged between gushing young matrons, and I myself witnessed the disappearance of a decidedly comfortable tea, to say nothing of sundry pints of porter discussed sub rosâ and free of expense to such as stood in need of sustenance; and indeed a good many seemed to stand in need of it. Small wonder, when the mammas were so forcibly reminded by the highly-developed British baby that, in Byron's own words, "our life is twofold."

It is certainly passing, not from the sublime to the ridiculous, but vice versâ, yet it is noting another testimony to the growing importance of the British baby, if one mentions the growth of crèches, or day-nurseries for working-men's children in the metropolis. Already an institution in Paris, they have been recently introduced into England, and must surely prove a boon to the wives of our working men. What in the world does become of the infants of poor women who are forced to work all day for their maintenance? Is it not a miracle if something almost worse than "farming"—death from negligence, fire, or bad nursing—does not occur to them? The good ladies who have founded, and themselves work, these crèches are surely meeting a confessed necessity. I paid a visit one day to 4, Bulstrode Street, where one of these useful institutions was in full work. I found forty little toddlers, some playing about a comfortable day-nursery, others sleeping in tiny cribs ranged in a double line along a spacious, well-aired sleeping-room; some, too young for this, rocked in cosy cradles; but all clean, safe, and happy. What needs it to say whether the good ladies who tended them wore the habit of St. Vincent de Paul, the poke-bonnet of the Puseyite "sister," or the simple garb of unpretending Protestantism? The thing is being done. The most helpless of all our population—the children of the working poor—are being kept from the streets, kept from harm, and trained up to habits of decency, at 4, Bulstrode Street, Marylebone Lane. Any one can go and see it for himself; and if he does—if he sees, as I did, the quiet, unostentatious work that is there being done for the British baby, "all for love and nothing for reward"—I shall be very much surprised if he does not confess that it is one of the best antidotes imaginable to baby-farming, and a sight more decorous and dignified than any Baby Show that could possibly be imagined.

CHAPTER VII.

A NIGHT IN A BAKEHOUSE.

Alarmed at the prospect of "a free breakfast table" in a sense other than the ordinary one—that is, a breakfast table which should be minus the necessary accompaniment of bread, or the luxury of French rolls—I resolved to make myself master, so far as might be possible, of the pros and cons of the question at issue between bakers and masters at the period of the anticipated strike some years ago. I confess to having greatly neglected the subject of strikes. I had attended a few meetings of the building operatives; but the subject was one in which I myself was not personally interested. I am not likely to want to build a house, and might manage my own little repairs while the strike lasted. But I confess to a leaning for the staff of life. There are sundry small mouths around me, too, of quite disproportionate capacities in the way of bread and butter, to say nothing at all of biscuits, buns, and tartlets. The possibility of having to provide for an impending state of siege, then, was one that touched me immediately and vitally. Should I, before the dreaded event, initiate the wife of my bosom in the mysteries of bread baking? Should I commence forthwith a series of practical experiments within the limited confines of my kitchen oven? To prevent the otherwise inevitable heaviness and possible ropiness in my loaves of the future, some such previous process would certainly have to be adopted. But, then, in order to calculate the probabilities of the crisis, an examination of the status in quo was necessary. Having a habit of going to head-quarters in such questions, I resolved to do so on the present occasion; so I took my hat, and, as Sam Slick says, "I off an' out."

The actual head-quarters of the men I found to be at the Pewter Platter, White Lion Street, Bishopsgate. Thither I adjourned, and, after drinking the conventional glass of bitter at the bar, asked for a baker. One came forth from an inner chamber, looking sleepy, as bakers always look. In the penetralia of the parlour which he left I saw a group of floury comrades, the prominent features of the gathering being depression and bagatelle. By my comatose friend I was referred to the Admiral Carter, in Bartholomew Close, where the men's committee sat daily at four. The society in front of the bar there was much more cheerful than that of the Pewter Platter, and the bakers were discussing much beer, of which they hospitably invited me to partake. Still I learned little of their movements, save that they were to a man resolved to abide by the now familiar platform of work from four to four, higher wages, and no Sunday bakings. These were the principal features of the demands, the sack money and perquisites being confessedly subsidiary. Nauseated as the public was and is with strikes, there are certain classes of the community with whom it is disposed to sympathize; and certainly one of those classes is that of journeymen bakers. Bread for breakfast we must have, and rolls we should like; but we should also like to have these commodities with as little nightwork as possible on the part of those who produce them. The "Appeal to the Public" put forth by the Strike Committee on the evening of the day concerning which I write was, perhaps, a trifle sensational; but if there was any truth in it, such a state of things demanded careful investigation—especially if it was a fact that the baker slept upon the board where the bread was made, and mingled his sweat and tears with the ingredients of the staff of life. Pardonably, I hope, I wished to eat bread without baker for my breakfast; but how could I probe this dreadful problem? I had it—by a visit to the bakehouse of my own baker, if possible, during the hours of work.

So I set out afresh after supper, and was most obligingly received by the proprietor of what one may well take as a typical West-end shop—neither very large nor very small—what is graphically termed a "snug" concern with a good connexion, doing, as the technical phrase goes, from sixteen to twenty sacks a week. The resources of this establishment were at once placed at my disposal for the night. Now, the advantage of conferring with this particular master was, that he was not pig-headed on the one hand, nor unduly concessive, as he deemed some of his fellow-tradesmen to be, on the other. He did not consider a journeyman baker's berth a bed of roses, or his remuneration likely to make him a millionaire; but neither did he lose sight of the fact that certain hours must be devoted to work, and a limit somewhere placed to wage, or the public must suffer through the employer of labour by being forced to pay higher prices. The staff of this particular establishment consisted of four men at the following wages: A foreman at 28s. and a second hand at 20s. a week, both of whom were outsiders; while, sleeping on the premises, and, at the time of my arrival, buried in the arms of Morpheus, were a third hand, at 16s., and a fourth, at 12s. Besides these wages they had certain perquisites, such as bread, butter, sugar, flour, sack-money, yeast-money, &c.; and the master, moreover, took his adequate share of day-work. He was seated outside his shop, enjoying the cool breezes, not of evening, but of midnight, when I presented myself before his astonished gaze. His wife and children had long since retired. The foreman and second "hand" had not arrived; the third and fourth "hands" were, as I said, sweetly sleeping, in a chamber on the basement, well out of range of the bakehouse, to which, like a couple of conspirators, we descended. It was not exactly the spot one would have selected for a permanent residence if left free to choose. It was, perhaps, as Mr. Dickens's theatrical gentleman phrased it, pernicious snug; but the ventilation was satisfactory. There were two ovens, which certainly kept the place at a temperature higher than might have been agreeable on that hot September night. Kneading troughs were ranged round the walls, and in the centre, like an altar-tomb, was the fatal "board" where, however, I sought in vain for the traces of perspiration or tears. All was scrupulously clean. In common phrase, you might have "eaten your dinner" off any portion of it.

Soon after midnight the outsiders turned in, first the second hand and then the foreman, and, plunging into the "Black Hole," made their toilettes du soir. Then active operations commenced forthwith. In one compartment of the kneading-trough was the "sponge," which had been prepared by the foreman early in the evening, and which now, having properly settled, was mixed with the flour for the first batch, and left to "prove." The process of making the dough occupied until about one o'clock, and then followed two hours of comparative tranquillity, during which the men adjourned to the retirement of certain millers' sacks hard by, which they rolled up cleverly into extempore beds, and seemed to prefer to the board. The proving takes about two hours, but varies with the temperature. If the dough is left too long, a sour batch, or a "pitch in," is the result. It is then cut out, weighed, and "handed up;" after which it stands while the dough for the second batch is being made, and those fatal rolls, around which so much of this contest is likely to turn, are being got forward. It must be understood that I am here describing what took place in my typical bakehouse. Proceedings will of course vary in details according to the neighbourhood, the season, and other circumstances. This makes, as my informant suggested, the race of bakers necessarily in some degree a varium atque mutabile genus, whom it is difficult to bind by rigid "hard and fast" lines. The first batch is in the oven at four, and is drawn about 5.30. During the intervals there has been the preparation of fancy bread and the "getting off" of the rolls. Then the "cottage" batch is moulded and got off, and comes out of the oven at eight. From three o'clock up to this hour there has been active work enough for everybody, and I felt myself considerably in the way, adjourning ever and anon to the master's snuggery above stairs to note down my experiences. As for the men, they must have fancied that I was an escaped lunatic, with harmless eccentricities; and the fourth hand, who was young, gazed at me all night with a fixed and sleepy glare, as though on his guard lest I should be seized with a refractory fit. At eight the close atmosphere of the bakehouse was exchanged for the fresh morning breeze by three out of the four hands, who went to deliver the bread. The foreman remained with the master to work at "small goods" until about one, when he prepares the ferment for the next night's baking. All concerned can get their operations over about one or half-past one; so that, reckoning them to begin at half-past twelve, and deducting two hours of "sweat and tears" from one to three, when they can sleep if they will, there are some eleven hours of active labour. After the delivery of the bread is over, it should be mentioned, each man has about half an hour's bakehouse work in the way of getting coals, cleaning biscuit tins, brushing up, &c. When this is done, all, with the exception of the foreman, who will have to look in and make the sponge at eight p.m., are free until the commencement of their most untimely work at midnight.

On Sunday, the work in this particular bakehouse is comparatively nil. The ovens have to be started on Sunday morning; but this the master does himself, and puts in the ferment, so that there is only the sponge to be made in the evening—a brief hour's job, taken on alternate Sundays by the foreman and the second hand. The "undersellers," my informant told me, made large sums by Sunday bakings, often covering their rent by them, so that their abandonment would be a serious question; but there was little in the way of Sabbath-breaking in my typical bakehouse. As there were no Sunday bakings, Saturday was a rather harder day than others, there being a general scrub-up of the premises. The work, my informant thought, could be condensed by judicious co-operation, and the "four to four" rule might be adopted in some establishments, but by no means in all—as, for instance, where there was a speciality for rolls and fancy bread. It seems, as usual, that the difficulties thicken, not about the necessaries, but about the luxuries and kickshaws of life. The master relieved my immediate fears by saying that he scarcely imagined matters would come to a crisis. There was this difference between the building and the baking trades, that all the master bakers had been journeymen themselves, and were thus able to sympathize with the men's difficulties. They were not, he seemed to think, disposed to haggle over a few shillings; but he added, "This is not a question of labour against capital only, but of labour against capital plus labour. I could," he said, "if my men left me on the 21st, make bread enough myself to supply all my customers, only they would have to fetch it for themselves."

Thus my worst fears were relieved. If it only came to going out for my loaf, and even foregoing French rolls, I could face that like a man; so I paced the streets gaily in the morning air and arrived home safely some time after the milk, and about the same hour as those rolls themselves whose hitherto unguessed history I had so far fathomed by my brief experiences in the bakehouse.

CHAPTER VIII.

A LONDON SLAVE MARKET.

There is a story called "Travellers' Wonders" in that volume which used to be the delight of our childhood, when the rising generation was more easily amused and not quite so wide-awake as at present. The point of the narrative is, that a facetious old gentleman named Captain Compass beguiles a group of juveniles—who must have been singularly gullible even for those early days—by describing in mysterious and alien-sounding terms the commonest home objects, such as coals, cheese, butter, and so on. It would almost seem as though Hood must have been perpetrating a kindred joke upon grown-up children when he wrote the lines—

It's O to be a slave

Along with the barbarous Turk,

Where woman has never a soul to save,

If this is Christian Work!

Was he aware that here, in the heart of Christian London, without going farther east than Bethnal Green, there had existed from time immemorial, as there exists still, a genuine Slave Market? Such there is, and actually so named; less romantic, indeed, than that we read of in "Don Juan," or used to see on the Adelphi boards in the drama of the "Octoroon"—but still interesting in its way to those who have a penchant for that grotesque side of London life where the sublime and the ridiculous sometimes blend so curiously.

With only the vague address of Bethnal Green and the date
of Tuesday morning to guide me, I set out for Worship
Street Police Court, thinking it possible to gain some
further particulars from the police. I found those
functionaries civil, indeed, but disposed to observe even
more than official reticence about the Slave Market. They
told me the locality precisely enough, but were even more
vague as to the hour than my own impressions. In fact, the
sum of what I could gain from them was, in slightly
Hibernian language, that there was nothing to see, and I
could see it any time on a Tuesday morning when I chose
to go down White Street, Bethnal Green. Leaving the
Court and inquiring my route to White Street, I found that
it ran off to the right some way down the Bethnal Green
Road from Shoreditch Station. Having turned out of the
main thoroughfare, you proceed down one of those
characteristic East End streets where every small
householder lives behind an elaborate bright green door
with portentous knocker, going on until an arch of the
Great Eastern Railway spans the road. Arriving at this
point any time between the hours of eight and half-past
nine on a Monday or Tuesday morning, you have no need
to be told that this is the East London Slave Market—
supposing you knew such a thing as a slave market was to
be seen in East London at all.

There was, indeed, nothing resembling Byron's graphic
description in "Don Juan." Our English slaves were all
apparently of one nation, and there were no slave
merchants. The hundred young ladies and gentlemen, of all
ages from seven to seventeen, were, as they would have
expressed it, "on their own hook." Ranged under the dead
brick wall of the railway arch, there was a generally
mouldy appearance about them. Instead of a picturesque
difference of colour, there was on every visage simply a

greater or less degree of that peculiar neutral tint, the unmistakable unlovely hue of London dirt. In this respect, too, they differed from the fresh country lads and lasses one sees at a hiring in the North. They were simply male and female City Arabs, with that superabundant power of combining business and pleasure which characterizes their race. The young gentlemen, in the intervals of business— and it seemed to be all interval and no business—devoted themselves to games at buttons. Each of the young ladies—I am afraid to say how young—had her cavalier, and applied herself to very pronounced flirtation. The language of one and all certainly fulfilled the baptismal promise of their sponsors, if the poor little waifs ever had any—for it was very "vulgar tongue" indeed; and there was lots of it. The great sensation of the morning was a broken window in an unoffending tradesman's shop—a far from unusual occurrence, as I learnt from the sufferer. This led to a slave hunt on the part of the single policeman who occasionally showed himself to keep as quiet as might be the seething mass of humanity; and the young lady or gentleman who was guilty of the damage was "off market" for the morning—while the suffering tradesman was assailed with a volley of abuse, couched in strongest Saxon, for meekly protesting against the demolition of his window-pane.

The scene was most characteristic—very unlike the genteel West End Servants' Registry, where young ladies and gentlemen's gentlemen saunter in to find places with high wages and the work "put out." It was on Tuesday morning, and a little late in the day, that I timed my visit; and I was informed that the Market was somewhat flat. Certainly, one could not apply to it the technicalities of the Stock Exchange, and say that little boys were "dull," or girls, big or little, "inactive;" but early on a Monday morning is, it appears, the time to see the Slave Market in full swing. Strangely enough, so far as I could judge, it was all slaves and no buyers—or, rather, hirers. I did not see the symptom of a bargain being struck, though I was informed that a good many small tradesmen do patronize the Market, for shop-boys, nurse-girls, or household drudges. I do not know whether my appearance was particularly attractive; but the number of offers I received from domestics of all kinds would have sufficed to stock half-a-dozen establishments. "Want a boy, sir?" "A girl for the childer, sir?" said the juveniles, while the offers of the adult ladies were more emphatic and less quotable. All, of course, was mere badinage, or, as they would have called it, "chaff," and it was meant good-humouredly enough; though, had I been a legitimate hirer, I do not know that I should have been tempted to add to my household from this source. Indeed, there were some not exactly pleasant reflections cast on the Slave Market by those whom I consulted as to its merits. It was not unusual, I was told, for slaves who were hired on a Monday to turn up again on Tuesday morning, either from incompatibility of temper on the part of domestic and superior, or from other causes unexplained. Tuesday morning is, in fact, to a large extent, the mere residuum either of Monday's unhired incapables, or of "returns." And yet, as I looked around, I saw—as where does one not see?—some fair young faces; girls who might have played with one's little children all the better because they were so nearly children themselves; and boys of preternatural quickness, up to any job, and capable of being useful—ay, and even ornamental—members of society, if only that dreadful Bethnal Green twang could have been eradicated. The abuse of the mother tongue on the part even of these children was simply frightful. If this were so in their playful moods, what—one could not help thinking—would it be if any dispute arose on a contested point of domestic economy: as, for instance, the too rapid disappearance of the cold mutton, or sudden absence of master's boots?

There was a garrulous cobbler whose stall bordered on the Market, and his panacea for all the evils the Slave Market brought with it was the London School Board. "Why don't the officers come down and collar some o' them youngsters, sir?" Why, indeed? At present the Slave Market is undoubtedly a nuisance; but there is no reason why, under proper police supervision, it should not become a local convenience. The ways of East London differ in all respects from those of the West, and Servants' Registries would not pay. Masters and servants are alike too poor to advertise; and there seems to be no reason why the Slave Market, under a changed name, and with improved regulations, may not as really supply a want as the country "hirings" do. The Arab, at present, is not to be trusted with too much liberty. Both male and female have odd Bedouin ways of their own, requiring considerable and judicious manipulation to mould them to the customs of civilized society. The respectable residents, tired of the existing state of things, look not unreasonably, as ratepayers, to the School Board to thin down the children, and the police to keep the adults in order. Under such conditions, the Bethnal Green Slave Market may yet become a useful institution.

CHAPTER IX.

TEA AND EXPERIENCE.

I was walking the other day in one of the pleasant western
suburbs, and rashly sought a short cut back; when, as is
generally the case, I found that the longer would have been
much the nearer way home. Before I knew it, I was
involved in the labyrinths of that region, sacred to
washerwomen and kindred spirits, known as Kensal New
Town; and my further progress was barred by the
intervention of the Paddington Canal, which is spanned at
rare intervals in this locality by pay-bridges, to the great
discomfort of the often impecunious natives. There was not
even one of these at hand, or my halfpenny would have
been paid under protest; so I had to wander like a lost
sprite among the network of semi-genteel streets that skirt
that most ungenteel thoroughfare, the Kensal New Town
Road, and forthwith I began to find the neighbourhood
papered with placards, announcing a "Tea and Experience
Meeting" at a local hall, under the presidency of the Free
Church pastor, for the following Monday evening. Bakers'
shops bristled with the handbills, and they studded the
multitudinous pork butchers' windows in juxtaposition
with cruel-looking black puddings and over-fat loin chops.
I determined I would go, if not to the tea, certainly to the
"Experience," for I like novel experiences of all kinds: and
this would certainly be new, whether edifying or not.

I got at length out of the labyrinth, and on the following
Monday ventured once more within its mazes, though not
exactly at six o'clock, which was the hour appointed for the
preliminary experience of tea. I had experienced that kind

of thing once or twice before, and never found myself in a position of such difficulty as on those occasions. In the first place I do not care about tea, when it is good; but loathe it when boiled in a washhouse copper, and poured out from a large tin can, of which it tastes unpleasantly. But, then again, the quantity as well as the quality of the viands to be consumed was literally too much for me. I might have managed one cup of decidedly nasty tea, or what passes muster for such, but not four or five, which I found to be the minimum. I could stomach, or secretly dispose of in my pockets, a single slice of leaden cake or oleaginous bread-and-butter; but I could not do this with multitudinous slabs of either. I never went to more than one tea-meeting where I felt at home, and that was at the Soirée Suisse, which takes place annually in London, where pretty Helvetian damsels brew the most fragrant coffee and hand round delicious little cakes, arrayed as they are in their killing national costume and chattering in a dozen different patois. I had a notion that tea at Kensal New Town would be very much less eligible, so I stopped away. Perhaps I was prejudiced. The tea might have been different from what I expected. The experiences certainly were.

I got there about half-past seven, having allowed an interval of an hour and a half, which I thought would be sufficient for the most inveterate tea-drinker, even among the Kensal Town laundresses, should such happen to be present. I took the precaution, however, of bespeaking a lad of fifteen to accompany me, in case any of the fragments of the feast should yet have to be disposed of, since I knew his powers to equal those of the ostrich in stowing away eatables, especially in the lumpy cake line. Arrived at the hall, however, I found no symptoms of the tea save a steamy sort of smell and the rattle of the retreating cups and saucers. Whether "to my spirit's gain or loss," I had escaped the banquet and yet got in good time for the subsequent experiences.

A motherly-looking woman stood at the door, and gave me a cheery invitation to come in. She looked rather askance at my boy, but finding him properly convoyed by my sober self, she admitted him within the portal. A good many young gentlemen of a similar age were evidently excluded, and were regaling themselves with pagan sports outside. The hall was partially filled with respectable-looking mechanics, their wives, and families, there being more wives than mechanics, and more families than either. Children abounded, especially babies in every stage of infantile development. Many were taking their maternal tea; and the boys and girls were got up in the most festive attire, the boys particularly shining with yellow soap. Most of the mammas wore perky hats, and many had follow-me-lads down the back, but all were exceedingly well-dressed and well-behaved, though evidently brimful of hilarity as well as cake and tea.

At the end of the hall was the inevitable platform, with chairs and a large cushion spread over the front rail for convenience of praying; since the "experiences" were to be interspersed with sacred song and prayer. Two gentlemen—I use the term advisedly—mounted the rostrum, one a long-bearded, middle-aged man, in a frock coat, who was the pastor, and another an aged minister, superannuated, as I afterwards discovered, and not altogether happy in his worldly lot. He was very old, grey-haired, and feeble, with a worn suit of clerical black, and a voluminous white tie. He sat humbly, almost despondingly, by the side of his younger brother in the ministry, while the latter delivered a merry little opening address, hoping all had made a good tea; if not, there was still about half a can left. Nobody wanted any more; so they had a hymn from the "Sacred Songster," a copy of which volume I purchased in the hall for twopence halfpenny. The tune was a martial one, well sung by a choir of men and women to the accompaniment of a harmonium, and bravely borne part in, you may depend upon it, by the whole assembly, I verily believe, except the babies, and one or two of these put in a note sometimes. The hymn was called, "Oh, we are Volunteers!" and was very Church-militant indeed, beginning thus:—

Oh, we are volunteers in the army of the Lord,

Forming into line at our Captain's word;

We are under marching orders to take the battle-field,

And we'll ne'er give o'er the fight till the foe shall yield.

Then came the chorus, repeated after every verse:—

Come and join the army, the army of the Lord,

Jesus is our Captain, we rally at His word:

Sharp will be the conflict with the powers of sin,

But with such a leader we are sure to win.

The poor old minister offered up a short prayer. The pastor read the 1st Corinthians, chapter 13, and explained briefly what charity meant there; adding that this gathering was very like one of the Agapæ of the early Christians—a remark I had not expected to hear in that assembly. Then there was another hymn, "Beautiful Land of Rest," when it did one good to hear the unction with which the second syllable of the refrain was given:—

Jerusalem, Jerusalem,

Beautiful land of rest.

After this the "Experiences" commenced in real earnest. Brothers and Sisters were exhorted to lay aside shyness and mount the platform. Of course no one would do so at first; and the poor shaky old minister had to come to the rescue.

He told us, at rather too great length, the simple story of his life—how he was a farmer's son, and had several brothers "besides himself." He had to learn verses of the Bible for his father, which used to go against the grain, until at last, instead of being "a wicked boy," he took up religion on his own account. He began to be afraid that, if he died, he should go to "a bad place," and therefore started saying his prayers. His brother George used to push him over when he was praying half-dressed in the bedroom, or occasionally vary proceedings by stirring him up with a sweeping brush. At last he found out a quiet place under a haystack, and there retired to pray. The old man drew a perfect picture of the first prayer thus offered, and told us he could remember every little detail of the spot, and the great oak tree spreading its branches over it.

"Here I am," he said, "a poor old pilgrim on the bright side of seventy now, and yet I can remember it all. I say the 'bright' side, for I know it is a bright home I am soon going to." Then he told us how God took his wife from him and all his worldly goods, and he was quite eloquent about the comfort his religion was to him now as he went to his little lonely lodging. He drew next too truthful a picture of the state of things he saw around him in Kensal New Town—mothers with infants in their arms crowding the tavern doors; and finished up with a story, of which he did not see the irrelevancy, about a fine lady going to the "theatre," and saying how much she had enjoyed the anticipation, then the play itself, and, lastly, the thought of it afterwards. She was overheard by a faithful pastor, who told her she had omitted one detail. "No," she said, "I have told you all." "You have told us how you enjoyed the thoughts of the theatre, and the performance, and the recollection of it afterwards; but you have not told us how you will enjoy the thoughts of it on your death-bed." Of course the "fine lady" was converted on the spot, as they always are in tracts; and the good old fellow brought his long-winded narrative of experiences to an end by-and-by, the pastor having omitted to pull his coat-tails, as he promised to do if any speaker exceeded the allotted time. "The people were certainly very attentive to hear him," and one man next my boy expressed his satisfaction by letting off little groans, like minute guns, at frequent intervals.

Then another hymn was sung, "The Beautiful Land on High," which, by the way, is a favourite with the spiritualists at their "Face Séances." I half expected to see a ghostly-looking visage peep out of some corner cupboard, as I had often done with my spiritual friends—that being another experience which I cultivate with considerable interest and curiosity. The hymn being over, a black-bearded, but soft-voiced man, in a velveteen coat, got upon the platform, and told us how the chief delight of his life was at one time making dogs fight. When the animals were not sufficiently pugnacious of themselves, his habit was to construct an apparatus, consisting of a pin at the end of a stick, and so urge them to the combat, until it proved fatal to one of them. It was, he said, dreadful work; and he now considered it the direct machination of Satan. Another favourite pursuit was interrupting the proceedings of open-air missionaries. One day after he had done so, he went home with a companion who had taken a tract from one of the missionaries. He had a quarrel with his "missis." "Not that missis sittin' there," he said, alluding to a smart lady in front, "but my first missis." In order to show his sulks against his missis, he took to reading the tract, and it soon made him cry. Then he went to chapel and heard a sermon on Lot's wife being turned into a pillar of salt. He was a little exercised by this, and saw the minister in the vestry, but soon fell back into bad habits again, singing canaries for 10s. 6d. a side. As he was taking his bird out one Sunday morning, the bottom of the cage came out, and the canary escaped. This he looked upon as "God's work," since it caused him to go to chapel that morning. His conversion soon followed, and he applied to that circumstance, in a very apposite manner, the Parable of the Prodigal, concluding with a stanza from the well-known hymn—

God moves in a mysterious way

His wonders to perform.

Another moustached man followed. He was exceedingly well-dressed, though he told us he was only a common labourer. He had long given up his "'art" to God, but to little purpose until he came to this chapel. "But there," he said, "down in that corner under the gas-lamp, I prayed for the first time. I prayed that God would take away my stony 'art and give me a 'art of flesh, and renew a right sperrit within me." From that time he led a new life. His fellow-workmen began to sneer at the change, and said ironically they should take to going to chapel too. "I wish to God you would," was his reply. He described the personal influence of the pastor upon him, which strengthened the good resolutions he had formed, and enabled him to say, "I will not let Thee go."

I could not help thinking, as I listened to the simple, earnest words of the speaker, that here was an element the National Church is too apt to ignore. The Roman Catholic Church would seize hold upon that man, and put him in a working men's guild or confraternity. The Free Church found him work to do, and gave him a chief seat in the synagogue, and an opportunity of airing his "experiences" on a platform. Surely better either one or the other, than sotting his life at a public-house, or turning tap-room orator. He ended by crying shame upon himself for having put off the change until so late in life, and added a wish that all the labouring classes could see, as he had been brought to see, where their chief interest as well as happiness lay.

A tall man from the choir followed, and was considerably more self-possessed than the other two speakers. He told us at the outset that he had been "a Christian" for fourteen years. It was generally laid down as a rule, he said, that big men were good-tempered. He was not a small man; but until he gave his heart to God he was never good-tempered. He had, for thirty-two years, been brought up in the Church of England, but had found no conversion there. He had no wish to speak against the Church, but such was the case. He wandered about a good deal in those years, from Roman Catholic to Old Methodist chapels; but the latter settled him. He was attending a class meeting in Kensal New Town one night, and suddenly a determination came over him that he would not sleep that night until he had kneeled down and prayed with his wife, though it would be the first time he had done so for thirty-two years. When it came to bedtime his courage failed him. He could not get into bed; and he did not like to tell his wife why. "That," he said, "was the devil worritin' me." His wife said, "I know what's the matter with you. You want to pray. We will see what we can do." His wife, he told us, was "unconverted," but still she "throwed open the door" on that occasion. He never knew happiness, he said, until he came to Jesus; and he added, "Oh, I do love my Jesus." He often talked to his fellow-workmen about the state of their souls, and they asked him how it was he was so certain of being converted (a question I fancy others than they would like to have solved), and he answered them, "I feel it. I was uncomfortable before; and now I am happy. I don't wonder so much at the old martyrs going boldly up to the stake, because I feel I could do anything rather than give up my Jesus."

Hereupon the pastor, anticipating the departure of some of the assembly—for the clock was pointing to ten—announced a Temperance Meeting for the following Monday, and also said he should like the congregation to get up these meetings entirely on their own account, without any "clerical" element at all, and to make the Tea Meeting a "Free and Easy" in the best sense of the word.

I went—shall I confess it?—to the experience meeting rather inclined to scoff, and I stopped, if not altogether to pray, at least to think very seriously of the value of the instrumentality thus brought to bear on such intractable material as the Kensal New Town population. The more cumbrous, even if more perfect or polished, machinery of the Established Church has notoriously failed for a long time to affect such raw material; and if it is beginning to succeed it is really by "taking a leaf out of the book" of such pastors as the one whose Tea-and-Experience Meeting I had attended. "Palmam qui meruit ferat."

Stiggins element, I must, in all justice, say there was none. The pastor was a simple but a refined and gentlemanly man; so was the poor broken old minister. There was no symptom of raving or rant; no vulgarity or bad taste. A gathering at a deanery or an episcopal palace could not have been more decorous, and I doubt if the hymns would have been sung as heartily. There was as little clerical starch as there was of the opposite element. Rubbing off the angles of character was one of the objects actually proposed by the pastor as the result of these gatherings; and I really felt as though a corner or two had gone out of my constitution. If a man is disposed to be priggish, or a lady exclusive, in religious matters, I would recommend the one or the other to avail themselves of the next opportunity to attend a Tea-and-Experience Meeting at Kensal New Town.

CHAPTER X.

SUNDAY LINNET-SINGING.

There is something very Arcadian and un-Cockney-like in
the idea of linnet-singing in Lock's Fields. Imagination
pictures so readily the green pastures and the wild bird's
song, and Corydon with his pipe and his Phyllis, that it
seems a pity to disabuse that exquisite faculty of our nature
so far as to suggest that the linnets of which we speak are
not wild, but tame and caged, and the fields very much less
rural than those of Lincoln's Inn. This was the
announcement that drew me to the New Kent Road on a
recent Sunday morning to hear what poor Cockney Keats
called the "tender-legged linnets:" "Bird-singing.—A
match is made between Thomas Walker (the Bermondsey
Champion) and William Hart (Champion of Walworth) to
sing two linnets, on Sunday, for 2l. a side; birds to be on
the nail precisely at two o'clock; the host to be referee. 10s.
is now down; the remainder by nine this evening, at the
Jolly Butchers, Rodney Road, Lock's Fields. Also a copper
kettle will be sung for on the same day by six pairs of
linnets; first pair up at half-past six o'clock in the evening.
Any person requiring the said room for matches, &c., on
making application to the host, will immediately be
answered."

Rodney Road, be it known, is anything but a romantic
thoroughfare, leading out of the New Kent Road, a little
way from the Elephant and Castle; and the caravanserai
bearing the title of the Jolly Butchers is an unpretending
beershop, with no outward and visible signs of especial
joviality. On entering I met mine host, rubicund and jolly

enough, who politely pioneered me upstairs, when I reported myself as in quest of the linnets. The scene of contest I found to be a largish room, where some twenty or thirty most un-Arcadian looking gentlemen were already assembled, the only adjunct at all symptomatic of that pastoral district being their pipes, at which they were diligently puffing. The whole of the tender-legged competitors, both for the money and the copper kettle, were hanging in little square green cages over the fireplace; and the one idea uppermost in my mind was how well the linnets must be seasoned to tobacco smoke if they could sing at all in the atmosphere which those Corydons were so carefully polluting. Corydon, besides his pipe, had adopted nuts and beer to solace the tedium of the quarter of an hour that yet intervened before the Bermondsey bird and its Walworth antagonist were to be "on the nail;" and ever and anon fresh Corydons kept dropping in, until some fifty or sixty had assembled. They were all of one type. There was a "birdiness" discernible on the outer man of each; for birdiness, as well as horseyness, writes its mark on the countenance and the attire. In the latter department there was a proclivity to thick pea-jackets and voluminous white comforters round the neck, though the day was springlike and the room stuffy. The talk was loud, but not boisterous, and garnished with fewer elegant flowers of speech than one would have expected. Five minutes before two the non-competing birds were carefully muffled up in pocket-handkerchiefs, and carried in their cages out of earshot, lest their twitterings might inspire the competing minstrels. Bermondsey and Walworth alone occupied the nails. Scarcely any bets were made. They seemed an impecunious assemblage, gathered for mere sport. One gentleman did, indeed, offer to stake "that 'ere blowsy bob," as though a shilling in his possession were a rarity of which his friends must be certainly aware. What was the occult meaning of the epithet "Blowsy" I could not fathom, but there were no takers; and, after the windows had been opened for a few minutes to clear the atmosphere, they were closed again; the door locked; the two markers took their place at a table in front of the birds, with bits of chalk in their hands; mine host stood by as referee in case of disputes; time was called; and silence reigned supreme for a quarter of an hour, broken only by the vocal performances of the Bermondsey and Walworth champions respectively. If a hapless human being did so far forget himself as to cough or tread incontinently upon a nutshell, he was called to silence with curses not loud but deep.

The Walworth bird opened the concert with a brilliant solo by way of overture, which was duly reported by the musical critic in the shape of a chalk line on the table. The length of the effusion did not matter; a long aria, or a brilliant but spasmodic cadenza, each counted one, and one only. The Bermondsey bird, heedless of the issue at stake, devoted the precious moments to eating, emitting nothing beyond a dyspeptic twitter which didn't count; and his proprietor stood by me evidently chagrined, and perspiring profusely, either from anxiety or superfluous attire. Nearly half the time had gone by before Bermondsey put forth its powers. Meanwhile, Walworth made the most of the opportunity, singing in a manner of which I did not know linnets were capable. There were notes and passages in the répertoire of Walworth which were worthy of a canary. The bird no doubt felt that the credit of home art was at stake, and sang with a vigour calculated to throw foreign feathered artistes into the shade. Bermondsey evidently sang best after dinner, so he dined like an alderman; yet dined, alas! not wisely, but too well, or rather too long. Then he sang, first, a defiant roulade or so, as much as to say, "Can you beat that, Walworth?" pausing, with his head wickedly on one side, for a reply. That reply was not wanting, for Walworth was flushed with success; and one could not help regretting ignorance of bird-language so as to gather exactly what the reply meant. Then came a protracted duet between the two birds, which was the pièce de résistance of the whole performance. The silence became irksome. I could not help congratulating myself on the fact that no Corydon had brought his Phyllis; for Phyllis, I am sure, would not have been able to stand it. Phyllis, I feel certain, would have giggled. We remained mute as mice, solemn as judges. The ghost of a twitter was hailed with mute signs of approval by the backers of each bird; but a glance at the expressive features of the host warned the markers that nothing must be chalked down that did not come up to his idea of singing. Had the destinies of empires hung upon his nod he could scarcely have looked more oracular. But Walworth could afford to take matters easily now. For the last five minutes the Bermondsey bird did most of the music; still it was a hopeless case. Success was not on the cards. By-and-by, time was again called. Babel recommenced, and the result stood as follows:

Walworth 3 score 18

Bermondsey 1 score 10

It was an ignominious defeat truly; and, had one been disposed to moralize, it had not been difficult to draw a moral therefrom. It was not a case of "no song, no supper;" but of supper—or, rather, dinner—and no song. Bermondsey had failed in the artistic combat, not from lack of powers, as its brilliant part in the duet and its subsequent soli proved, but simply from a Sybaritic love for creature comforts. I ventured to suggest it might have been expedient to remove the seed, but was informed that, under those circumstances, the creature—its proprietor called it an uglier name—would not have sung at all. The remarkable part of the business to me was that they did sing at the proper time. They had not uttered anything beyond a twitter until silence was called, and from that moment one or the other was singing incessantly. I suppose it was the silence. I have noticed not only caged birds, but children—not to speak ungallantly of the fair sex—generally give tongue most freely when one is silent, and presumably wants to keep so.

The contest, however, was over, the stakes paid, and Corydon sought his pastoral pipe again—not without beer. It was a new experience, but not a very exciting one—to me, at least. It evidently had its attractions for the very large majority of attendants. In fact, Rodney Road is generally a "birdy" neighbourhood. Its staple products, to judge by the shops, seemed birds and beer. I was much pressed by mine host to stay for the evening entertainment, when six birds were to sing, and the attendance would be more numerous. As some five hours intervened I expressed regret at my inability to remain, reserving my opinion that five hours in Lock's Fields might prove the reverse of attractive, and Corydon in greater force might not have an agreeable effect on that already stuffy chamber. So I took myself off, wondering much, by the way, what strange association of ideas could have led any imaginative man to propose such an incongruous reward as a copper kettle by way of præmium for linnet-singing.

CHAPTER XI.

A WOMAN'S RIGHTS DEBATE.

There never was a time when, on all sorts of subjects, from
Mesmerism to Woman's Rights, the ladies had so much to
say for themselves. There is an ancient heresy which tells
us that, on most occasions, ladies are prone to have the last
word; but certain it is that they are making themselves
heard now. On the special subject of her so-called "Rights"
the abstract Woman was, I knew, prodigiously emphatic—
how emphatic, though, I was not quite aware, until having
seen from the top of a City-bound omnibus that a lady
whom I will describe by the Aristophanic name of
Praxagora would lecture at the Castle Street Co-operative
Institute. I went and co-operated so far as to form one of
that lady's audience. Her subject—the "Political Status of
Women"—was evidently attractive, not only to what we
used in our innocence to call the weaker sex, but also to
those who are soon to have proved to them the fallacy of
calling themselves the stronger. A goodly assemblage had
gathered in the fine hall of the Co-operators to join in
demolishing that ancient myth as to the superiority of the
male sex. My first intention was to have reported verbatim
or nearly so the oration of Praxagora on the subject; and if
I changed my scheme it was not because that lady did not
deserve to be reported. She said all that was to be said on
the matter, and said it exceedingly well too; but when the
lecture, which lasted fifty minutes, was over, I found it was
to be succeeded by a debate; and I thought more might be
gained by chronicling the collision of opinion thence
ensuing than by simply quoting the words of any one
speaker, however eloquent or exhaustive.

I own with fear and trembling—for it is a delicate, dangerous avowal—that, as a rule, I do not sympathize with the ladies who declaim on the subject of Woman's Rights. I do not mean to say I lack sympathy with the subject—I should like everybody to have their rights, and especially women—but they are sometimes asserted in such a sledge-hammer fashion, and the ladies who give them utterance are so prone to run large and be shrill-voiced that their very physique proves their claim either unnecessary or undesirable. I feel certain that in whatever station of domestic life those ladies may be placed, they would have their full rights, if not something more; and as for Parliamentary rights, I tremble for the unprotected males should such viragos ever compass the franchise; or, worse still, realize the ambition of the Ecclesiazusæ of Aristophanes, and sit on the benches of St. Stephen's clad in the nether garments of the hirsute sex. There was nothing of that kind on Tuesday night. In manner and appearance our present Praxagora was thoroughly feminine, and, by her very quietude of manner, impressed me with a consciousness of power, and determination to use it. Her voice was soft and silvery almost as that of Miss Faithfull herself; and when, at the outset of her lecture, she claimed indulgence on the score of never having spoken in a public hall before, we had to press forward to the front benches to catch the modulated tones, and men who came clumping in with heavy boots in the course of the lecture were severely hushed down by stern-visaged females among the audience.

Disclaiming connexion with any society, Praxagora still adopted the first person plural in speaking of the doctrines and intentions of the down-trodden females. "We" felt so and so; "we" intended to do this or that; and certainly her cause gained by the element of mystery thus introduced, as well as by her own undoubted power of dealing with the subject. When the "we" is seen to refer to the brazen-voiced ladies aforesaid, and a few of the opposite sex who appear to have changed natures with the gentle ones they champion, that plural pronoun is the reverse of imposing, but the "we" of Praxagora introduced an element of awe, if only on the omne ignotum pro magnifico principle. In the most forcible way she went through the stock objections against giving women the franchise, and knocked them down one by one like so many ninepins. That coveted boon of a vote she proved to be at the basis of all the regeneration of women. She claimed that woman should have her share in making the laws by which she was governed, and denied the popular assertion that in so doing she would quit her proper sphere. In fact, we all went with her up to a certain point, and most of the audience beyond that point. For myself I confess I felt disheartened when, having dealt in the most consummate way with other aspects of the subject, she came to the religious phase, and begging the question that the Bible and religion discountenanced woman's rights, commenced what sounded to me like a furious attack on each.

Now I happen to know—what perhaps those who look from another standpoint do not know—that this aggressive attitude assumed so unnecessarily by the advocates of woman's rights is calculated to keep back the cause more than anything else; and matter and manner had been so much the reverse of hostile up to the moment she plunged incontinently into the religious question, that it quite took me by surprise. I have known scores of people who, when they came under vigorous protest to hear Miss Emily Faithfull on the same fertile subject, went away converted because they found no iconoclasm of this kind in her teaching. They came to scoff and stopped, not indeed to pray, but to listen very attentively to a theme which has so much to be said in its favour that it is a pity to complicate its advocacy by the introduction of an extraneous and most difficult question. So it was, however; with pale, earnest face, and accents more incisive than before, Praxagora said if Bible and religion stood in the way of Woman's Rights, then Bible and religion must go. That was the gist of her remarks. I need not follow her in detail, because the supplementary matter sounded more bitterly still; and, had she not been reading from MS. I should have thought the lecturer was carried away by her subject; but no, she was reading quite calmly what were clearly enough her natural and deliberate opinions. I said I was surprised at the line she took. Perhaps I ought scarcely to have been so, for she was flanked on one side by Mr. Bradlaugh, on the other by Mr. Holyoake! but I never remember being so struck with a contrast as when at one moment Praxagora pictured the beauty of a well-regulated home, and the tender offices of woman towards the little children, and then shot off at a tangent to fierce invectives against the Bible and religion, which seemed so utterly uncalled for that no adversary who wanted to damage the cause could possibly have invented a more complete method of doing so.

The lecture over, the chairman invited discussion, and a fierce little working man immediately mounted the platform and took Praxagora to task for her injudicious onslaught. But, as usual, this gentleman was wildly irrelevant and carried away by his commendable zeal. Over and over again he had to be recalled to the question, until finally he set his whole audience against him, and had to sit down abruptly in the middle of a sort of apotheosis of Moses—as far as I could hear, for his zeal outran his eloquence as well as his discretion, and rendered him barely audible. A second speaker followed, and, though cordially sympathizing with the address, and tracing woman's incapacity to her state of subjugation, regretted that such a disturbing element as religion had been mixed up with a social claim. He considered that such a subject must inevitably prove an apple of discord. For this he was at once severely handled by Mr. Bradlaugh, who, consistently enough, defended the line Praxagora adopted towards the religious question, and justified the introduction of the subject from the charge of irrelevance. He also deprecated the surprise which the last speaker had expressed at the excellent address of Praxagora by pointing out that in America about one-third of the press were females, a fact which he attributed to the plan of Mixed Education. Then a new line was opened up by a speaker— it was as impossible to catch their names as to hear the stations announced by porters on the Underground Railway. He predicted that if women did get the franchise, Mr. Bradlaugh's "Temple" would be shut up in six months, as well as those of Messrs. Voysey and Conway and Dr. Perfitt. The ladies, he said, were swayed by Conventionalism and Priestcraft, and until you educated them, you could not safely give them the franchise.

A youthful Good Templar mounted the rostrum, for the purpose of patting Praxagora metaphorically on the back, and also ventilating his own opinions on the apathy of the working man in claiming his vote. Then somebody got up and denied that ladies were by nature theological. Their virtues were superior to those of men just as their voices were an octave higher. He was for having a Moral Department of the State presided over by ladies. Only one lady spoke; a jaunty young woman in a sailor's hat, who said that in religious persecutions men, not women, had been the persecutors; and then Praxagora rose to reply. She first of all explained her position with regard to the Bible, which she denied having unnecessarily attacked. The Bible forbade a woman to speak; and, that being so, the Bible must stand on one side, for "we" were going to speak. That the highest intellects had been formed on Bible models she denied by instancing Shelley. If she thought that this movement was going to destroy the womanhood of her sex she would not move a finger for its furtherance. She only thought it would give a higher style of womanhood. As to women requiring to be educated before they would know how to use the franchise, she pointed triumphantly to the Government which men had placed in power. It was significant, she said, that the first exercise of the working men's franchise had been to place a Conservative Government in office.

I daresay I am wrong, but the impression left on my mind by the discussion was that the liberty of thought and action claimed was the liberty of thinking as "we" think and doing what "we" want to have done—a process which has been before now mistaken for absolute freedom. Stripped of its aggressive adjuncts, Praxagora's advocacy of her main subject would be telling in the extreme from the fact of her blending such thorough womanliness of person, character, and sentiment with such vigorous championship of a doctrine against which I do not believe any prejudice exists. Drag in the religious difficulty, however, and you immediately array against it a host of prejudices, whether reasonable ones or the reverse is not now the question. I am only concerned with the unwisdom of having called them into existence. I own I thought that Christianity had been the means of raising woman from her state of Oriental degradation to the position she occupies in civilized countries. But I was only there to listen, not to speak; and I confess I came away in a divided frame of mind. I was pleased with the paper, but irritated to think that a lady, holding such excellent cards, should risk playing a losing game.

CHAPTER XII.

AN OPEN-AIR TICHBORNE MEETING.

When Sydney Smith, from the depths of his barbarian ignorance, sought to rise to the conception of a Puseyite, he said in substance much as follows:—"I know not what these silly people want, except to revive every obsolete custom which the common sense of mankind has allowed to go to sleep." Puseyism is not to our present purpose; but Tichborne-ism is—for it has attained to the dignity of a veritable ism—and we may define it much after the same method, as an attempt, not, indeed, to revive the claims of, but to restore to society a person, who, after a trial of unexampled length, was consigned by the verdict of a jury, and the consequent sentence of the Lord Chief Justice, to the possibly uncongenial retirement of Millbank Penitentiary. With the rights or wrongs of such an event I have simply nothing to do. I abandoned the Tichborne Trial at an early stage in a condition of utter bewilderment; and directly an old gentleman sought to button-hole me, and argue that he must be the man, or he couldn't be the man, I made off, or changed the conversation as rapidly as I could.

But when the question had at length been resolved by wiser heads than mine, and when, too, I felt I could write calmly, with no fear of an action for contempt of court before my eyes, I confess that a poster announcing an open-air Tichborne meeting in Mr. Warren's cricket-field, Notting Hill, was too fascinating for me. I had heard of such gatherings in provincial places and East End halls; but this invasion of the West was breaking new ground. I would go; in fine I went. On the evening of an exceptionally hot July day, I felt there might be worse places than Mr. Warren's breezy cricket ground alongside Notting Barn Farm; so six o'clock, the hour when the chair was to be taken, found me at the spot—first of the outer world—and forestalled only by a solitary Tichbornite. How I knew that the gentleman in question deserved that appellation I say not; but I felt instinctively that such was the case. He had a shiny black frock-coat on, like a well-to-do artisan out for a holiday, and a roll of paper protruding from his pocket I rightly inferred to be a Tichborne petition for signature. As soon as we got on the ground, and I was enjoying the sensation of the crisp well rolled turf beneath my feet, a man hove in sight with a table, and this attracted a few observers. A gentleman in a light coat, too, who was serenely gazing over the hedge at the Kensington Park Cricket Club in the next ground, was, they informed me, Mr. Guildford Onslow. The presiding genius of the place, however, was Mrs. Warren, who, arrayed in a gown of emerald green—as though she were attending a Fenian meeting—bustled about in a state of intense excitement until the greengrocer's cart, which was to serve as a rostrum, had arrived. When this occurred, the table and half a dozen Windsor chairs were hoisted into it; another table was arranged below the van, with the Tichborne Petition outspread upon it; and I fancied that arrangements were complete.

Not so, however. The gentleman in the shiny coat and emerald green Mrs. Warren between them tin-tacked up a long scroll or "legend" along the rim of the van, consisting of the text from Psalm xxxv. 11:—"False witnesses did rise up against me. They laid to my charge things that I knew not." The association of ideas was grotesque, I know, but really as Mrs. Warren and the shiny artisan were nailing this strip to the greengrocer's van, they put me very much in mind of a curate and a lady friend "doing decorations" at Christmas or Eastertide. Nor was this all. When the "strange device" was duly tin-tacked, some workmen brought four long pieces of quartering, and a second strip of white calico with letters stuck on it was nailed to these; and when the stalwart fellows hoisted it in air and tied the two centre pieces of wood to the wheels of the greengrocer's cart, I found that it consisted of the Ninth Commandment. The self-sacrificing carpenters were to hold—and did hold—the outside poles banner-wise during the entire evening; and, with one slight exception, this banner with the strange device, No. 2, formed an appropriate, if not altogether ornamental background for the greengrocer's van. Knots of people had gathered during these proceedings; and I was confused to find that I was being generally pointed out as Mr. Onslow, that gentleman having retired to the privacy of Mr. Warren's neighbouring abode. Later on I was taken for a detective, because, in my innocence, I withdrew ever and anon from the crowd, and, sitting on a verdurous bank, jotted down a note in my pocket-book; but this got me into such bad odour by-and-by that I felt it better to desist, and trust to memory. Some of the smaller boys also averred that I was Sir Roger himself, but their youthful opinions were too palpably erroneous to carry weight.

In due course the van was occupied by Mr. Onslow, the Rev. Mr. Buckingham (about whom I felt, of course, very curious), my shining artisan, and a few others. A thin-faced gentleman, whose name I could not catch, was voted to the chair, and announced to us that he should go on talking awhile in order that Messrs. Onslow and Buckingham might "refresh," as they had each come from the country. This they did coram publico in the cart, while the chairman kept us amused. The wind, too, was blowing pretty freshly, and was especially hard on the Ninth Commandment, which gave considerable trouble to the holders of the props. It was directly in the teeth of the speaker, too—an arrangement which Mrs. Warren, in her zeal, had overlooked; and it was decided by common consent to "reverse the meeting"—that is, to turn the chairs of the speakers round, so that the Ninth Commandment was nowhere, and looked like an Egyptian hieroglyph, as the reversed letters showed dimly through the calico. The chairman eventually read to the meeting, which was now a tolerably full one, the form of petition which was to serve as the single resolution of the evening. I was struck with this gentleman's departure from conventional legal phraseology on this occasion. Instead of naming the cause célèbre "The Queen versus Castro" (it being written, as Sam Weller says, with a "wee") he termed it "The Queen via Castro!" The petition was as follows:—

"That in the trial at Bar in the Court of Queen's Bench, on an indictment of the Queen v. Castro, alias Arthur Orton, alias Sir Roger Charles Doughty Tichborne, Bart., for perjury, the jury, on the 28th day of February, 1874, brought in a verdict of guilty against him, declaring him to be Arthur Orton, and he was sentenced to fourteen years' penal servitude, which he is now undergoing.

"That your petitioners have reason to know and believe and are satisfied, both from the evidence produced at the trial and furnished since, and from their own personal knowledge that he is not Arthur Orton.

"That though 280 witnesses were examined at the said trial in his behalf, a very large number more, as your petitioners have been informed and believe, were also ready to be examined, but that funds were not available for the purpose, the defendant having been entirely dependent on the voluntary subscriptions of the public for his defence.

"That your petitioners submit that such a large number as 280 witnesses, most of whom gave positive evidence that the defendant was not Arthur Orton, and whose testimony in two instances only was questioned in a court of law—as against about 200 witnesses for the prosecution, whose evidence was chiefly of a negative character—was of itself enough to raise a doubt in the defendant's favour, of which doubt he ought to have had the benefit, in accordance both with the law and the custom of the country.

"That, under the circumstances, your petitioners submit that he had not a fair trial, and they pray your honourable House to take the matter into your serious consideration, with a view to memorialize her Majesty to grant a free pardon."

The Rev. Mr. Buckingham, a cheery gentleman who bore a remarkable resemblance to the celebrated Mr. Pickwick, rose to move the resolution; and I could not help noticing that, not content with the ordinary white tie of clerical life, he had "continued the idea downwards" in a white waistcoat, which rather altered the state of things. He spoke well and forcibly I should think for an hour, confining his remarks to the subject of "Sir Roger" not being Arthur Orton. He (Mr. Buckingham) belonged to some waterside mission at Wapping, and had known Arthur Orton familiarly from earliest boyhood. His two grievances were that his negative evidence had not been taken, and that he was now being continually waited on by "Jesuits," who temptingly held out cheques for 1000l. to him if he would only make affidavit that the man in Millbank was Arthur Orton.

Mr. Onslow, who seconded the resolution, however, made the speech of the evening, and was so enthusiastically received that he had to recommence several times after glowing perorations. The burden of Mr. Onslow's prophecy was the unfairness of the trial; and his "bogies" were detectives, just as Mr. Buckingham's were Jesuits. The Jean Luie affair was the most infernal "plant" in the whole case; and he read records of conflicting evidence which really were enough to make one pack up one's traps and resolve on instant emigration. He was, however, certainly right on one point. He said that such meetings were safety-valves which prevented revolution. No doubt this was a safety-valve. It amused the speakers, and Mrs. Warren and the glazed artisan; and it could do nobody any possible harm. Whether it was likely to do the man of Millbank any good was quite another matter, and one which, of course, it was quite beside my purpose to discuss. There was a deal of—to me—very interesting speaking; for I gained new light about the case, and stood until my legs fairly ached listening to Messrs. Buckingham and Onslow.

When the editor of the Tichborne Gazette claimed an innings it was another matter; and—perhaps with lack of esprit de corps—I decamped. I only saw this gentleman gesticulating as I left the field; but the rate at which he was getting up the steam promised a speech that would last till nightfall.

As I went off the ground I was struck with the clever way in which a London costermonger will turn anything and everything to account. One of them was going about with a truck of cherries, crying out, "Sir Roger Tichborne cherries. Penny a lot!"

There was no symptom of overt opposition, though opponents were blandly invited to mount the waggon and state their views; but there was a good deal of quiet chaff on the outskirts of the crowd, which is the portion I always select on such occasions for my observation. On the whole, however, the assembly was pretty unanimous; and though it never assumed the dimensions of a "monster meeting," the fact that even so many people could be got together for such a purpose seemed to me sufficiently a sign of the times to deserve annotation in passing.

CHAPTER XIII.

SUNDAY IN A PEOPLE'S GARDEN.

I have often thought that an interesting series of articles might be written on the subject of "London out of Church," dealing with the manners and customs of those people who patronize no sort of religious establishment on the Sunday.

I have seen pretty well all the typical phases of religious London and London irreligious; but these would rather be characterized as non-religious than as irreligious folks. They do not belong to any of the varied forms of faith; in fact faith is from their life a thing apart. It is in this negative way that they are interesting. Sunday is with them only a regularly recurring Bank Holiday. It would be interesting to know what they do with it. A special difficulty, however, exists for me in any such inquiry, resulting from the fact that, in my capacity of clerical casual, I am pretty generally engaged on the Sunday; and when I am not, my Day of Rest is too valuable to be devoted to any of the manifold forms of metropolitan Sabbath-breaking. I have a great idea that parsons ought to be frequently preached at; and so I generally go to some church or chapel when out of harness myself; and if "hearing sermons" constitute the proper carrying out of the things promised and vowed on my behalf at baptism I must have undergone as complete a course of Christian discipline as any man in Christendom, for I have been preached at by everybody from Roman Catholics down to Walworth Jumpers and Plumstead Peculiars!

But impressed with anxiety to know about the doings of the non-Church-goers, I have for a long time cast sheep's eyes at the Sunday League, and more than once definitely promised to join one of their Sunday outings; but I am strongly of Tom Hood's opinion that—

The man who's fond precociously of stirring

Must be a spoon.

The Sunday League commence their excursions at untimely hours; and it is a cardinal point in my creed that Sunday ought to be a Day of Rest, at all events in the matter of breakfast in bed. I missed the excursion to Shakspeare's House in this way, and the paper on the Bard of Avon, full of the genius loci, must have been as edifying as a sermon. So, too, on a recent Sunday, when the Sunday League on their way to Southend got mixed up with the Volunteer Artillery going to Shoebury, I was again found wanting. But still the old penchant remained, and Sunday was my last free one for a long time. How could I utilize it? I had it; I would go to the People's Garden at Willesden. I had heard that certain very mild forms of Sabbath breaking prevailed there. I would go and see for myself.

I had been at the People's Garden twice before; once on the occasion of a spiritualistic picnic, and once, more recently, at a workmen's flower show; and felt considerable interest in the place, especially as the People had been polite enough to send me a season ticket, so that I was one of the People myself.

This People's Garden was not exactly a Paradise yet, though it is in a fair way of becoming one. It is a spot of some fifty acres reclaimed from the scrubbiest part of Wormwood Scrubbs, and made the focus of a club of working men, of whom I am very proud indeed to be one. Indeed, I do not see why throughout the remainder of this article I should not use the first person plural. I will. Well, then, we secured this spot, and we have got in the first place one of the finest—I believe the finest—dancing platforms in England, for we as a community are Terpsichorean, though I, as an individual, am not. I felt it necessary to give up dancing when my weight turned the balance at fourteen stone odd. Then we can give our friends refreshments from a bottle of champagne down to tea and cresses. We have all sorts of clubs, dramatic and otherwise, and rather plume ourselves on having put up our proscenium ourselves, that is with our own hands and hammers and nails. There is the great advantage of being a Working Man or one of the People. If you had been with me that Sunday you would have seen a glow of conscious pride suffusing my countenance as I read the bills of our last amateur performance, consisting of the "Waterman" and "Ici on parle Français," played on the boards which I, in my corporate capacity, had planed, and sawn, and nailed. My route last Sunday lay across the crisp sward of the Scrubbs; and it was quite a pleasure to be able to walk there without danger of falling pierced by the bullet of some erratic volunteer; for there are three butts on Wormwood Scrubbs, which I examined with minuteness on Sunday, and was exercised to see by marks on the brickwork how very wide of the target a volunteer's shot can go. I wonder there is not a wholesale slaughter of cattle in the neighbouring fields. The garden lies on the other side of the Great Western Railway, across which I had to trespass in order to get to it. But the man in charge regarded me with indulgence, for was I not a working man and a "mate?" The portion of the garden abutting on the rail is still unreclaimed prairie. The working men have begun at the top of the hill, and are working downwards.

There is a good-sized refreshment-room at the entrance, with all the paraphernalia of secretary's office, &c.; and this large room, which is exceedingly useful in wet weather, opens right on to the dancing-platform, in the centre of which is a pretty kiosk for the band. We have no gas; but tasty paraffin lamps at frequent intervals give sufficient light, and, at all events, do not smell worse than modern metropolitan gas. There is a large tent standing en permanence during the summer for flower shows, and terrace after terrace of croquet lawns, all of which it will, I fear, shock some Sabbatarian persons to learn were occupied on that Sunday afternoon, and the balls kept clicking like the week-day shots of the erratic riflemen on the Scrubbs. I had a young lady with me who was considerably severe on the way in which we workmen male and female, handled our mallets. There was, I confess, something to be desired in the way of position; and one group of German artisans in the corner lawn made more noise than was necessary, howling and uttering all sorts of guttural interjections, as though they were playing polo at least, or taking part in a bull-fight, instead of in croquet—beloved of curates.

And then the flowers. We are making the desert blossom like the rose. It is really marvellous to see what has been done in so short a time. We might have been a society of market gardeners. We don't get so many flowers along the walk of life, we working men; so that we want to see a bit of green sward and a flower or two on Sundays. There is a capital gymnasium, and our observation of the young men who disport themselves there would lead an uninitiated observer to form the opinion that the normal condition of humanity was upside down. The way one youthful workman hung by his legs on the trapeze was positively Darwinian to behold. Swings attracted the attention of the ladies; and I regret to say that the particular young lady I escorted—who was of the mature age of twelve—passed most of the afternoon in a state of oscillation, and was continually adjuring me to push her.

An interesting addition to the gardens—our gardens— since I was last there, consisted of a cage of meditative monkeys, four in number, who were stationed so near the gymnasium as inevitably to suggest the Darwinian parallel. They had their gymnasium too, and swung gaily on their tree-trunks at such times as they were not engaged in eating or entomological researches. I could not help thinking what a deprivation it was to the gymnasts that, in course of evolution, we have lost our tails. They would have been so convenient on the horizontal bar, where that persevering young workman was still engaged in the pursuit of apoplexy by hanging head downwards. Soon after we got there an excellent band commenced playing, not in the kiosk, lest we should be beguiled into dancing. The first piece was a slow movement, which could scarcely have been objected to by any Sabbatarian, unless he was so uncompromising as to think all trumpets wrong. The second was the glorious march from "Athalie;" and then— my blood runs cold as I write it—a sort of pot pourri, in the midst of which came the "Dutchman's Little Wee Dog," considerably disguised in the way of accompaniment and variation, I own, but the "Little Wee Dog" beyond a doubt. Then I understood why the band was not in the kiosk; for, fourteen stone though I be, I felt all my toes twiddling inside my boots at that time as wickedly as though it had been Monday morning. There were fourteen or fifteen loud brass instruments, with a side and bass drum and cymbals. All these were playing the "Little Wee Dog" to their brazen hearts' content, and only one gentleman on a feeble piccolo-flute trying to choke their impiety by tootling out a variation, just as the stringed instruments in the glorious "Reformation Symphony" of Mendelssohn try in vain to drown with their sensuous Roman airs the massive chords of the old Lutheran chorale—"Ein feste Burg ist unser Gott." I really could not bear it any longer, and was rising to go when they stopped; and as the gentleman who played the circular bass got outside his portentous instrument, I found he had a little wee dog of his own who retired into the bell of the big trumpet when his master laid it on the grass. Perhaps it was in honour of this minute animal the air was selected. However, I could not lend myself to such proceedings; so I bribed my youthful charge with a twopenny bottle of frothless ginger beer to come out of her swing and return to the regions of orthodoxy. The Teutonic gentlemen were still hooting and yelling as we crossed the corner of their croquet lawn, until I expected to see them attack one another with the mallets and use the balls for missile warfare; but it was only their peculiar way of enjoying themselves.

My little friend described the action of our working men in the croquet lawn as "spooning," and also drew my attention to the fact that two lovers were doing the same on a seat, in the approved fashion prevalent among us workmen, with the manly arm around the taper waist coram publico. This arrangement is quite a necessity with us. We should often like to forego it, especially when little boys make rude remarks about us in the street; but it is expected of us, and we submit.

The sun was beginning to sink grandly over that magnificent panorama of country visible from Old Oak Common as we passed down the hill and again violated the bye-laws of the Great Western Railway Company. The spires of the West End churches were bathed in the soft glow of departing day; and in the distance the Crystal Palace glittered like a fairy bower. We got back after making a little détour on account of some gentlemen who were bathing in a very Paradisiacal way indeed—we actually got back in time to go to church like good Christians; and I do not think either of us felt much the worse for the hours we had spent in the People's Garden— save and except the wicked Little Wee Dog!

CHAPTER XIV.

UTILIZING THE YOUNG LADIES.

Time was when it was accepted as an axiom that young ladies had no object in life but to be ornamental—no mission but matrimony. The "accomplishments" were the sum total of a genteel education, though charged as "extras" on the half-yearly accounts; and all the finished creature had to do, after once "coming out," was to sit down and languidly wait for an eligible suitor.

Times changed. And, in England, when we make a change, we always rush violently into an opposite extreme. Woman had a mission, and no mistake. Now it was the franchise and Bloomer costume, just as aforetime it was the pianoforte and general fascination. Blue spectacles rose in the market. We had lady doctors and female lawyers. The only marvel is that there was no agitation for feminine curates.

Then came reaction again. It was discovered that woman could be educated without becoming a bluestocking, and practical without wearing bloomers or going in for the suffrage. Still holding to the wholesome principle that "woman is not undeveloped man, but diverse," the real friends of the gentler sex discovered a hundred and one ways in which it could employ itself usefully and remuneratively. It was no longer feared lest, as Sydney Smith puts it, if a woman learnt algebra she would "desert her infant for a quadratic equation;" and the University of Cambridge soon fell in with the scheme for the Higher Education of Women; while Miss Faithfull, and several others, organized methods for employing practically the talents which education could only develope in a general way. It was to one of these methods—not Miss Faithfull's—my attention was drawn a short time since by a letter in the daily papers. The Victoria Press and International Bureau are faits accomplis, and it is well that efforts should be made for utilizing in other ways that interesting surplus in our female population. Mrs. Fernando, of Warwick Gardens, Kensington, has set herself to the solution of the problem, and the shape her method takes is a Technical Industrial School for Women.

The object and aim of the institution is to examine, plan, and organize such branches of industrial avocation as are applicable to females, and open up new avocations of useful industry compatible with the intellectual and mechanical capabilities of the sex, not forgetting their delicacy, and the untutored position of females for practical application in all industrial labour: to give the same facilities to females as are enjoyed by males, in collective classes for special training or special preparation for passing examinations open to women, thereby to enable them to earn their livelihood with better success than is attainable by mere school education only: to give special training to females to qualify them to enter special industrial avocations with such competency as will enable them to be successful in obtaining employment: to apprentice females, or to employ them directly into trades where such employers will receive them beyond the limits of the industrial school and where females can be constantly employed, such as in composing, embossing, illuminating, black-bordering, ticket-writing, circular-addressing, flower-making, flower-cultivating, &c.

Being a determined sceptic in the matter of prospectuses, I determined to go and see for myself the working of this scheme, which looked so well on paper. The Institution occupies a large house exactly opposite Dr. Punshon's chapel: and there is no chance of one's missing it, for it is placarded with announcements like a hoarding at election time. I found Mrs. Fernando an exceedingly practical lady, doing all the work of the institution herself, with the exception of a few special subjects such as botany, &c., which are conducted by her husband. There are no "assistants," therefore, or deputed interests, the bane of so many high-priced schools.

These classes are held in the evening from seven to nine o'clock, and are intended for ladies above the age of fifteen years, who may be engaged through the day in various occupations, and for such as suffer from neglected education, and who wish conveniently and economically to improve themselves, without being necessitated to mix with their juniors in day-schools. These classes prepare ladies to meet the qualifications necessary to enter clerkships and other official departments; to bring them also to a standard to meet the qualifications for post offices and telegraph departments; and also to pass certain examinations open to them. The charge is only 2s. per week—8s. per month—1l. 4s. per quarter. The first course embraces spelling, reading, writing, arithmetic, history, geography, and grammar. The second course consists of advanced arithmetic, book-keeping and commercial instruction, so as to qualify women to take posts of responsibility with marked success. The third course consists of French, for practical usefulness. The fourth course embraces simple or technical training in such departments as are available within the limits of the class-room—to qualify women to enter industrial avocations with competency, and to make them successful in obtaining employment. This department will be extended to greater usefulness as conveniences arise, by apprenticing the girls or employing them directly in trades beyond the limits of the class-room, where employers will receive them, or where women could be consistently engaged—as, for instance, in the work of compositors, ticket-writers, embossers, &c. &c.

The two classes with which I was brought into contact were the book-keeping and embossing. In the former, more than a dozen young ladies were being initiated in the mysteries of single and double entry, and they posted up their books in a way that made me feel very much ashamed of myself, when I thought how incapable I should be of doing anything half so useful. Many girls go from this department to be book-keepers at large hotels, places of business, &c.

I then went to the embossing room, where six presses were being worked by as many young ladies, one in an adjoining room being reserved for Mrs. Fernando, who not only tells her pupils what to do, but shows them how to do it. The gilding and colouring of the stamps was most elaborate; two monograms of the Queen's name and that of the Empress Eugénie being perfect marvels of artistic and intricate workmanship. Every process, from mixing the colours up to burnishing the gold, was gone through in detail by this practical lady and her intelligent pupils for my special edification, and I passed out a much wiser and certainly not a sadder man than I entered this veritable hive of human bees.

No expense was spared in the education of these girls, low as are the terms they pay. I saw quite a ruinous heap of spoilt envelopes and fashionable sheets of thick cream-laid; for they have to make their experiments on the best material, and the slightest alteration in the position of a pin where the stamping process has to be several times repeated spoils the whole result. Mrs. Fernando has also introduced envelope and circular addressing by women, as a department of female industrial work in the Technical Industrial School for Women, where a number of females are employed between the hours of ten and four o'clock, receiving satisfactory remuneration. She provides the females employed in this department evening classes free of charge, to improve themselves in general education.

I am an intense admirer of the female sex in general, and young ladies in particular, but really when I came away, leaving my pretty book-keepers and embossers to resume their normal work, and saw the numbers of young ladies sitting listlessly over misnamed "work" at the window, or walking languidly nowhither in the streets, I thought that, without losing any of their attractions, nay, adding a new claim to the many existing ones on our regard, they might with great advantage take a turn at Mrs. Fernando's sixpenny lessons in technical education.

CHAPTER XV.

FAIRLOP FRIDAY.

Amongst those customs "more honoured in the breach than
the observance" which are rapidly being stamped out by
the advancing steps of civilization, are the institutions
which we can yet remember as so popular in the days of
our childhood, called pleasure fairs. Like that social dodo
in a higher section of society, the "three-bottle man," with
the stupid Bacchanalian usages of which he was the
embodiment, these fairs are slowly but surely disappearing
as education spreads among the masses of the people. In
the country a fair is a simple and a necessary thing enough.
At certain seasons of the year, according to the staple
commodities for the sale of which the assemblage was
originally instituted, our bucolic friends gather at early
morning with the products of their farms; a good deal of
noisy buying, selling, and barter takes place. Later in the
day the ladies invest their profits in a little mild finery, or
in simple pleasures; and, later still, when the public-houses
have done their work, comes a greater or lesser amount of
riot, rude debauchery, and vice; and then, voilà tout—the
fair is over for a year. One can easily imagine the result of
the transition when, from the quiet country, the fair
removes to the city or suburb. In such places every
utilitarian element is wanting, and the gilt ginger-bread and
gewgaws are only a speciously innocent attraction towards
the drinking and dancing booth where the mischief is done.
Well-wishers to society are unromantic enough not to
regret the decidedly waning glories of these gatherings,
from the great Bartholomew Fair itself down to that which,
on the Friday of which I write, converted many miles of

thoroughfare at the East End of London, as well as one of the prettiest forest scenes still surrounding the metropolis, into a vast al fresco tavern, where the "worship of Bacchus" was as freely indulged as in any heathen temple of ancient times.

Fairlop Fair—which has not yet died out, though beginning to show satisfactory signs of decay—commenced its existence, innocently enough, about a century ago. At that time Mr. Day, a shipbuilder, wishing to have a day's outing in the forest with his friends and employés, fitted up a vessel on wheels, fully rigged, in which he conveyed his picnic party to Hainault Forest, on the outskirts of which, some distance from Ilford, stood the famous Fairlop Oak. The holiday became an annual custom, and gradually changed its character from the simple gathering of a master and his men into regular saturnalia; during which, each year, from the first Friday in July, over the ensuing Saturday and Sunday, riot and debauchery reigned supreme in the glades of the forest and the eastern districts of London. The example set by Mr. Day was followed by other ship, boat, and barge builders, but of late years, more particularly by the mast and block makers, riggers, shipwrights, and shipyard labourers; and more recently still by the licensed victuallers. Finding the custom good for trade, the publicans formed a society for building or hiring these boats on wheels, which, covered with flags, and provided each with a band of music and filled with revellers, annually make their progress into Hainault Forest. They go no longer, alas! to Fairlop Oak—for that is numbered with the things of the past—but now to Barking side, where, at the Maypole Inn, the festivities of Fairlop Fair are still kept up.

These ship and boat cars attract immense multitudes along
the Mile End, Bow, and Whitechapel Roads, down as far
as Aldgate; the crowd assemble in the morning to see the
holiday people start on their expedition. The most
remarkable sight, however, is at night, when the "boats"
return lighted with coloured lanterns, red and green fires,
&c.; and at every public-house along the road similar fires
are burnt, and brass bands stationed to strike up as the cars
pass, and stop at certain favoured establishments "for the
good of the house." Anxious to witness the fading glories
of Fairlop Friday myself, before the advancing tide of
civilization shall have done their inevitable work upon
them, I sallied forth to the East End, and walking along one
of the finest approaches to London, from Aldgate, by
Whitechapel, to Bow and Stratford Churches, succeeded in
realizing more completely than ever before two facts: first,
how gigantic is the population of the East End of London;
and, secondly, how little is required to amuse and attract it.
There were only two of the "boats" sent to the Forest that
year. Their return could gratify the sight of these people
but for a single instant; yet there, from early dusk almost to
succeeding daylight, those working men, literally "in their
thousands"—and not in the Trafalgar Square diminutive of
that expression—gathered to gratify themselves with the
sight of the pageant. In comparison, the "Bœuf Gras,"
which annually sends the gamins of Paris insane, is really a
tasteful and refined exhibition. Yet there they were,
women, men, and children—infants in arms, too, to a
notable extent—swarming along that vast thoroughfare,
boozing outside the public-houses, investing their pence in
"scratch-backs" and paper noses, feathers and decorations,
as do their betters on the course at Epsom, under the feeble
excuse of "waiting for the boats." The first arrived en
retour at Stratford Church about ten o'clock; and certainly
the appearance of the lumbering affair as it moved along,

with its rigging brought out by means of coloured fires, lanterns, and lamps, was odd enough. As soon as it passed me at Stratford, I jumped outside one of the Bow and Stratford omnibuses, and so had an opportunity of following, or rather joining in, the procession as far as Whitechapel, where the "boat" turned off into Commercial Road. For the whole of that space the footway was filled with one seething mass of humanity, and the publicans were driving a rattling trade outside and inside their establishments. As the glare of the coloured fires lighted up the pale faces of the crowd with a ghastly hue, and I heard the silly and too often obscene remarks bandied between the bystanders and the returning revellers, I could not help agitating the question, whether it would not be possible to devise some innocent recreation, with a certain amount of refinement in it, to take the place of these—to say the best—foolish revelries. In point of fact, they are worse than foolish. Not only was it evident that the whole affair from beginning to end, as far as adults were concerned, was an apotheosis of drink; but amongst another section of the populace, the boys and girls, or what used to be boys and girls—for, as the Parisians say, "Il n'y a plus de garçons"—one must have been blind indeed not to see the mischief that was being done on those East End pavements; done more thoroughly perhaps, certainly on a vastly larger scale, than in the purlieus of the forest. It is an uninviting subject to dwell upon; but one could understand all about baby farms, and Lock Hospitals, and Contagious Diseases Acts, out there that July night, in the crowded streets of East London.

It would be unfair to dilate upon these evils, and not to mention an organization which, for the last ten years, has been seeking to remedy the mischief. Some hundreds of working men of a more serious stamp, aided by a few gentlemen and ministers of various denominations, form themselves into small bands of street preachers, and sallying forth in a body, hold services and preach sermons at the most populous points of the Fairlop route. Being curious to see the effect of their bold labours—for it requires immense "pluck" to face a Whitechapel mob—I joined one of these detachments, where the Rev. Newman Hall was the preacher. Before starting, this gentleman gave it as the result of his long experience with the British workman that there is no use in waiting for him to come to church. If the church is to do anything with him, it must go out and meet him in the streets and fields, as it originally did. Mr. Hall gave some amusing illustrations of his experience at Hastings, where, for several weeks, he had been preaching on the beach to large congregations. He was idling there, he said, for health's sake, and one evening, seeing a number of men loafing about, he proposed to one of them that he should give them an address. This gentleman declined the address, but added, characteristically enough, "If ye'll gie me some beer I'll drink it." Two others, being asked if they would listen, "didn't know as they would." Under these unpromising auspices Mr. Hall began, and, attracting a crowd, was "moved on" by a policeman. A gentleman who recognised him proposed an adjournment to the beach, and there a sermon was preached, and has been repeated by Mr. Hall on several occasions, with a congregation of thousands. He has a peculiar knack of speaking in a tongue "understanded of the people," and his address to the Fairlop crowd on that Friday night "told" considerably. At its conclusion he quietly put on his hat, dropped into the crowd, and went his way; but the tone of criticism amongst his hearers was very favourable, and I quite agree with the critics that it's a pity we haven't "more parsons like that." It is not, however, simply by religious zeal such a want as that to which I allude is to be supplied, but by the substitution of some sensible recreation for the low attractions of the beershop and gin-palace. It is a problem worthy of our deepest thinkers: "What shall we offer our huge populations in exchange for the silly pageant even now being enacted in the outskirts of the metropolis—which may well be taken to embody the pastime of the lower orders—Fairlop Fair?"

CHAPTER XVI.

A CHRISTMAS DIP.

There are few more exhilarating things, on a breezy spring morning, than a spurt across that wonderful rus in urbe— Kensington Gardens and Hyde Park—for a prospective dip in the Serpentine, where, at specified hours every morning and evening, water-loving London is privileged to disport itself in its congenial element. So congenial is it, in fact, that some enthusiastic individuals do not limit themselves to warm summer mornings, or the cooler ones of springtide and autumn, but bathe all the year round—even, it is said, when a way for their manœuvres has to be cut through the ice. Skirting the north bank of the Serpentine at morning or evening in the summer, the opposite shore appears absolutely pink with nude humanity, the younger portion dancing and gambolling very much after the manner of Robinson Crusoe's cannibals. The bathers occasionally look a great deal better out of their integuments than in them. Not from this class, however, do your all-the-year-round bathers come. The Arab is an exotic—a child of the Sun, loving not to disport himself in water the temperature of which shocks his tentative knuckles, as he dips them in the unaccustomed element. His wardrobe, again, is too much after the fashion of that pertaining to Canning's needy knife-grinder to make an al fresco toilette other than embarrassing. From the all-the-year-round bathers, as a nucleus, there has grown up, within the last few years, the Serpentine Swimming Club; and on Christmas-day in the morning they have an annual match open to all comers—though, it need scarcely be said, patronized only by those whom, for brevity's sake, we may term all-rounders.

Now, I had often heard of this Christmas-day match, and as often, on Christmas-eve, made up my mind to go; but the evening's resolution faded away, as such resolutions have only too often been known to do, before the morning's light. This year, however—principally, I believe, because I had been up very late the previous night—I struggled out of bed before dawn, and steered for the Serpentine. A crescent moon was shining, and stars studded the clear spaces between ominous patches of cloud. A raw, moist wind was blowing, and on the muddy streets were evident traces of a recent shower. I had no notion that the gates of Kensington Gardens were open so early; and the sensation was novel as I threaded the devious paths in morning dawn, and saw the gas still alight along the Bayswater Road. A solitary thrush was whistling his Christmas carol as I struggled over the inundated sward; presently the sun threw a few red streaks along the East, over the Abbey Tower; but, until I had passed the Serpentine Bridge, not a single human being met my gaze. There, however, I found some fifty men, mostly with a "sporting" look about them. The ubiquitous boy was there, playing at some uncomfortable game in the puddles round the seats. The inevitable dog stood pensively by the diving board; and when, by-and-by straggling all-rounders came and took their morning header, the quadruped rushed after them to the very edge of the water, as though he had been a distinguished member of the Humane Society. He shirked the element itself, however, as religiously as though he had been one of London's great unwashed. In the pause which preceded the race, I learned, from the Honorary Secretary of the Serpentine Swimming Club, particulars of its history and of the race itself. For six years it had been merely a club race; but last year it was thrown open. Strangely enough the race had never been won twice by one man, though the competitors had been pretty much the same every year. I also conversed with one of the intending competitors, who showed me on his breast with pardonable pride, five medals of the Royal Humane Society, awarded for saving life in cases of danger from drowning. The wearer was a Professor of Natation, and told me that, among his pupils, he had an old lady sixty-seven years of age, who had just commenced, and was able to swim some twenty yards already. The brave old lady's example may do good; though it is to be hoped that she may not, at her time of life, be compelled to exert her art for her own protection.

Names were now called, and fourteen competitors presented themselves—a motley group, clad for the most part in trousers, horse-rug, and wide-awake, or, more simply still, in Ulster frieze coat only. The group of spectators had by this time grown to some hundreds, nearly all directly interested in the noble art; and the dips became fast and frequent. Two flags were placed in the water at the distance of 100 yards from the diving board; on this slender platform fourteen shivering specimens of humanity ranged themselves, and at the word of the starter plunged into the water with that downward plunge so incomprehensible to the uninitiated. A short, sharp struggle followed, the competitors swimming with the sidelong movement and obstreperous puffing which likens the swimmer so closely to the traditional grampus. Eventually one of the group is seen heading the others, and breasting the water with calm and equable stroke in the old-fashioned style. He reaches the flag a full yard before his nearest antagonist. Numbers two and three, following, are about half a yard apart. The others come in pretty much in a group. All were picked men, and there were no laggards. The names of the winners were as follows:—1. Ainsworth; 2. Quartermain; 3. H. Coulter. The time occupied in the race was 1 min. 24 sec. Immediately after the race there was a rapid re-assumption of rugs and Ulsters, though some of the more hardy walked about in the garb of Nature, making everybody shiver who looked at them. Finally, the prizes, consisting of three handsome medals, were distributed by Mr. H. Bedford, who stood on a park seat and addressed a few genial words to each of the successful candidates; then, with a cheer, and frequent wishes for a Merry Christmas, the assembly resolved itself into its component parts.

I had taken my accustomed cold tub before coming out, yet each of these fourteen devoted men appeared to me as a hero. They were not Herculean individuals: several of them were mere youths. Some of the all-rounders were grey-headed men, but there was about them all a freshness and ruddiness which showed that their somewhat severe regimen agreed with them. Fresh from such a Spartan exhibition, everything seemed very late and Sybaritic in my domestic establishment, and I could not help revolving in my mind the question, what would one of these hardy all-the-year-rounders think of me if he knew I was ever guilty of such a malpractice as breakfast in bed? It is a novel method; but there are many worse ways of inaugurating the Great Holiday than by taking—what it had been a novel sensation for me even to witness—a Christmas Dip in the Serpentine.

CHAPTER XVII.

BOXING-DAY ON THE STREETS.

Boxing-day in the London streets, and especially a wet Boxing-day, can scarcely fail to afford us some tableaux vivants illustrative of English metropolitan life. In a metaphorical and technical sense, Boxing-day is always more or less "wet"—generally more, and not less; but this year the expression is used climatically, and in its first intention. Christmas-eve of the year about which I write was bright and springlike; Christmas-day dismal, dark, and un-Christmas-like; but Boxing-day that year was essentially muggy, sloppy, drizzly, and nasty. A day to avoid the London streets if you want to take a romantic Rosa-Matilda view of London life; but the very day of all others, if you wish to see real London as it is. Boxing-day will inevitably be "wetter" in every sense than usual this year, internally and externally. So let us commence our series of living pictures at ten o'clock in the morning.

Suppose we begin with something that shall bear reference to the past festival—the eve and the day of the Great Birth, recollect. See, here is Grotto Passage, Marylebone, and at its extremity Paradise Street—the names sound promising, but alas for the reality! We are going to turn for a moment into the Marylebone Police Court, where Mr. D'Eyncourt is dispensing summary justice to the accumulations of the last two days. These are the people who have been spending Christmas-eve, Christmas-day, and some portion of Boxing-day already in the police-cells. Let us take one as a typical case. Let that poor little eight-year-old Arab step down from the dock and go off with his mother, who, we hope, will take the magistrate's excellent advice, and keep the child from begging—that is why he has spent Christmas in the cells—lest he be sent to a school for eight years, and she have to pay for him—God help her! she does not look as though she could afford very high terms. A bruised and bleeding woman, not young or good-looking, enters the box with her head bound up. Her lord and master confronts her in the dock. It is the "old, old story." A drop of drink yesterday—the day of the Great Nativity, never forget—series of "drops of drink" all day long; and, at five o'clock, just when gentility was beginning to think of dinner, the kitchen poker was used with frightful effect. A triangular cut over the right eye, and another in the dangerous neighbourhood of the left ear, administered with that symbol of domestic bliss, the kitchen poker, sends the wife doubled up into a corner, with an infant of two years old in her arms. The head of the family goes out for a walk after his exertions. The woman lies there bleeding until the neighbours hear her "mourning," as she terms it—the result being that the lord and master's "constitutional" is cut short by a policeman, and the happy pair are this morning separated for six months, at the expiration of which period Paterfamilias is to find surety for another six months' good behaviour. Such, starred round with endless episodes of "drunk and disorderly," "foul language," and so on, is our first tableau this Boxing-day. It is not a pleasant one. Let us pass on.

Along Oxford Street, despite the Bank Holidays Act, many shops are open, chiefly those devoted to the sale of articles eatable, drinkable, and avoidable; these last being in the shape of chemists' shops, and shops for Christmas presents—to be shunned by miserly old bachelors. Let us turn into the British Museum and see sensible, decorous Boxing-day there. At the corner of Museum Street there is a lively itinerant musician, evidently French, who plays the fiddle until his bow tumbles all to pieces, but he goes on playing with the stick as though nothing had happened. When his instrument has come entirely to grief he turns to a clarionet, which he carries under his arm, and plays "Mourir pour la Patrie" with extraordinary vocal effect and irreverent gestures. Punch-and-Judy is largely attended at the other end; Punch is kitchen-pokering his wife, too, like the gentleman we have just left; but we pass in with the crowds to the Museum itself. Halting a moment in the reading-room, to jot down there a few notes, one is struck with the scanty show of students. They are spending Boxing-day somewhere else. Passing through the little knot of people who are permitted by special order to come as far as the door of the reading-room, and who evidently regard the readers as some curious sort of animal exhibited for their special delectation—perhaps the book-"worm" of which they have heard so much—we go up the stairs, now thronged with crowds in unwonted broadcloth and fragrant with the odour of the inevitable orange. Next to the drinking fountain, which is decidedly the chief attraction, comes the gorilla, and then the extinct animals. One stout old lady, contemplating the megatherium and mastodon, inquires in what parts "them creeturs" are to be found, and seems considerably damped by being informed that Nature has been "out" of such articles for several æons. The mummies, with the bones of their toes sticking out, also come in for a large share of admiration. There is a good deal of rough flirtation going on; but, on the whole, the pleasure is rather of a placid order, though still contrasting favourably with the settled gloom visible on the faces of the attendants in the various galleries. How well we can understand such gloom! How utterly hateful must that giant elk and overgrown extinct armadillo be to a man condemned to spend a lifetime in their close contemplation!

But let us pass on to the artistic Boxing-day keepers at the National Gallery. The walk will take us through the Seven Dials, and can scarcely fail to be suggestive. It is now one o'clock, the traditional hour of dinner; and in Broad Street, St. Giles's, I see, for the first time to-day, the human barometer evidently standing at "much wet." A gentleman in a grey coat and red comforter, who bears palpable signs of having been more than once on his back, has just reached that perplexing point of inebriety when he can walk quickly or run, but cannot stand still or walk steadily. He is pursued by small children, mostly girls, after whom, every now and then, he runs hopelessly, to their intense gratification. The poultry and bird shops in the Seven Dials are objects of some attraction, though they savour too much of "business" to be in very great force. The National Gallery is crowded with unaccustomed art students. There is about the visitors a quiet air of doing their duty, and being determined to go through with it at any price. One brazen-faced quean speculates audibly—in fact, very audibly—as to which "picter" she should choose if she had her "pick," and decent matrons pass the particularly High

Art of the old masters with half-averted gaze, as though they were not quite sure of doing right in countenancing such exhibitions. Hogarth's evergreen "Marriage à la Mode" is a great centre of attraction, and the youngsters never tire of listening, as "with weeping and with laughter still is the story told" over and over again by their elders. Gainsborough's likeness of Mrs. Siddons is also a great favourite; but perhaps the picture that attracts most attention is Van Eyck's "John Arnolfini, of Lucca, and his Wife." The gentleman wears a portentous hat, which tickled the fancy of the Boxing-day people immensely. There were great speculations too among them as to whether the curious Tuscan pictures at the top of the stairs were "needlework" or not. Still, who shall say that these visitors were not the better for their visit, surrounded as they were by forms of beauty on every side, even if they did not examine them with the eyes of connoisseurs?

Boxing-day on the river: The silent street is almost deserted. There is no rush for the Express boat to-day. It is literally the streets—muddier and sloppier than the Thames itself—that are the attraction. Some little boys are making the trip from Westminster to London Bridge as a treat; and it is an intense joke with them to pretend to be dreadfully seasick. Boxing-day in the City is synonymous with stagnation. It is a howling wilderness, with nobody to howl. On the Metropolitan Railway I verily believe travellers were tripping it like the little boys on board the penny boat. And so theatre time draws on, and the interest of Boxing-day grows to a climax. Soon after five o'clock groups furtively collect outside the playhouses, half-ashamed of being so early, but gathering courage from numbers to form the disorderly queue, so unlike that of a Parisian theatre. Boxing-night in the theatres others will describe. It is too much to expect of one whose mission has been the whole day long on the streets.

CHAPTER XVIII.

THE VIGIL OF THE DERBY.

In those days—happily now gone by—when public strangulation was the mode in Merry England, there was always an evident fascination appertaining to the spot where, on the morrow, some guilty wretch was to expiate his crimes on the gallows. Long before the erection of that elegant apparatus commenced, and generally on a Sunday evening, when decent citizens had newly come from houses of God, where they had heard the message of life, crowds began to collect on that central spot in the heart of the great City dedicated to sudden and violent death. The coming event seemed to cast its shadow before; and throughout the night the roisterer or belated traveller made a détour to visit the human shambles. I confess to having felt the attraction. I could not then bring myself to be present at the strangulation proper; so, as the nearest approach to a "sensation," sometimes visited Newgate on the eve of the victim elect's last morrow. In the same way, being unfortunate enough to be London-bound on the day of our great annual holiday, and having heard graphic accounts of the Downs on the eve of the Derby, I determined that year, as I could not go to the race by day, to visit the racecourse by night. Let me own the soft impeachment: I am not a racing man—not in any degree "horsey." When I do go to the Derby it is to see the bipeds rather than the quadrupeds; to empty the hamper from Fortnum and Mason's, rather than to study the "names, weights, and colours of the riders" on the "c'rect card." If you prefer to have the sentiment in Latin—and there is no doubt Latin does go much farther than English—I am not one of those "quos pulverem Olympicum collegisse juvat," except in so far that "homo sum; nihil humanum alienum a me puto." It was to see humanity under a new aspect, I took the last train to Epsom on the eve of the Derby.

In order to combine business with pleasure, and economy with both, I took a third-class ticket at Victoria, and was fortunate enough to find a compartment already partially occupied by a nigger troupe. In this, which under ordinary circumstances I should have avoided, I took my seat, and was regaled all the way down with choice morceaux from the répertoire of my musical friends. The "talking man" of the party, too, enlivened the proceedings by anxiously inquiring of the porters at the different stations what they would take in the way of refreshment, and issuing unlimited orders to imaginary waiters on their behoof. It was a strange sensation, being whirled away from home and bed down to a wild heath towards midnight; and as we neared our destination, the air began to "bite shrewdly," and the sky to look uncommonly like rain—a contretemps which would have been fatal to my proposed experience. We had to change carriages at Sutton, and here a sociable Aunt-Sally-man, struggling under the implements of his craft, sought to beguile me from my African friends by offers of a shake-down in his tent, with which he proposed to walk across from Ewell and erect, instead of journeying on to Epsom. My Ethiopian friends jumped at the proposal, and forthwith fraternized with Aunt Sally. I determined to follow out my previous plans; so having drunk to our next merry meeting, we parted, ostensibly until to-morrow, but, I fear, for ever.

I had been led to expect "high jinks" at Epsom—a sort of Carnival in the quiet town. Nothing could have been farther from the truth. The town, so far as outward semblance went, was almost as quiet as ever. A few sporting men thronged the bar of the principal hotel, and stragglers hung about the low beer-shops; but there was nothing at all to indicate the imminence of the great event. So I fell back on my usual expedient of applying to the executive, and found not only an active and intelligent but exceedingly civil sergeant of police, to whom I told my errand. He was pleased with the novelty of the idea, and as he happened to be then going the round of the town previously to visiting the course, I cast in my lot with him for the night. We first visited what he termed the "German Opera," on Epsom Common. This is an encampment of organ-grinders, hurdy-gurdy-players, German bands, &c., who pitch their tents here instead of going to the Downs. It was, however, rather late when we reached the spot where these artists were bivouacking, and they had retired for the night, so we could not form much idea of them beyond their numbers, which seemed considerable, and their odour, which was unfragrant. Thence we passed down a short alley to a railway arch, which was aglow with many fires, and rang with the sounds of many voices. Bidding me make no observation, whatever might be said, and requesting me to try and look like an officer in plain clothes, my cicerone led me into the strange arcade, which I certainly could not have entered without his protection. Hundreds of men, women, and boys were gathered in groups round coke fires, some partaking of coffee, others singing, the majority sleeping. After satisfying himself that the fires were legitimate ones, and not composed of broken fences, my guide left this teeming hive unmolested. We then steered for the course, not by the high road, but skirting it along the fields. The policeman, like myself, carried a stout stick, which really seemed to be endowed with creative powers that night. Wherever he poked that staff—and he did poke it everywhere—a human being growled, or snored, or cursed. Every bush along the hedgerow bore its occupant—often its group of four or five, sometimes a party of a dozen or a score. One shed filled with carts yielded at least a hundred, though the sergeant informed me it must have been already cleared several times that evening, as he had a file of men along the road, besides a cordon inside the Park palings, which border a great portion of it. It is with these palings the tramps chiefly do mischief, pulling them down to make fires along their route. Wherever my guide found these, he trampled the fires remorselessly out, and kicked the burning embers over the sleepers in a manner that must have been uncomfortable. The men submitted in comparative silence; but the ladies—where there happened to be any—exerted the privilege of their sex, and treated us to some choice specimens of the vernacular. In one case, a female cried out that he was kicking the fire over the "childer;" and, sure enough, we found half-a-dozen little ones huddled up asleep. The policeman remonstrated with her for bringing them to such a place; but she informed us it was to "make their living." In what way, she did not add. To us, it seemed very much like reversing the process, and causing their death. Fancy young children camping out on the road to the Downs at midnight! Boys of thirteen and fourteen abounded, sleeping in large groups along the hedgerows, and sometimes out in the open fields, where the dew lay thick.

At length, after many windings, we reached the Downs. The white booths, following the direction of the course in their sinuous lines, looked like stately white marble streets and crescents in the dim, uncertain light of that hour which, between May 31 and June 1, is neither day nor night. Under the stands and around the booths, tabernacling beneath costermongers' barrows, and even lying out openly sub dio, were still the hundreds of human beings. In one small drinking booth was a sight the policeman said he had never seen equalled in his twenty years' experience. A long, narrow table ran down the centre, with benches on each side. The table itself was occupied with recumbent figures; on the benches the sleepers sat, bending forward over it, and under the benches sleepers sprawled upon the grass. The whole of the front of the booth was open, and exposed to the biting wind; but there they snored as calmly as though on eider-down. We climbed the steps of the stand above the ring, and waited for the day, which slowly broke to the song of the lark and nightingale over that strange scene. With the first suspicion of dawn the sleepers awoke and got up; what for I cannot imagine. It was barely two o'clock, and how they were going to kill the next twelve hours I could not guess. Rise they did however, and an itinerant vendor of coffee, who was literally up with the lark, straightway began to drive a roaring trade. I saw no stronger drink than this consumed; nor did I witness a single case of drunkenness during the whole night. But this was before the Derby! At this juncture we were all surprised by the apparition of a hansom-lamp toiling up the hill. Two adventurous gentlemen from Liverpool, it appeared, had arrived at the Euston Station, and insisted upon being driven at once to an hotel on Epsom Downs. The Jehu, secure of a fabulous fare, drove them accordingly; and, of course, had to drive them back again to Epsom—the hotels on the Downs quietly but firmly declining to be knocked up at that untimely hour even by gentlemen from Liverpool. As the sun showed his first up-slanting rays above the horizon, with the morning star hanging impertinently near, the two gipsy encampments began to exhibit signs of life. The Zingari encamp exclusively by themselves, and some picturesque specimens of the male sex, looking remarkably like the lively photograph of the Greek brigands, showed themselves on the outskirts. The ladies reserved themselves for later in the day. My guide cautioned me not to attempt to enter the encampment, as the men are dangerous, and their position on the Downs a privileged one. It was only when the tramps were trespassing, or evidently bent on mischief, that they were disturbed. On the Downs they were monarchs of all they surveyed.

When the sun was fairly up, and the morning mists rolled away from those glorious Downs, I felt my mission accomplished. I had seen the sun rise on Epsom course. As it was many hours before a train would return, and I still felt fresh, I resolved to give the coup de grace to my night's adventure by walking home—at least, walking to the radius of workmen's trains. The vanguard of the Derby procession now began to show strongly in the shape of the great unwashed climbing the ridge of the hill by the paddock; and I felt I should see some characteristic sights along the road. Bidding good-bye, therefore, to my guide at Epsom, I set out on foot along the now-populous road, mine being the only face turned London-wards. Carts laden with trestles and boards for stands now began to be in force. By-and-by the well-known paper bouquets and outrageous head-gear showed themselves as forming the cargo of costermongers' carts. The travellers were all chatty, many of them chaffy. Frequent were the inquiries I had to answer as to the hour and the distance to the course. Occasionally a facetious gentleman anxiously inquired whether it was all over, as I was returning? I believe the majority looked upon me as a harmless lunatic, since I was travelling away from Epsom on the Derby morning, and pitied me accordingly. An Irishman aptly illustrated the genial character of Hibernian chaff as compared with English. "Good day to your honner!" he said. "It does me good to see your honner's happy face again;" though, of course, he had never seen it before. As I passed on with a brief salutation, he took the trouble to run after me, and slapping me on the shoulder, added, in a beautiful brogue: "Wait a minnit; I don't want to ax you for anything, but only to tell you how glad I am to see yer honner's happy face agin. Good mornin'!"

So through Ewell, Cheam, and Morden, up to Tooting; the throng increasing at every mile. At Balham, finding no train for an hour, I footed it again. I found preparations for endless Aunt Sally already being made on Clapham Common. Soon after six, I jumped into a train on the London, Chatham, and Dover, and came home "with the milk;" having not only had a healthy night's exercise—for the weather had all along been splendid—but having added to my experiences of London life one new "wrinkle" at least: I had seen the life of St. Giles's kitchen and Bethnal Green lodging-house à la campagne. What I had already seen under the garish candlelight of the Seven Dials and Commercial Road I saw gilded into picturesqueness by that glorious and never-to-be-forgotten sunrise on Epsom Downs which ushered in the Derby Day.

CHAPTER XIX.

THE WIFESLAYER'S "HOME."

There is something very weird and strange in that
exceptional avocation which takes one to-day to a Lord
Mayor's feast or a croquet tournament, to-morrow to a
Ritualistic service, next day to the home of a homicide. I
am free to confess that each has its special attractions for
me. I am very much disposed to "magnify my office" in
this respect, not from any foolish idea that I am "seeing
life," as it is termed, but still from a feeling that the proper
study of mankind is man in all his varied aspects.

It need not always be a morbid feeling that takes one to the
scene of a murder or other horrible event, though, as we
well know, the majority of those who visit such localities
do go out of mere idle curiosity. It may be worth while,
however, for some who look a little below the surface of
things, to gauge, as it were, the genius loci, and see
whether, in the influences surrounding the spot and its
inhabitants there be anything to afford a clue as to the
causes of the crime.

In summing up the evidence concerning a certain tragedy
at Greenwich, where a man killed his wife by throwing a
knife, the coroner "referred to the horrible abode—a coal
cellar—in which the family, nine in number, had resided,
which was unfit for human habitation, and ought to have
been condemned by the parish authorities." Having seen
and described in these pages something of how the poor
are housed in the cellars of St. Giles's and Bethnal Green,
and traced the probable influences of herding together the

criminal and innocent in the low lodging-houses, it occurred to me to visit the scene of this awful occurrence, and see how far the account given before the coroner's jury was correct.

With this view I took the train to Greenwich, and, consulting the first policeman I met, was by him directed to Roan Street as the scene of the tragedy. Roan Street I found to be a somewhat squalid by-street, running out of Skelton Street, close—it seemed significantly close—to the old parish church. One could not help thinking of the familiar proverb, "The nearer the church, the farther from God." The actual locality is called Munyard's Row, being some dozen moderate-sized houses in Roan Street, let out in lodgings, the particular house in question being again, with a horrible grotesqueness, next door but one to a beer-shop called the "Hit or Miss!" I expected to find Roan Street the observed of all observers, but the nine days' wonder was over since what Dickens called the "ink-widge." Indeed, a homicide has ceased to be a nine days' wonder now. This only happened on Saturday; and when I was there, on the following Wednesday, Roan Street had settled down into its wonted repose. A woman with a child was standing on the door-step, and, on my inquiring if I could see the kitchen, referred me to Mrs. Bristow at the chandler's shop, who farms the rent of these populous tenements; for Munyard's Row is peopled "from garret to basement," and a good way underground too.

Mrs. Bristow, a civil, full-flavoured Irishwoman, readily consented to act cicerone, and we went through the passage into the back garden, where all the poor household furniture of the homicide's late "home" was stacked. It did not occupy a large space, consisting only of the bedstead on which the poor woman sat when the fatal deed was done, two rickety tables, and two chairs. These were all the movables of a family of nine. The mattress was left inside—too horrible a sight, after what had taken place, to be exposed to the light of day.

We passed—Honora Bristow and myself—with a "gossip" or two, who had come to see what I was after, into the back kitchen, for the wifeslayer had two rooms en suite, though the family elected to occupy only one. The floor of this apartment was either mother earth, or, if flagged, so grimed with filth as to be a very fair resemblance of the soil. Here stood only that terrible memento, the drenched mattress. In the front kitchen—which, let me state, would have been palatial in comparison with the Seven Dials or Spitalfields, had it been only clean—there was very little light, for the window, which was well down below the surface of the pavement, had not a whole pane in it, and the broken ones had been stuffed up with old rags which were very protuberant indeed. That window alone would show that the ménage had not been a judicious one.

"He was a quiet man," said Honora, "and gave trouble to no one. He and his wife never had a word." The gossips all believed that the story of the throwing the knife was true, notwithstanding the medical evidence went against it. The boy of twelve, who provoked the father to throw the knife, was evidently the incubus of the wretched home. "Almost before the breath was out of his mother, that boy was searching about the bed to see if he could find any ha'pence," said Honora. That boy was evidently not satisfactory. His evidence was refused by the Coroner, because he could not read or write. But then what had been the child's surroundings? They have been described above. The man himself had a patriarchal family of seven, from a girl of seventeen down to a baby of two, and all, as we have seen, slept in one room, though there were two, and though a bucket of whitewash would have made the pair habitable, besides giving the lad some useful employment.

The father was of no particular occupation, picking up odd jobs, and leaning largely to the shrimp trade. He stood high in Honora Bristow's regards as having regularly paid his 1s. 9d. a week for five years, or, at least, being some 5s. behind now; a sum which will probably be covered by the chattels in the back garden. The poor home was silent then. The mother lay calmly in the dead-house, after the post-mortem examination, "terrible cut and hacked about," said the one gossip who had ventured to go and see her quondam friend. The father was in Maidstone Gaol. The little children were being taken care of by the grandmother until such time as the mother should have been buried, when they would gravitate to the workhouse.

In the meantime the boy, æt. twelve, the cause of all the mischief, disports himself in Munyard's Row as though nothing had happened. Perhaps he is the most difficult part of the problem; but the whole question of the home is a puzzling one. The boy is evidently the product of the home. It very much concerns the community that such produce should become extinct; and therefore the sooner some improvements can be introduced into such homes the better. In the first place, there is decidedly too little light. Sunshine, under any circumstances, would have been impossible there. The advisability of human beings burrowing underground may be questioned, whether in cellars or genteel underground kitchens.

Then again, one bedroom—nay, one bedstead—for father, mother, and seven children ranging from seventeen to two is decidedly deficient. This sounds almost too horrible to be true; but I was careful to ascertain that the eldest girl, though in domestic service in Greenwich, slept at the "home." More horrible still is the fact disclosed, that they had a second room, yet had not the decency to use it. "De mortuis nil nisi bonum." They lived according to their light; but they had very little light, literally or figuratively. Surely we want to teach our poor the simple rules of hygiene. One of the gossips, a clean, healthy little woman, with a fine baby at her breast, referred with pride to her poor kitchen, identical in all respects, save dirt, with the home.

Then, again, there was one thing that struck me forcibly, and that was the sort of qualified reprobation with which these good gossips—really decent people in their way— spoke of the habit of throwing knives. Honora had once thrown one at her daughter of eighteen, but never meant to do so again. And all this under the bells of the old parish church of Greenwich in the year of grace 1870!

Clearly, however, the first question is what to do with the boy, æt. twelve. Comporting himself as he did in the face of the awful tragedy he had caused, this young gentleman must clearly not be lost sight of, or it will be the worse for himself and those with whom he is brought into contact. Nay, in a few years, he will become a centre of influence, and radiate around him another such "home," worse, perhaps, than the first.

Let our Social Science so far break through the programme it may have laid down as to touch on this very appropriate subject of squalid homes, and its next sitting may be a very useful one indeed.

CHAPTER XX.

BATHING IN THE FAR EAST.

Visions of Oriental splendour and magnificence float across the imagination at the mere mention of the storied East. Soaring above all the routine of ordinary existence and the commonplaces of history, that creative faculty within us pictures Pactolus with its golden sands; or recalls from the legendary records of childhood the pomp of Aladdin's Princess going to her luxurious bath; or brings back to mind the almost prosaic minuteness with which the Greek poet describes the bath of Ulysses when he returned from his wanderings. In the East the bath has ever been an institution—not merely a luxury, but a necessity; and it is a proof of the eclectic tendencies of our generation that we have domesticated here in the West that great institution, the Hammam, or Turkish bath, which the Romans were wise enough to adopt, after their Eastern experience, more than two thousand years ago. Of none of these Oriental splendours, however, has the present narrative to tell. I ask those interested in social questions to take a very early Sunday expedition to the East End of London, and catch a glimpse of those whom, after what I have to relate, it would be libel to call the "Great Unwashed." We will look at East London engaged in the interesting process of performing its ablutions.

Very enjoyable is a Saturday afternoon stroll in Victoria Park. Those gentlemen of London who sit at home at ease are apt to think of the East End as a collection of slums, with about as much breathing space for its congregated thousands as that supplied to the mites in a superannuated

Cheshire cheese. Let us pass through Bethnal Green Road, and, leaving behind the new Museum, go under a magic portal into the stately acres which bear the name of our Sovereign. On our right is the Hospital for Diseases of the Chest, of which the foundation-stone was laid by the Prince Consort, and the new wing of which our Orientals hope one day to see opened by her Majesty in person. Most convincing test of all is the situation of this Consumptive Hospital—showing the salubrity of the Eastern breezes. Inside the imposing gate the visitor will find extensive cricket-grounds interspersed with broad pastures, whose flocks are the reverse of Arcadian in hue. Cricket-balls whiz about us like shells at Inkermann; and the suggestive "Thank you" of the scouts forces the passer-by into unwonted activity as he shies the ball to the bowler. Then there are roundabouts uncountable, and gymnasia abundant. There are bosquets for the love-makers, and glassy pools, studded with islands innumerable, over which many a Lady of the Lake steers her shallop, while Oriental sailor-boys canoe wildly along. There are flower-beds which need not blush to be compared with Kew or the Crystal Palace. But it is not with such that we are now concerned. On one of those same lakes over which, on Saturday evening, sailors in embryo float their mimic craft—and one young gentleman, slightly in advance of the rest, directs a very miniature steamship—we see boards suggesting that daily, from four to eight a.m., the Orientals may immerse themselves in the limpid and most tempting waters. The depth, they are paternally informed, increases towards the centre, buoys marking where it is six feet; so that our Eastern friends have no excuse for suicide by drowning.

East London birds are early birds, and to catch them at their bath you must be literally up with the lark. Towards six o'clock is the most fashionable hour for our metropolitan Pactolus; and, as it is some miles distant from what can, by any stretch of courtesy, be called the West End, and as there are no workmen's trains on a Sunday morning, a long walk or cab drive is inevitable for all who would witness the disporting of our amphibious Orientals. Rising thus betimes on a recent "Sunday morning before the bells did ring," I sped me to the bathing pond, judiciously screened off by shrubs from the main path. It was between the appointed hours that I arrived; and, long before I saw anything, the ringing laughter of the young East reached me through the shrubs. Threading the path which led to the lake, I found the water literally alive with men, boys, and hobbledehoys, revelling in the water like young hippopotami on the Nile. Boys were largely in the ascendant—boys from ten to fifteen years of age swam like young Leanders, and sunned themselves on the bank, in the absence of towels, as the preparative to dressing, or smoked their pipes in a state of nature. It is only just to say that while I remained, I heard little if any language that could be called "foul." Very free and easy, of course, were the remarks, and largely illustrative of the vulgar tongue; not without a share of light chaff directed against myself, whose presence by the lake-side puzzled my young friends. I received numerous invitations to "peel" and have a dip; and one young urchin assured me in the most patronizing way possible that he "wouldn't laugh at me" if I could not get on. The language may not have been quite so refined as that which I heard a few days before from the young gentlemen with tall hats and blue ties at Lord's; but I do say advisedly that it would more than bear comparison with that of the bathers in the Serpentine, where my ears have often been assailed with something far worse than anything I heard in East London. In the matter of clothes, too, the apparel of our young friends was indeed Eastern in its simplicity; yet they left it unprotected on the bank with a confidence that did honour to our common humanity in general, and to the regulations of Victoria Park in particular. Swimming in some sort was almost universal among the bathers, showing that their visit to the water was not an isolated event in their existence, but a constant as it is a wholesome habit. The Oriental population were for the most part apparently well fed; and one saw there lithe and active frames, either careering gracefully along in the old style of swimming, or adopting the new and scientific method which causes the human form divine to approach very nearly to the resemblance of a rather excited grampus.

But inexorable Time warns the youthful bathers that they must sacrifice to the Graces; and some amusing incidents occur during the process. Generally speaking, though the amount of attire is not excessive, considerable effort in the way of pinning and hitching is required to get things in their proper places. A young gentleman was reduced to inexpressible grief, and held up to the scorn of his fellow-bathers, by the fact that, in the course of his al fresco toilette, one of his feet went through his inexpressibles in an honourable quarter, instead of proceeding by the proper route; the error interested his friends vastly—for they are as critical as the most fastidious could be of any singularity in attire, and they held the unfortunate juvenile in his embarrassing position for a long time, to his intense despair, until he was rescued from his ignoble position by some grown-up friend. Then, the young East is prone to the pleasures of tobacco. It was, I presume, before breakfast with most of the bathers, and smoking under those conditions is a trial even to the experienced. Some, pale from their long immersion—for theirs was no transient dip—grew paler still after they had discussed the pipe or cigar demanded of them by rigorous custom.

Fashion reigns supreme among the gamins of the East as well as among the ladies of the West. Off they went, however, cleaner and fresher than before—tacitly endorsing by their matutinal amusement the motto that has come down from the philosopher of old, and even now reigns supreme from Bermondsey to Belgravia, that "water is a most excellent thing."

The day may arrive perhaps when, having embanked the Thames, we shall follow suit to the Seine and the Rhine, by tenanting it with cheap baths for the many. Until we do so, the stale joke of the "Great Unwashed" recoils upon ourselves, and is no less symptomatic of defective sanitary arrangements than the possibility of a drought in Bermondsey. But we are forgetting our bathers. They have gone, leaving the place to solitude—some, I hope, home to breakfast, others out among the flower-walks or on the greensward. It is a gloomy, overcast, muggy, unseasonable July morning; and the civil attendant by the lake-side tells me that the gathering has not been so large as usual. The young Orientals—as is the custom of their race—love sunshine. They get little enough of it, Heaven knows. The next bright Sunday morning, any one who happens to be awake between the hours mentioned, and who would like to add to his experiences of metropolitan existence, may do a worse thing, and see many a less pleasant sight, than if he hailed a hansom and drove by the principal entrance of Victoria Park to our Eastern Bath.

CHAPTER XXI.

AMONG THE QUAKERS.

There is no more engaging or solemn subject of contemplation than the decay of a religious belief. Right or wrong, by that faith men have lived and died, perhaps for centuries; and one cannot see it pass out from the consciousness of humanity without something more than a cursory thought as to the reasons of its decadence. Being led by exceptional causes to take a more than common interest in those forms of belief which lie beyond the pale of the Church of England, I was attracted by a notice in the public journals that on the following morning the Society of Friends would assemble from all parts of England and open a Conference to inquire into the causes which had brought about the impending decay of their body. So, then, the fact of such decay stood confessed. In most cases the very last persons to realize the unwelcome truth are those who hold the doctrines that are becoming effete. Quakerism must, I felt, be in a very bad condition indeed when its own disciples called together a conference to account for its passing away. Neither men nor communities, as a rule, act crowner's 'quest on their own decease. That faith, it was clear, must be almost past praying for which, disbelieving, as our modern Quietism does, the efficacy of assemblies, and trusting all to the inward illumination of individuals, should yet summon a sort of Quaker Œcumenical Council. I thought I should like to probe this personal light myself, and by inquiring of one or two of the members of the body, learn what they thought of the matter. I was half inclined to array myself in drab, and tutoyer the first of the body I chanced to encounter in my walks abroad. But then it occurred to me how very seldom one did meet a Quaker nowadays except in the "month of Maying." I actually had to cast about for some time before I could select from a tolerably wide and heterogeneous circle of acquaintance two names of individuals belonging to the Society of Friends; though I could readily remember half a dozen of every other culte, from Ultramontanes down to Jumpers. These two, at all events, I would "interview," and so forestall the Conference with a little select synod of my own.

It was possible, of course, to find a ludicrous side to the question; but, as I said, I approached it seriously. Sydney Smith, with his incorrigible habit of joking, questioned the existence of Quaker babies—a position which, if proven, would, of course, at once account for the diminution of adult members of the sect. It was true I had never seen a Quaker infant; but I did not therefore question their existence, any more than I believed postboys and certain humble quadrupeds to be immortal because I had never seen a dead specimen of either. The question I acknowledged at once to be a social and religious, not a physiological one. Why is Quakerism, which has lived over two hundred years, from the days of George Fox, and stood as much persecution as any system of similar age, beginning to succumb to the influences of peace and prosperity? Is it the old story of Capua and Cannæ over again? Perhaps it is not quite correct to say that it is now beginning to decline; nor, as a fact, is this Conference the first inquiry which the body itself has made into its own incipient decay. It is even said that symptoms of such an issue showed themselves as early as the beginning of the eighteenth century; and prize essays have been from time to time written as to the causes, before the Society so far fell in with the customs of the times as to call a council for the present very difficult and delicate inquiry. The first prize essay by William Rountree attributes the falling off to the fact that the early Friends, having magnified a previously slighted truth—that of the Indwelling Word—fell into the natural error of giving it an undue place, so depriving their representations of Christian doctrine of the symmetry they would otherwise have possessed, and influencing their own practices in such a way as to contract the basis on which Christian fellowship rests. A second prize essay, called "The Peculium," takes a still more practical view, and points out in the most unflattering way that the Friends, by eliminating from their system all attention to the arts, music, poetry, the drama, &c., left nothing for the exercise of their faculties save eating, drinking, and making money. "The growth of Quakerism," says Mr. T. Hancock, the author of this outspoken essay, "lies in its enthusiastic tendency. The submission of Quakers to the commercial tendency is signing away the life of their own schism. Pure enthusiasm and the pursuit of money (which is an enthusiasm) can never coexist, never co-operate; but," he adds, "the greatest loss of power reserved for Quakerism is the reassumption by the Catholic Church of those Catholic truths which Quakerism was separated to witness and to vindicate."

I confess myself, however, so far Quaker too that I care little for the written testimony of friends or foes. I have, in all my religious wanderings and inquiries, adopted the method of oral examination; so I found myself on a recent November morning speeding off by rail to the outskirts of London to visit an ancient Quaker lady whom I knew very slenderly, but who I had heard was sometimes moved by the spirit to enlighten a little suburban congregation, and was, therefore, I felt the very person to enlighten me too, should she be thereunto moved. She was a venerable,

silver-haired old lady, clad in the traditional dress of her
sect, and looking very much like a living representation of
Elizabeth Fry. She received me very cordially; though I
felt as if I were a fussy innovation of the nineteenth
century breaking in upon the sacred, old-fashioned quiet of
her neat parlour. She "thee'd and thou'd" me to my heart's
content: and—to summarize the conversation I held with
her—it was to the disuse of the old phraseology and the
discarding of the peculiar dress that she attributed most of
the falling off which she was much too shrewd a woman of
the world to shut her eyes to. These were, of course, only
the outward and visible signs of a corresponding change
within; but this was why the Friends fell off, and
gravitated, as she confessed they were doing, to steeple-
houses, water-dipping, and bread-and-wine-worship. She
seemed to me like a quiet old Prophetess Anna chanting a
"Nunc Dimittis" of her own on the passing away of her
faith. She would be glad to depart before the glory had
quite died out. She said she did not hope much from the
Conference, and, to my amazement, rather gloried in the
old irreverent title given by the Independents to her
forefathers from their "quaking and trembling" when they
heard the Word of God, though she preferred still more the
older title of "Children of the Light." She was, in fact, a
rigid old Conservative follower of George Fox, from the
top of her close-bordered cap to the skirts of her grey silk
gown. I am afraid my countenance expressed incredulity as
to her rationale of the decay; for, as I rose to go, she said,
"Thou dost not agree, friend, with what I have said to
thee—nay, never shake thy head; it would be wonderful if
thou didst, when our own people don't. Stay; I'll give thee a
note to my son in London, though he will gainsay much of
what I have told thee." She gave me the letter, which was
just what I wanted, for I felt I had gained little beyond a
pleasant experience of old-world life from my morning's

jaunt. I partook of her kindly hospitality, was shown over her particularly cosy house, gardens, and hothouses, and meditated, on my return journey, upon many particulars I learnt for the first time as to the early history of Fox; realizing what a consensus there was between the experiences of all illuminati. I smiled once and again over the quaint title of one of Fox's books which my venerable friend had quoted to me—viz., "A Battle-door for Teachers and Professors to learn Plural and Singular. You to Many, and Thou to One; Singular, One, Thou; Plural, Many, You." While so meditating, my cab deposited me at the door of a decidedly "downy" house, at the West End, where my prospective friend was practising in I will not mention which of the learned professions. Both the suburban cottage of the mother and the London ménage of the son assured me that they had thriven on Quakerism; and it was only then I recollected that a poor Quaker was as rare a personage as an infantile member of the Society.

The young man—who neither in dress, discourse, nor manner differed from an ordinary English gentleman— smiled as he read his mother's lines, and, with a decorous apology for disturbing the impressions which her discourse might have left upon me, took precisely the view which had been latent in my own mind as to the cause of the Society's decay. Thoroughly at one with them still on the doctrine of the illuminating power of the Spirit in the individual conscience, he treated the archaic dress, the obsolete phraseology, the obstinate opposition to many innocent customs of the age, simply as anachronisms. He pointed with pride to the fact that our greatest living orator was a member of the Society; and claimed for the underlying principle of Quakerism—namely, the superiority of a conscience void of offence over written scripture or formal ceremony—the character of being in

essence the broadest creed of Christendom. Injudicious
retention of customs which had grown meaningless had, he
felt sure, brought down upon the body that most fatal of all
influences—contempt. "You see it in your own Church,"
he said. "There is a school which, by reviving obsolete
doctrines and practices, will end in getting the Church of
England disestablished as it is already disintegrated. You
see it even in the oldest religion of all—Judaism. You see,
I mean, a school growing into prominence and power
which discards all the accumulations of ages, and by going
back to real antiquity, at once brings the system more into
unison with the century, and prevents that contempt
attaching to it which will accrue wherever a system sets its
face violently against the tone of current society." He
thought the Conference quite unnecessary. "There needs no
ghost come from the dead to tell us that, Horatio," he said,
cheerily. "They will find out that Quakerism is not a
proselytizing religion," he added; "which, of course, we
knew before. They will point to the fashionable attire, the
gold rings, and lofty chignons of our younger sisters as
direct defiance of primitive custom. I am unorthodox
enough"—and he smiled as he used that word—"to think
that the attire is more becoming to my younger sisters, just
as the Society's dress is to my dear mother." That young
man, and the youthful sisters he told me of, stood as
embodied answers to the question I had proposed to
myself. They were outward and visible evidences of the
doctrine of Quaker "development." The idea is not dead.
The spirit is living still. It is the spirit that underlies all real
religion—namely, the personal relation of the human soul
to God as the source of illumination. That young man was
as good a Quaker at heart as George Fox or William Penn
themselves; and the "apology" he offered for his
transformed faith was a better one than Barclay's own. I am
wondering whether the Conference will come to anything

like so sensible a conclusion as to why Quakerism is declining.

CHAPTER XXII.

PENNY READINGS.

Who has ever penetrated beneath the surface of clerical society—meaning thereby the sphere of divinities (mostly female) that doth hedge a curate of a parish—without being sensible of the eligibility of Penny Readings for a place in Mystic London? When the Silly Season is at its very bathos; when the monster gooseberries have gone to seed and the showers of frogs ceased to fall; after the matrimonial efforts of Margate or Scarborough, and before the more decided business of the Christmas Decorations, then there is deep mystery in the penetralia of every parish. The great scheme of Penny Readings is being concocted, and all the available talent of the district—all such as is "orthodox" and "correct"—is laid under contribution.

It is true to a proverb that we English people have a knack of doing the best possible things in the worst possible way; and that not unfrequently when we do once begin doing them we do them to death. It takes some time to convince us that the particular thing is worth doing at all; but, once persuaded, we go in for it with all our British might and main. The beard-and-moustache movement was a case in point. Some years ago a moustache was looked upon by serious English people as decidedly reckless and dissipated. A beard was fit only for a bandit. Nowadays, the mildest youth in the Young Men's Christian Association may wear a moustache without being denounced as "carnal," and paterfamilias revels in the beard of a sapeur, no misopogon daring to say him nay. To no "movement," however, does the adage "Vires acquirit eundo" apply more thoroughly than to that connected with "Penny Readings." Originally cropping up timidly in rustic and suburban parishes, it has of late taken gigantic strides, and made every parish where it does not exist, rural or metropolitan, very exceptional indeed. There was a sound principle lying at the bottom of the movement, in so far as it was designed to bring about a fusion of classes; though, perhaps, it involved too much of an assumption that the "working man" had to be lectured to, or read to, by his brother in purple and fine linen. Still the theory was so far sound. Broad cloth was to impart to fustian the advantages it possessed in the way of reading, singing, fiddling, or what not; and that not gratuitously, which would have offended the working man's dignity, but for the modest sum of one penny, which, whilst Lazarus was not too poor to afford, Dives condescended to accept, and apply to charitable purposes.

Such being, in brief, the theory of the Penny Reading movement, it may be interesting to see how it is carried out in practice. Now, in order to ascertain this, I availed myself of several opportunities afforded by the commencement of the Penny Reading season, which may be said to synchronize very nearly with the advent of London fogs, and attended the opening of the series in several widely different localities. In describing my experiences it would perhaps be invidious to specify the exact locality where they were gathered. I prefer to collate those experiences which range from Campden Hill to Camden Town inclusive. Amid many distinguishing traits there are common elements traceable in all, which may enable us to form some estimate of the working of the scheme, and possibly to offer a few words of advice to those interested therein.

In most cases the Penny Readings are organized by the parochial clergy. We will be orthodox, and consider them so to be on the present occasion. In that case, the series would probably be opened by the incumbent in person. Some ecclesiastical ladies, young and middle-aged, who, rightly or wrongly, believe their mission is music, and to whom the curate is very probably an attraction, aid his efforts. Serious young men read, and others of a more mundane turn of mind sing doleful "comic" songs, culled from the more presentable of the music-hall répertoire. In many cases skilled amateurs or professionals lend their valuable assistance; and it is not too much to say that many a programme is presented to the audience—ay, and faithfully carried out too—which would do credit to a high-priced concert-room. But, then, who make up the audience? Gradually the "penny" people have been retiring into the background, as slowly but as surely as the old-fashioned pits at our theatres are coyly withdrawing under the boxes to make way for the stalls. The Penny Readings have been found to "draw" a higher class of audience than those for whom they were originally intended. The curate himself, if unmarried, secures the whole spinsterhood of the parish. His rendering of the lines, "On the receipt of my mother's picture out of Norfolk," is universally acknowledged to be "delightful;" and so, in course of time, the Penny Readings have been found to supply a good parochial income; and the incumbent, applying the proceeds to some local charity, naturally wishes to augment that income as much as possible. The consequence is that the penny people are as completely nowhere at the Penny Readings as they are in the free seats at their parish church. The whole of the body of the room is "stalled off," so to say, for sixpenny people, and the penny folk are stowed away anywhere. Then, again, in several programmes I have been at the pains to analyse, it is palpable that, whilst the bulk of the extracts fire over the heads of the poor people, one or two are inserted which are as studiously aimed at them as the parson's remarks in last Sunday's sermon against public-house loafing. Still "naming no names," I attended some readings where one of the clergy read a long extract from Bailey's "Festus," whilst he was succeeded by a vulgar fellow, evidently put in for "the gods," who delivered himself of a parody on Ingoldsby, full of the coarsest slang—nay, worse than that, abounding in immoralities which, I hope, made the parochial clergy sit on thorns, and place the reader on their "Index Expurgatorius" from henceforth.

Excellent in its original design, the movement is obviously degenerating into something widely different. First, I would say, Let your Penny Readings be really Penny Readings, and not the egregious lucus a non they now are. If there is any distinction, the penny people should have the stalls, and then, if there were room, the "swells" (I must use an offensive term) could come in for sixpence, and stand at the back. But there should be no difference at all. Dives and Lazarus should sit together, or Dives stop away if he were afraid his fine linen may get soiled. Lazarus, at all events, must not be lost sight of, or treated to second best. The experiment of thus mingling them has been tried, I know, and succeeds admirably. Dives and Lazarus do hobnob; and though the former occasionally tenders a silver coin for his entrée, he does not feel that he is thereby entitled to a better seat. The committee gets the benefit of his liberality; and when the accounts are audited in the spring, Lazarus is immensely pleased at the figure his pence make. Then, again, as to the quality of the entertainment. Let us remember Lazarus comes there to be elevated. That was the theory we set out with—that we, by our reading, or our singing, or fiddling, or tootle-tooing on the cornet, could civilize our friend in fustian. Do not let us fall into the mistake, then, of descending to his standard. We want to level him up to ours. Give him the music we play in our own drawing-rooms; read the choice bits of fiction or poetry to his wife and daughters which we should select for our own. Amuse his poor little children with the same innocent nonsense with which we treat our young people. Above all, don't bore him. I do not say, never be serious, because it is a great mistake to think Lazarus can only guffaw. Read "The Death of Little Nell" or of Paul Dombey, and look at Mrs. Lazarus's eyes. Read Tom Hood's "Song of the Shirt," and see whether the poor seamstress out in the draughty penny seats at the back appreciates it or not. I did hear of one parish at the West End—the very same, by the way, I just now commended for sticking to the "penny" system—where Hood's "Nelly Gray," proposed to be read by the son of one of our best known actors, was tabooed as "unedifying." Lazarus does not come to be "edified," but to be amused. If he can be at the same time instructed, so much the better; but the bitter pill must be highly gilded, or he will pocket his penny and spend it in muddy beer at the public-house. If the Penny Reading can prevent this—and we see no reason why it should not—it will have had a mission indeed. Finally, I feel sure that there is in this movement, and lying only a very little way from the surface, a wholesome lesson for

Dives too; and that is, how little difference there is, after all, between himself and Lazarus. I have been surprised to see how some of the more recherché "bits" of our genuine humorists have told upon the penny people, and won applause which the stalest burlesque pun or the nastiest music-hall inanity would have failed to elicit. Lazarus must be represented on the platform then, as well as comfortably located in the audience. He must be asked to read, or sing, or fiddle, or do whatever he can. If not, he will feel he is being read at, or sung to, or fiddled for, and will go off to the Magpie and Stump, instead of bringing missus and the little ones to the "pa'son's readings." Let the Penny Reading teach us the truth—and how true it is—that we are all "working men." What matters it whether we work with head or with hand—with brain or muscle?

CHAPTER XXIII.

DARWINISM ON THE DEVIL.

It has been said—perhaps more satirically than seriously—that theology could not get on without its devil. Certain it is that wherever there has been a vivid realization of the Spirit of Light, there, as if by way of antithesis, there has been an equally clear recognition of the Power of Darkness. Ormuzd—under whatever name recognised—generally supposes his opponent Ahriman; and there have even been times, as in the prevalence of the Manichean heresy, when the Evil Spirit has been affected in preference to the good—probably only another way of saying that morals have been held subordinate to intellect. But I am growing at once prosy and digressive.

The announcement that the "Liberal Social Union" would devote one of their sweetly heretical evenings at the Beethoven Rooms, Harley Street, to an examination of the Darwinian development of the Evil Spirit, was one not to be scorned by an inquirer into the more eccentric and erratic phases of theology. Literary engagements stood in the way—for the social heretics gather on a Friday—but come what might, I would hear them discuss diabolism. Leaving my printer's devil to indulge in typographical errors according to his own sweet will (and I must confess he did wander), I presented myself, as I thought in good time, at the portals of the Harley Street room, where his Satanic Majesty was to be heretically anatomized. But, alas! I had not calculated aright the power of that particular potentate to "draw." No sooner had I arrived at the cloak-room than the very hats and umbrellas warned me of the number of his votaries. Evening Dress was "optional;" and I frankly confess, at whatever risk of his displeasure, that I had not deemed Mephistopheles worthy of a swallow-tailed coat. I came in the garb of ordinary life; and at once felt uncomfortable when, mounting the stairs, I was received by a portly gentleman and an affable lady in violent tenue de soir. The room was full to the very doors; and as soon as I squeezed into earshot of the lecturer (who had already commenced his discourse) I was greeted by a heterodox acquaintance in elaborate dress-coat and rose-pink gloves. Experience in such matters had already told me—and thereupon I proved it by renewed personal agony—that an Englishman never feels so uncomfortable as when dressed differently from his compeers at any kind of social gathering. Mrs. T—— asks you to dinner, and you go clad in the correct costume in deference to the prandial meal, but find all the rest in morning dress. Mrs. G——, on the contrary, sends you a rollicking note to feed with a few friends—no party; and you go straight from office to find a dozen heavily-got-up people sniggering at your frock coat and black tie. However, as I said, on this occasion the lecturer, Dr. Zerffi, was in the thick of what proved to be a very attractive lecture; so I was not the observed of all observers for more than two or three minutes, and was able to give him my whole attention as soon as I had recovered from my confusion. Dr. Zerffi said:—

Dr. Darwin's theory of evolution and selection has changed our modern mode of studying the inorganic and organic phenomena of nature, and investigating the realities of truth. His theory is not altogether new, having been first proclaimed by Leibnitz, and followed up with regard to history by Giovanni Battista Vico. Oken and Goethe amplified it towards the end of the last, and at the beginning of the present century. Darwin, however, has systematized the theory of evolution, and now the branches of human knowledge can only be advantageously pursued if we trace in all phenomena, whether material or spiritual, a beginning and a gradual development. One fact has prominently been established, that there is order in the eternal change, that this order is engendered by law, and that law and order are the criterions of an all-wise ruling Spirit pervading the Universe. To this positive spirit of law a spirit of negation, an element of rebellion and mischief, of mockery and selfishness, commonly called the Devil, has been opposed from the beginning.

It appeared, till very lately, as though God had created the world only for the purpose of amusing the Devil, and giving him an abundance of work, all directed to destroying the happiness of God's finest creation—man. Treating the Devil from a Darwinian point of view, we may assert that he developed himself from the protoplasm of ignorance, and in the gloomy fog of fear and superstition grew by degrees into a formidable monster, being changed by the overheated imaginations of dogmatists into a reptile, an owl, a raven, a dog, a wolf, a lion, a centaur, a being half monkey, half man, till, finally, he became a polite and refined human being.

Man once having attained a certain state of consciousness, saw sickness, evil, and death around him, and as it was usual to assign to every effect some tangible cause, man developed the abstract notion of evil into a concrete form, which changed with the varying impressions of climate, food, and the state of intellectual progress. To the white man the Devil was black, and to the black man white. Originally, then, the Devil was merely a personification of the apparently destructive forces of nature. Fire was his element. The Indians had their Rakshas and Uragas, the Egyptians their Typhon, and the Persians their Devas. The Israelites may claim the honour of having brought the theory of evil into a coarse and sensual form, and the Christians took up this conception, and developed it with the help of the Gnostics, Plato, and the Fathers dogmatically into an entity.

I shall not enter on a minute inquiry into the origin of this formidable antagonist of common sense and real piety; I intend to take up the three principal phases of the Devil's development, at a period when he already appears to us as a good Christian Devil, and always bearing in mind Mr.

Darwin's theory of evolution, I shall endeavour to trace
spiritually the changes in the conceptions of evil from the
Devil of Luther to that of Milton, and at last to that of
Goethe.

The old Jewish Rabbis and theological doctors were
undoubtedly the first to trace, genealogically, the pedigree
of the Christian Devil in its since general form. If we take
the trouble to compare chap. i. v. 27 of Genesis with chap.
ii. v. 21, we will find that two distinct creations of man are
given. The one is different from the other. In the first
instance we have the clear, indisputable statement, "So
God created man in his own image:" and to give greater
force to this statement the text goes on, "in the image of
God created he him; male and female created he them."
Both man and woman were then created. Nothing could be
plainer. But as though no creation of man had taken place
at all, we find, chap. ii. v. 7: "And the Lord formed man of
the dust of the ground, and breathed into his nostrils the
breath of life." This was evidently a second man,
differently created from the first, who is stated to have
been made "in the image of God himself." This second
creature was entrusted with the nomination and
classification of all created things; that is, with the
formation of language, and the laying down of the first
principles of botany and zoology. After he had performed
this arduous task it happened that "for Adam there was not
found an help meet for him" (verse 20), and chap. ii. v. 21
tells us, "The Lord God caused a deep sleep to fall upon
Adam, and he slept; and He took one of his ribs and closed
up the flesh instead thereof;" and verse 22, "And of the rib
which the Lord God had taken from man made He a
woman, and brought her unto man." Adam then joyfully
exclaims (verse 23), "This is now bone of my bones, and
flesh of my flesh." This cannot but lead to the conclusion

that this woman was an altogether different creature from the first. The contradiction was most ingeniously explained by the learned Jewish Rabbis, who considered the first woman the organic germ from which the special Hebrew-Christian devils were evolved. The Rabbis discovered that the name of the first woman was "Lilith" [1] (the nightly); they knew positively—and who can disprove their assertion?—that she was the most perfect beauty, more beautiful than Eve; she had long waving hair, bright eyes, red lips and cheeks, and a charmingly finished form and complexion; but having been created at the same moment as the first man, and like him, in the image of God, she refused to become man's wife; she objected to being subordinate to the male part of creation—she was, in fact, the first strong-minded woman, claiming the same rights as man, though a woman in body and form. Under these circumstances the existence of the human race was deemed to be an impossibility, and therefore the Lord had to make good his error, and He created Eve as the completing part of man. The first woman left her co-equally created male, and was changed into an enormous, most beautiful, and seducing "She Devil," and her very thoughts brought forth daily a legion of devils—incarnations of pride, vanity, conceit, and unnaturalness. Happily these devils were so constituted that they devoured one another. But in their rage they could take possession of others, and more especially entered little children—boys under three days old, girls under twenty days—and devoured them. This myth, by means of evolution and the law of action and re-action, engendered the further legend about the existence of three special angels who acted as powerful antidotes to these devils, and whose names, "Senoi, Sansenoi, and Sanmangeloph," if written on a piece of parchment suspended round the neck of children afforded certain protection against them.

The origin of the Devil may thus be traced to the first vain contempt for the eternal laws of nature. The woman, refusing to be a woman, engenders devils; the man, trying to be a God, loses paradise and his innocence, for the element of the supernatural intruded upon him and abstracted his thoughts from this earth. These were the half idealistic and half realistic elements from which the three greatest spiritual incarnations of the Evil Spirit sprung up. Luther took the Evil Spirit as a bodily entity, with big horns, fiery eyes, a reddish, protruding tongue, a long tail, and the hoof of a horse. In this latter attribute we trace at once the Kentaur element of ancient times. Through nearly one thousand three hundred years from Tertullian and Thaumaturgus down to Luther, every one was accustomed to look upon life as one great battle with tens of thousands of devils, assaulting, harassing, annoying, and seducing humanity. All fought, quarrelled, talked, and wrestled with the Devil. He was more spoken of in the pulpits of the Christian Churches, written about in theological and scientific books, than God or Christ. All misfortunes were attributed to him. Thunder and lightning, hailstorms and the rinderpest, the hooping cough and epileptic fits were all the Devil's work. A man who suffered from madness was said to be possessed by a legion of Evil Spirits. The Devil settled himself in the gentle dimples of a pretty girl with the same ease and comfort as in the wrinkles of an old woman. Everything that was inexplicable was evil. Throughout the Middle Ages the masses and the majority of their learned theological teachers believed the Greek and Latin classics were inspired by Evil Spirits; that sculptures or paintings, if beautiful, were of evil; that all cleverness in Mathematics, Chemistry, or Medicine proved the presence of the corrupting Evil Spirit working in man. Any bridge over a chasm or a rapid river was the work of the Devil; even the most beautiful Gothic cathedrals, like those of Cologne and St. Stephen at Vienna were constructed by architects who served their apprenticeship in the infernal regions. The Devil sat grinning on the inkstands of poets and learned men, dictating to the poor deluded mortals, as the price for their souls, charming love-songs or deep theological and philosophical essays. It was extremely dangerous during this period of man's historical evolution to be better or wiser than the ignorant masses. Learning, talent, a superior power of reasoning, love for truth, a spirit of inquiry, the capacity of making money by clever trading, an artistic turn of mind, success in life, even in the Church, were only so many proofs that the soul had been sold to some dwarfish or giant messenger from Lucifer, who could appear in a thousand different forms. Man was, since his assumed Fall, the exclusive property of the coarse and vulgar conception of the Evil Spirit. Luther was full of these ideas, he was brought up in this belief, and though he unconsciously felt that the Devil ought to be expelled from our creed, he did not dare to attempt the reform of humanity by annihilating the mischief-maker: he could not rob man of his dearest spiritual possession; had he thought of consigning the Devil to the antediluvian period of our moral and social formation, he never could have succeeded in his reform. The Devil, in fact, was his strongest helpmate; he could describe the ritual of the Romish Church as the work of the Evil Spirit, produced to delude mankind. The Devil had his Romish prayers, his processions, his worship of relics, his remission of sins, his confessional, his infernal synods; he was to Luther an active, rough, and material incarnation of the roaring lion of the Scriptures in the shape of the Romish Church, walking about visibly, tangibly, bodily amongst men, devouring all who believed in the Pope, and who disbelieved in this stupid phantom of a dogmatically blinded imagination.

The Evolution-theory may be clearly traced in the two next conceptions: Milton's Satan and Goethe's Mephistopheles. They differ as strongly as the periods and the poems in which they appear. Milton's Satan loses the vulgar flesh and bone, horn and hoof nature—he is an epic character; whilst Goethe's Devil is an active dramatic entity of modern times. Milton's representative of evil is a very powerful conception—it is evil in abstracto; whilst Mephistopheles is evil in concreto—the intelligible, tangible Devil, evolved by the power of selection from an antediluvian monster, and transformed through a civilizing process of at least six thousand years into its present form. Milton's Satan is a debased intellect who in his boundless ambition is still a supernatural being. Mephistopheles is the incarnation of our complicated modern social evils, full of petty tricks and learned quotations; he piously turns up his eyes, he lies, doubts, calumniates, seduces, philosophizes, sneers, but all in a polite and highly educated way; he is a scholar, a divine, a politician, a diplomatist. Satan is capable of wild enthusiasm, he sometimes remembers his bright sinless past; "from the lowest deep," he yearns, "once more to lift himself up, in spite of fate, nearer to his ancient seat;"—he hopes to re-enter heaven, "to purge off his gloom;" some remnant of heavenly innocence still clings to him, for, though fallen, he is still an angel! Mephistopheles in his real nature is without any higher aspirations, he argues with a sarcastic smile on his lips, he is ironical with sophisticated sharpness. Satan has unconsciously gigantic ideas, he is ready to wrestle with God for the dominion of heaven. Mephistopheles is perfectly conscious of his littleness as opposed to our better intellectual nature, and does evil for evil's sake. Satan is sublime through the grandeur of his primitive elements, pride and ambition. Mephistopheles is only grave in his pettiness; he does not refuse an orgie with drunken students, indulges in jokes with monkeys, works miracles in the witch's kitchen, delights in the witch's "one-time-one;" distributes little tracts "to stir up the witch's heart with special fire." Satan has nothing vulgar in him: he is capable of melancholy feelings, he can be pathetic and eloquent. Mephistopheles laughs at the stupidity of the world, and at his own. Satan believes in God and in himself, whilst Mephistopheles is the "Spirit that denies;" he believes neither in God nor in heaven nor in hell; he does not believe in his own entity—he is no supernatural, fantastic being, but man incarnate: he is the evil part of a good whole, which loses its entity when once seen and recognised in its real nature; for Mephistopheles in reality is our own ignorant, besotted, animal nature, cultivated and developed at the expense of our intellectual part.

Luther's devil is the outgrowth of humanity in long-clothes. Man, ignorant of the forces of the Cosmos, blinded by theological dialectics and metaphysical subtleties, incapable of understanding the real essence of our moral and intellectual nature, philosophically untrained to observe that evil is but a sequence of the disturbed balance between our double nature—spirit and matter—attributed all mischief in the intellectual as well as in our social spheres to an absolute powerful being who continually tormented him.

Milton's Satan is the poetical conception of man developed from an infant in long-clothes into a boisterous but dreamy youth, ascribing to every incomprehensible effect an arbitrary, poetical cause. Goethe's Mephistopheles, lastly is the truthful conception of evil as it really exists in a thousand forms, evolved from our own misunderstood and artificially and dogmatically distorted nature.

Goethe in destroying the Devil as such, consigned him to the primeval myths and legends of ignorance and fear, and has shown us the real nature of the evil.

What then is the Devil?

The Devil took, as I said in the beginning, his origin in our blinded senses, in an undue preponderance of that which is material in us over that which is intellectual. The moment we look the Evil Spirit in the face, he vanishes as an absolute being and becomes—

A portion of that power

Which wills the bad and works the good at every hour.

After having been exposed during several periods of generations to new conditions, thus rendering a great amount of variation possible, the Devil has developed from a monster into a monkey, and from a monkey into a man endowed with the nature of a monkey and the propensities of a monster. In the State and in the Church, in Arts and Sciences, the Devil is the principle of injustice, hypocrisy, ugliness, and ignorance. Goethe has annihilated the ideal poetical grandeur of Milton's Satan; he has stripped Luther's Devil of his vulgar realism; Goethe has driven Satan from an imaginary hell, where he preferred to rule instead of worshipping and serving in heaven, and with the sponge of common sense he wiped the horned monster, drawn by the imagination of dogmatists, from the black board of ignorance. In banishing the Evil Spirit into the dominion of myths, Goethe showed him in his real nature. Darwin displaced man from the exalted pedestal of a special creation, and endeavoured to trace him as the development of cosmical elements. Darwin enabled us to look upon man as the completing link in the great chain of the gradual evolution of the life-giving forces of the Universe, and he rendered thus our position more comprehensible and natural. Goethe, in proving that the Evil Spirit of ancient and Hebrew-Christian times was a mere phantom of an ill-regulated fantasy, taught us to look for the real origin of evil. What was a metaphysical incomprehensibility became an intelligible reality. The Demon can be seen in "Faust" as in a mirror, and in glancing into it we behold our Darwinian progenitor, the animal, face to face. Before the times of Goethe, with very few exceptions, the Evil Spirit was an entity with whom any one might become familiar—in fact, the "spiritus familiaris" of old. The Devil spoke, roared, whispered, could sign contracts. We were able to yield our soul to him; and he could bodily enter our body. The Devil was a corporeal entity. The rack, water, and fire were used to expel him from sorcerers and witches, and to send him into all sorts of unclean animals. Goethe, in unmasking this phantom, introduced him not as something without, but as an element within us. The service rendered to humanity in showing us the true nature of evil is as grand as the service rendered by Mr. Darwin in assigning to man his place in nature, and not above nature. It is curious that those who have most of the incorrigible and immovable animal nature in them should protest with the greatest vehemence and clamour against this theory. They think by asserting their superiority, based on a special creation, to become at once special and superior beings, and prefer this position to trying, through a progressive development in science and knowledge, in virtue and honesty, to prove the existence of the higher faculties with which man has been endowed through his gradual development from the lowest phases of living creatures to the highest. In assuming the Devil to be

something absolute and positive, and not something
relative and negative, man hoped to be better able to
grapple with him. Mephistopheles is nothing personal; he
can, like the Creator himself, be only traced in his works.
The Devil lurks beneath the venerable broadcloth of an
intolerant and ignorant priest; he uses the seducing smiles
of a wicked beauty; he stirs the blood of the covetous and
grasping; he strides through the gilded halls of ambitious
emperors and ministers, who go with "light hearts" to kill
thousands of human beings with newly-invented infernal
machines; he works havoc in the brains of the vain. The
Devil shuffles the cards for the gambler, and destroys our
peace whether he makes us win or lose on the turf; he sits
joyfully grinning on the tops of bottles and tankards filled
with alcoholic drinks; he entices us on Sundays to shut our
museums and open our gin-palaces; to neglect the
education of the masses; and then prompts us to accuse
them with hypocritical respectability of drunkenness and
stupidity. It is the Devil who turns us into friends of
lapdogs and makes us enemies of the homeless. The Devil
is the greatest master in dogmatism; he creates sects who,
in the name of love and humility, foster hatred and pride;
the Devil encloses men in a magic circle on the barren
heath of useless speculation; drives them round and round
like blinded horses in a mill, starting from one point, and
after miles and miles of travel and fatigue, leading us to the
point, sadder but not wiser, from which we set out. The
Devil makes us quarrel whether we ought to have schools
with or without bigoted religious teachings; he burns
incense to stupefy our senses, lights candles to obscure our
sight, amuses the masses with buffooneries to prevent them
from thinking, draws us away from common-sense
morality, and leads us, under the pretext of a mystic and
symbolic religion, to the confessional, the very hothouse of
mischief. Satan in all his shapes and forms as he rules the

world has been described by Goethe as Egotism. Selfishness is his element and real nature. Selfishness not yet realizing the divine, because so entirely humane command—"Do unto others as you wish that they should do unto you." Selfishness is the only essence of evil. Selfishness has divided men into different nations, and fosters in them pride, envy, jealousy, and hatred. Mr. Darwin has shown that one animal preys on the other, that the weaker species has to yield to the stronger. Goethe again has shown us how the Evil Spirit drags us through life's wild scenes and its flat unmeaningness, to seek mere sensual pleasures and to neglect altogether our higher and better nature, which is the outgrowth of our more complicated, more highly developed organization. Were we only to recognise this, our real nature, we should leave less to chance and prejudices; were we to study man from a physiological, psychological, and honestly historical point of view, we should soon eliminate selfishness from among us, and be able to appreciate what is really the essence of evil. The more nearly we approach Darwin's primitive man, the ape, the nearer do we draw to the Mephistopheles who shows us his exact nature with impudent sincerity in Goethe's "Faust."

That which changes our Psyche, that is our intellectual faculty with its airy wings of imagination, its yearnings for truth, into an ugly, submissive, crawling worm, is heartless selfishness. Not without reason is poor guileless Margaret horrified at Mephistopheles. She shudders, hides herself on the bosom of Faust, like a dove under the wings of an eagle, and complains that the Evil Spirit—

... Always wears such mocking grin,

Half cold, half grim,

One sees that nought has interest for him;

'Tis writ on his brow, and can't be mistaken,

No soul in him can love awaken.

When all goes wrong, when religious, social, and political animosities and hatred disturb the peace; when unintelligible controversies on the inherited sin, the origin of evil, justification, and transubstantiation, "grace and free will," the creative and the created, mystic incantations, real and unreal presences, the like but not equal, the affirmative and the negative natures of God and man confuse the finite brains of infinite talkers and repeaters of the same things; when they quarrel about the wickedness of the hen who dared to lay an egg on the Sabbath; when the glaring torch of warfare is kindled by the fire of petty animosities, then the Evil Spirit of egotism celebrates its most glorious festivals.

What can banish this monster, this second and worse part of our nature? To look upon it from a Darwinian point of view. Goethe saves his fallen Faust through useful "occupation," through honest hard work for the benefit of mankind. The more we make ourselves acquainted with evil, the last remnant of our animal nature, in a rational and not mystic dogmatical sense, the less we exalt ourselves as exceptional creatures above nature, the easier it must be for us to dry up the source of superstition and ignorance which serves to nourish this social monster.

Let our relations to each other be based on "mutual love," for God is love, and selfishness as the antagonist of love, and the Devil as the antagonist of God, will both vanish.

Let us strive to vanquish our unnatural social organization
by a natural, social, but at the same time, liberal union of
all into one common brotherhood, and the roaring lion will
be silenced for ever.

Let us purify society of all its social, or rather unsocial,
iniquities and falsehoods, of all ingratitude and envy, in
striving for an honest regeneration of ourselves, and
through ourselves of humanity at large, convincing one
another that man has developed by degrees into earth's
fairest creature, destined for good and happiness, and not
for evil and wretchedness, and there will be an end of the
Devil and all his devilries.

FOOTNOTES:

[1] The word is found in Isaiah xxxiv. 14. Translated in the
Vulgate as "Lamia;" in Luther's translation as "Kobold;" in
the English version as "screech-owl;" and in others as "an
ugly night-bird."

CHAPTER XXIV.

PECULIAR PEOPLE.

In this title, be it distinctly understood, no reference is
intended to those anti-Æsculapian persons who, from time
to time, sacrifice to Moloch among the Essex marshes. It is
not necessary to journey even as far as Plumstead in search
of peculiarity, since the most manifold and ever-varying
types of it lie at one's very doors. And here, at the outset,
without quite endorsing the maxim that genius is always
eccentric, let it be confessed that a slight deviation from
the beaten track is generally apt to be interesting. When we
see the photograph of some distinguished artist, musician,
or poet, and find the features very like those of the pork
butcher in the next street, or the footman over the way, we
are conscious of a feeling of disappointment almost
amounting to a personal grievance. Mr. Carlyle and
Algernon Swinburne satisfy us. They look as we feel
graphic writers and erotic poets ought to look. Not so the
literary females who affect the compartment labelled "For
ladies only," in the reading room of the British Museum or
on the Metropolitan Railway. They are mostly like one's
maiden aunts, and savour far less of the authoress than
some of the charming girls who studiously avoid their
exclusive locale, and evidently use their reading ticket only
to cover with an appearance of propriety a most
unmistakable flirtation. This they carry on sotto voce with
ardent admirers of the male sex, who, though regular
frequenters of the reading room, are no more literary than
themselves. One might pick out a good many peculiar
people from that learned retreat—that poor scholar's club
room; but let us rather avoid any such byways of life, and

select our peculiars from the broad highway. Hunting there, Diogenes-wise, with one's modest lantern, in search—not of honest—but eccentric individuals.

And first of all, having duly attended to the ladies at the outset, let there be "Place for the Clergy." There is my dear friend the Rev. Gray Kidds, the best fellow breathing, but, from a Diogenes point of view, decidedly eccentric. Gray Kidds is one of those individuals whose peculiarity it is never to have been a boy. Kidds at fifteen had whiskers as voluminous as he now has at six-and-twenty, and as he gambolled heavily amongst his more puerile schoolfellows, visitors to the playground used to ask the assistant masters who that man was playing with the boys. They evidently had an uneasy notion that a private lunatic asylum formed a branch of the educational establishment, and that Gray Kidds was a harmless patient allowed to join the boys in their sports. Gray Kidds was and is literally harmless. He grew up through school and college, innocently avoiding all those evils which proved the ruin of many who were deemed far wiser than himself. He warbled feebly on the flute, and was adored as a curate, not only for his tootle-tooings, but for his diligent presence at mothers' meetings, and conscientious labours among the poor. A preacher Kidds never pretended to be; but he had the singular merit of brevity, and crowded more harmless heresies into ten minutes' pulpit oratory than Colenso or Voysey could have done in double the time. The young ladies made a dead set at him, of course, for Kidds was in every respect eligible; and he let them stroke him like a big pet lamb, but there matters ended. Kidds never committed himself. He is now the incumbent of a pretty church in the suburbs, built for him by his aunt, and, strange to say, the church fills. Whether it is that his brevity is attractive, or his transparent goodness compensates for his other peculiarities, certainly he has a congregation; and if you polled that congregation, the one point on which all would agree, in addition to his eligibility or innocence, would be that the Rev. Gray Kidds was "so funny."

And now, for our second type of peculiarity, let us beat back for one moment to the fair sex again. Mrs. Ghoul is the reverse of spirituelle; but she is something more—she is spiritualistic. She devoutly believes that the spirits of deceased ancestors come at her bidding, and tilt the table, move furniture insanely about, or write idiotic messages automatically. She is perfectly serious. She does "devoutly" believe this. It is her creed. It is a comfort to her. It is extremely difficult to reconcile such a source of comfort with any respect for one's departed relatives, but that is Mrs. Ghoul's peculiarity and qualification for a niche amongst our originals.

Miss Deedy, on the other hand, is ecclesiastical to the backbone. Miss Deedy ruins her already feeble health with early mattins (she insists on the double t) and frequent fasts. Beyond an innocuous flirtation with the curate at decorations, or a choral meeting, Miss Deedy has as few sins as most of us to answer for; but, from her frequent penances, she might be a monster of iniquity. She is known to confess, and is suspected of wearing sackcloth. Balls and theatres she eschews as "worldly," and yet she is only just out of her teens. She would like to be a nun, she says, if the habits were prettier, and they allowed long curls down the back, and Gainsboroughs above the brow. As it is, Miss Deedy occupies a somewhat abnormal position, dangling, like Mahomet's coffin, between the Church and the world. That, again, is Miss Deedy's peculiarity.

Miss Wiggles is a "sensitive." That is a new vocation struck out by the prolific ingenuity of the female mind. Commonplace doctors would simply call her "hysterical;" but she calls herself magnetic. She is stout and inclined to a large appetite, particularly affecting roast pork with plenty of seasoning; but she passes readily into "the superior condition" under the manipulations of a male operator. She makes nothing, save notoriety, by her clairvoyance and other peculiarities; but she is very peculiar, though the type of a larger class than is perhaps imagined in this highly sensational age of ours.

Peculiar boys, too—what lots of them there are! What is called affectation in a girl prevails to quite as large an extent in the shape of endless peculiarities among boys. A certain Dick (his name is Adolphus, but he is universally, and for no assignable reason, known as Dick) rejoices in endorsing Darwinism by looking and acting like a human gorilla. Dick is no fool, but assumes that virtue though he has it not. To see him mumbling his food at meals, or making mops and mows at the wall, you would think him qualified for Earlswood; but if it comes to polishing off a lesson briskly or being mulct of his pudding or pocket-money, Master Dick accomplishes the polishing process with a rapidity that gives the lie to his Darwinian assumption.

Well, they are a source of infinite fun, these eccentrics— the comets of our social system. They have, no doubt, an object in their eccentricity, a method in their madness, which we prosaic planetary folks cannot fathom. At all events, they amuse us and don't harm themselves. They are uniformly happy and contented with themselves. Of them assuredly is true, and without the limitation he appends, Horace's affirmation, Dulce est desipere, which Mr.

Theodore Martin translates, "'Tis pleasing at times to be slightly insane."

CHAPTER XXV.

INTERVIEWING AN ASTROLOGER.

For several years—in fact ever since my first acquaintance with these "occult" matters whereinto I am now such a veteran investigator—my great wish has been to become practically acquainted with some Professor of Astral Science. One friend, indeed, I had who had devoted a long lifetime to this and kindred subjects, and of whom I shall have to speak anon; but he had never utilized his knowledge so as to become the guide, philosopher, and friend of amorous housemaids on the subject of their matrimonial alliances, or set himself to discover petty larcenies for a fee of half-a-crown. He assured me, however, that the practice of astrology was as rife as ever in London at this moment, and that businesses in that line were bought and sold for sterling coin of the realm, just as though they had been "corner" publics, or "snug concerns" in the cheesemongery line. All this whetted my appetite for inquiry, and seeing one Professor Wilson advertise persistently in the Medium to the effect that "the celebrated Astrologer may be consulted on the events of life" from two to nine p.m., I wrote to Professor Wilson asking for an interview; but the celebrated astrologer did not favour me with a reply.

Foiled in my first attempt I waited patiently for about a year, and then broke ground again—I will not say whether with Professor Wilson, or some other practitioner of astral science. I will call my Archimago Professor Smith, of Newington Causeway, principally for the reason that this is neither the real name nor the correct address. I have no wish to advertise any wizard gratuitously; nor would it be fair to him, since, as will be seen from the sequel, his reception of me was such as to make it probable that he would have an inconvenient number of applicants on the conditions observed at my visit.

Availing myself, then, of the services of my friend above-mentioned, I arranged that we should together pay a visit to Professor Smith, of Newington Causeway, quite "permiscuous," as Mrs. Gamp would say. My companion would go with his own horoscope already constructed, as he happened to know the exact hour and minute of his birth—particulars as to which I only possessed the vaguest information, which is all I fancy most of us have; though there was one circumstance connected with my own natal day which went a long way towards "fixing" it.

It was on a Monday evening that I visited this modern Delphic oracle; and, strangely enough, as is often the case, other events seemed to lead up to this one. The very lesson on Sunday evening was full of astrology. It was, I may mention, the story of the handwriting on the wall and the triumph of Daniel over the magicians. Then I took up my Chaucer on Monday morning; and instead of the "Canterbury Tales," opened it at the "Treatise on the

Astrolabe," which I had never read before, but devoured
then as greedily as no doubt did "Little Lowis," to whom it
is addressed. All this tended to put me in a proper frame of
mind for my visit to Newington; so, after an early tea, we
took my friend's figure of his nativity with us, and went.

Professor Smith, we found, lived in a cosy house in the
main road, the parlours whereof he devoted to the purposes
of a medical magnetist, which was his calling, as inscribed
upon the wire blinds of the ground floor front. We were
ushered at once into the professor's presence by a woman
who, I presume, was his wife—a quiet respectable body
with nothing uncanny about her. The front parlour was
comfortably furnished and scrupulously clean, and the
celebrated Professor himself, a pleasant elderly gentleman,
was sitting over a manuscript which he read by the light of
a Queen's reading lamp. There was not, on the one hand,
any charlatan assumption in his get-up, nor, on the other,
was there that squalor and neglect of the decencies of life
which I have heard sometimes attaches to the practitioners
in occult science. Clad in a light over-coat, with spectacles
on nose, and bending over his MS., Professor Smith might
have been a dissenting parson en déshabille "getting off"
his Sunday discourse, or a village schoolmaster correcting
the "themes" of his pupils. He was neither; he was a
nineteenth century astrologer, calculating the probabilities
of success for a commercial scheme, the draft prospectus
of which was the document over which he pored. As he
rose to receive us I was almost disappointed to find that he
held no wand, wore no robe, and had no volume of mystic
lore by his side. The very cat that emerged from
underneath his table, and rubbed itself against my legs was
not of the orthodox sable hue, but simple tabby and white.

My friend opened the proceedings by producing the figure of his nativity, and saying he had come to ask a question in horary astrology relative to a certain scheme about which he was anxious, such anxiety constituting what he termed a "birth of the mind." Of course this was Dutch to me, and I watched to see whether the Professor would be taken off his guard by finding he was in presence of one thoroughly posted up in astral science. Not in the least; he greeted him as a brother chip, and straightway the two fell to discussing the figure. The Professor worked a new one, which he found to differ in some slight particulars from the one my friend had brought. Each, however, had worked it by logarithms, and there was much talk of "trines" and "squares" and "houses," which I could not understand; but eventually the coveted advice was given by the Professor and accepted by my friend as devoutly as though it had been a response of the Delphic oracle itself. The business would succeed, but not without trouble, and possibly litigation on my friend's part. He was to make a call on a certain day and "push the matter" a month afterwards; all of which he booked in a business-like manner. This took a long time, for the Professor was perpetually making pencil signs on the figure he had constructed, and the two also discussed Zadkiel, Raphael, and other astrologers they had mutually known. Continual reference had to be made to the "Nautical Almanack;" but by-and-by my friend's innings was over and mine commenced. I have said that I did not know the exact hour and minute of my birth, and when, with appropriate hesitation, I named the 1st of April as the eventful day, the Professor looked at me for a moment with a roguish twinkle of the eye as though to ascertain that I was not poking fun at him. I assured him, however, that such was the inauspicious era of my nativity, and moreover that I was born so closely on the confines of March 31—I do not feel it necessary to specify the year—as to make it almost dubious whether I could claim the honours of April-Fooldom. This seemed enough for him—though he warned me that the absence of the exact time might lead to some vagueness in his communications—and he proceeded forthwith to erect my figure; which, by the way, looked to me very much like making a "figure" in Euclid; and I peered anxiously to see whether mine bore any resemblance to the Pons Asinorum!

I feared I had led my philosopher astray altogether when the first item of information he gave me was that, at about the age of twenty-one, I had met with some accident to my arm, a circumstance which I could not recall to memory. Several years later I broke my leg, but I did not tell him that. Going further back, he informed me that about the age of fourteen, if I happened to be apprenticed, or in any way placed under authority, I kicked violently over the traces, which was quite true, inasmuch as I ran away from school twice at that precise age, so that my astrologer scored one. At twenty-eight I married (true), and at thirty-two things were particularly prosperous with me—a fact which I was also constrained to acknowledge correct. Then came a dreadful mistake. If ever I had anything to do with building or minerals, I should be very successful. I never had to do with building save once in my life, and then Mr. Briggs's loose tile was nothing to the difficulties in which I became involved. Minerals I had never dabbled in beyond the necessary consumption of coals for domestic purposes. I had an uncle who interested himself in my welfare some years ago—this was correct—and something was going to happen to my father's sister at Midsummer, 1876. This, of course, I cannot check; but I trust, for the sake of my venerable relation, it may be nothing prejudicial. I was also to suffer from a slight cold about the period of my birthday in that same year, and was especially to beware of damp feet. My eldest brother, if I had one, he said, had probably died, which was again correct; and if my wife caught cold she suffered in her throat, which piece of information, if not very startling, I am also constrained to confess is quite true. Then followed a most delicate piece of information which I blush as I commit to paper. I wished to marry when I was twenty-one, but circumstances prevented. Then it was that memories of a certain golden-haired first love came back through the vista of memory. I was then a Fellow of my College, impecunious except as regarded my academical stipend, so the young lady took advice and paired off with a well-to-do cousin. Sic transit gloria mundi! We are each of us stout, unromantic family people now; but the reminiscence made me feel quite romantic for the moment in that ground floor front in Newington Causeway; and I was inclined to say, "A Daniel come to judgment!" but I checked myself and remarked, sotto voce, in the vernacular, "Right again, Mr. Smith!"

Before passing on to analyse me personally he remarked that my wife's sister and myself were not on the best of terms. I owned that words had passed between us; and then he told me that in my cerebral development there was a satisfactory fusion of caution and combativeness. I was not easily knocked over, or, if so, had energy to get up again. This energy was to tell in the future. This, I believe, is a very usual feature of horoscopic revelation. Next year was to be particularly prosperous. I should travel a good deal— had travelled somewhat this year, and was just now going to take a short journey; but I should travel a great deal more next year. I own to asking myself whether this could bear any reference to the Pontigny Pilgrimage in which I shared this year, and the possible pilgrimage to Rome next summer, and also a projected journey to Scotland by the

Limited Mail next Tuesday evening! On the whole, my astrologer had scored a good many points.

The most marvellous revelation of all yet remains to be made, however. When we rose to go we each of us endeavoured to force a fee on Professor Smith, but nothing would induce him to receive a farthing! I had got all my revelations, my "golden" memories of the past, my bright promises of the future free, gratis, for nothing! It will be evident, then, why I do not give this good wizard's address lest I inundate him with gratuitous applicants, and why I therefore veil his personality under the misleading title of Professor Smith of Newington Causeway.

CHAPTER XXVI.

A BARMAID SHOW.

The present age, denounced by some ungenial censors as the age of shams, may be described by more kindly critics as emphatically an age of "shows." Advancing from the time-honoured shows of Flora and Pomona—if not always improving on the type—and so on from the cattle show, suggestive of impending Christmas fare, we have had horse shows, dog shows, and bird shows. To these the genius of Barnum added baby shows; and, if we are not misinformed, a foreign firm, whose names have become household words amongst us, originated, though not exactly in its present form, the last kind of show which has been acclimatized in England—an exhibition of barmaids. We had two baby shows in one year—one at Highbury Barn by Mr. Giovannelli, the other at North Woolwich Gardens by Mr. Holland; and it is to the talent of this latter gentleman in the way of adaptation that we owe the exhibition of young ladies "practising at the bar." From babies to barmaids is indeed a leap, reversing the ordinary process of going from the sublime to the ridiculous, for while to all but appreciative mammas those infantile specimens of humanity savour largely of the ridiculous, there can be no question that the present generation of dames de comptoir is a very sublime article indeed. I do not say this in derision, nor am I among those who decry the improvements introduced during the last few years, both into refreshment bars themselves, and notably into the class of ladies who preside over them. The discriminating visitor will decidedly prefer to receive his sandwich and glass of bitter at the hands of a pretty barmaid rather than from an oleaginous pot-man in his shirt-sleeves; and the sherry-cobbler acquires a racier flavour from the arch looks of the Hebe who dispenses it. If silly young men do dawdle at the bar for the sake of the sirens inside, and occasionally, as we have known to be the case, take unto themselves these same sirens "for better or for worse," we can only cite the opinion of well-informed authorities, that very possibly the young gentlemen in question might have gone farther and fared worse, and that it is not always the young lady who has, in such a case, the best of the bargain.

So, then, the "Grand Barmaid Contest" opened; and in spite of the very unmistakable appearance put in by Jupiter Fluvius, a numerous assemblage gathered in the North Woolwich Gardens to inaugurate a festival which, whatever else we may think of it, is at all events sui generis. Prizes to the value of 300l. were to be presented to the successful candidates, varying from a purse of twenty sovereigns and a gold watch and chain, down to "a purse of two sovereigns," with "various other prizes, consisting of jewellery, &c."

Among the conditions it was required, that every young lady should be over sixteen years of age; that she should be dressed in plain but good articles of attire, "in which a happy blending of colours without prominent display is most suitable;" and it was moreover stipulated that each "young lady" should "ingratiate herself with the public in the most affable manner at her command, without undue forwardness or frivolity, but still retaining a strict attention to business." No young lady was permitted to take part in the contest unless she had been in the refreshment business for twelve months, and could produce good testimonials of character.

Upwards of 700 applications were made, out of which Mr. Holland selected fifty. Whence the large number of rejections "deponeth sayeth not." Of these twenty-eight actually put in an appearance at three p.m. on the opening day and four were expected to join in a day or two. Every visitor is provided with a voting ticket, which he hands to the lady of his admiration, and which counts towards the prize. Each young lady also receives 5 per cent. on what she sells at her bar. The places are awarded by lot; and, by a freak of fortune, the two most attractive demoiselles happened to come together. These were Numbers One and Fourteen. The former young lady—who desires to be known by her number only, true genius being ever modest—was certain to stand Number One in popular esteem; and, if chignons are taken into account, she ought literally to "head" the list by a very long way. The room was tastefully decorated by Messrs. Defries, and an excellent band enlivened the proceedings. As evening drew on the meeting grew more hilarious, but there was not the slightest impropriety of any kind, the faintest approach thereto leading to immediate expulsion.

Many persons may be disposed to ask, in respect of such exhibitions, Cui bono? But at all events there was nothing which the veriest Cato could denounce as demoralizing. The "young ladies" were all most modestly attired in "sober livery;" and certainly—though comparisons are odious—not so pressing in their attentions as we have seen some other young ladies at Dramatic Fêtes, or even some dévouées at charitable bazaars. If we may judge from the large numbers that visited North Woolwich, "in spite of wind and weather," Mr. Holland was likely to reap an abundant harvest from this latest "idea," excogitated from his fertile brain. As the babies have had their "show," and the stronger sex is not likely to be equal to the task of being exhibited just yet, there seems only one section of society open to the speculations of a skilful entrepreneur. Why does not some one, in a more serious line than Mr. Holland, try what Sydney Smith calls the "third sex," and open an exhibition of curates, with a genuine competition for prizes? There could be no possible doubt as to the success of such a display, and the instruction to be derived from it would be equally beyond question. In the meantime we have advanced one step towards such a consummation. The adult human being has taken the place of the baby; and people evidently like it. Where will the rage for exhibitions stop? Who can say to the advancing tide of shows, "Thus far shalt thou go, and no farther?" Other classes of society will probably have their turn, and may think themselves fortunate if they show up as well as Mr. Holland's "young ladies."

CHAPTER XXVII.

A PRIVATE EXECUTION.

I was quietly fiddling away one evening in the Civil Service band at King's College, as was my custom while my leisure was larger than at present, when the gorgeous porter of the college entered with a huge billet which he placed on my music-stand with a face of awe. It was addressed to me, and in the corner of it was written "Order for Execution." The official waited to see how I bore it, and seemed rather surprised that I went on with my fiddling, and smilingly said, "All right." I knew it was an order from the authorities of Horsemonger Lane Gaol admitting me to the private execution of Margaret Waters, the notorious baby-farmer.

If anything is calculated to promote the views of those who advocate the abolition of capital punishment, it is the fact of a woman meeting her death at the hands of the common hangman. There is something abhorrent, especially to the mind of the stronger sex, in the idea of a female suffering the extreme penalty of the law. On the other hand, the crime for which Margaret Waters suffered—which is too much a cause célèbre to need recapitulation—is exactly the one that would exile her from the sympathy of her own sex. Whilst therefore her case left the broad question much in the same position as before, we are not surprised to find that strenuous efforts had been made to obtain a commutation of the sentence. Mr. Gilpin, Mr. Samuel Morley, and Mr. Baines had been conspicuous for their efforts in the cause of mercy. All, however, had been to no purpose. Margaret Waters was privately executed within the walls of Horsemonger Lane Gaol at nine o'clock.

It was a thankless errand that called one from one's bed whilst the moon was still struggling with the feeble dawn of an October morning, and through streets already white with the incipient frost of approaching winter, to see a fellow-creature—and that a woman—thus hurried out of existence. On arriving at the gloomy prison-house I saw a fringe of roughs lounging about, anxious to catch a glimpse, if only of the black flag that should apprize them of the tragedy they were no longer privileged to witness. Even these, however, did not muster in strong force until the hour of execution drew near. On knocking at the outer wicket, the orders of admission were severely scrutinized, and none allowed to pass except those borne by the representatives of the press, or persons in some way officially connected with the impending "event." There was an air of grim "business" about all present, which showed plainly that none were there from choice, nor any who would not feel relief when the fearful spectacle was over. After assembling, first of all, in the porter's lodge, we were conducted by the governor, Mr. Keene, to the back of the prison, through courtyards and kitchen gardens; and in a corner of one of the former we came upon the ghastly instrument of death itself. Here half-a-dozen warders only were scattered about, and Mr. Calcraft was arranging his

paraphernalia with the air of a connoisseur. I remember—
so strangely does one's mind take in unimportant details at
such a crisis—being greatly struck with the fine leeks
which were growing in that particular corner of the prison
garden where the grim apparatus stood, and we—some
five-and-twenty at most, and all in the way of "business"—
stood, too, waiting for the event!

Then ensued a quarter of an hour's pause, in that cold
morning air, when suddenly boomed out the prison bell,
that told us the last few minutes of the convict's life had
come. The pinioning took place within the building; and on
the stroke of nine, the gloomy procession emerged, the
prisoner walking between the chaplain and Calcraft, with a
firm step, and even mounting the steep stair to the gallows
without needing assistance. She was attired in a plaid dress
with silk mantle, her head bare, and hair neatly arranged.

As this was my first experience in private hanging, I do not
mind confessing that I misdoubted my powers of
endurance. I put a small brandy-flask in my pocket, and
stood close by a corner around which I could retire if the
sight nauseated me; but such is the strange fascination
attaching to exhibitions even of this horrible kind, that I
pushed forward with the rest, and when the governor
beckoned me on to a "good place," I found myself standing
in the front rank with the rest of my confrères, and could
not help picturing what that row of upturned,
unsympathizing, pitiless faces must have looked like to the
culprit as contrasted with the more sympathetic crowds
that used to be present at a public execution.

One of the daily papers in chronicling this event went so
far as to point a moral on the brutalizing effect of such
exhibitions from my momentary hesitation and subsequent

struggle forward into the front rank. The convict's perfect sang froid had a good deal to do with my own calmness, I expect.

When the executioner had placed the rope round her neck, and the cap on her head ready to be drawn over the face, she uttered a long and fervent prayer, expressed with great volubility and propriety of diction, every word of which could be distinctly heard by us as we circled the scaffold. She could not have rounded her periods more gracefully or articulated them more perfectly, if she had rehearsed her part beforehand! Though most of the spectators were more or less inured to scenes of horror, several were visibly affected, one kneeling on the bare ground, and another leaning, overcome with emotion, against the prison wall. At last she said to the chaplain, "Mr. Jessopp, do you think I am saved?" A whispered reply from the clergyman conveyed his answer to that momentous question. All left the scaffold except the convict. The bolt was withdrawn, and, almost without a struggle, Margaret Waters ceased to exist. Nothing could exceed the calmness and propriety of her demeanour, and this, the chaplain informed us, had been the case throughout since her condemnation. She had been visited on one occasion by a Baptist minister, to whose persuasion she belonged; but he had, at her own request, forborne to repeat his visit. The prisoner said he was evidently unused to cases like hers, and his ministrations rather distracted than comforted her. The chaplain of the gaol had been unremitting in his attentions, and seemingly with happy effect. Though she constantly persisted in saying she was not a murderess in intent, she was yet brought to see her past conduct in its true light; and on the previous Saturday received the Holy Communion in her cell with one of her brothers. Two of them visited her, and expressed the strongest feelings of attachment. In fact, the unhappy woman seemed to have been deeply attached to and beloved by all the members of her family. She had, since her condemnation, eaten scarcely anything, having been kept alive principally by stimulants. Although this, of course, induced great bodily weakness, she did not from the first exhibit any physical fear of death. On the night before her execution—that peaceful moonlit night—when so many thoughts must have turned to this unhappy woman, she slept little, and rose early. The chaplain had arranged to be with her at eight, but she sent for him an hour earlier, and he continued with her until the end. On Monday night she penned a long statement addressed to Mr. Jessopp. This was written with a firm hand on four sides of a foolscap sheet, expressed with great perspicuity, and signed with the convict's name. Whilst still repudiating the idea of being a murderess in intent, she pleaded guilty to great deceit, and to having obtained money under false pretences. If she had not given proper food, that, she contended, was an error of judgment. It was hard, she thought, that she should be held accountable for the child who died in the workhouse. She dwelt much upon the difficulties brought upon her by her dread of the money-lender—that fungus growth of our so-called civilization, who has brought so many criminals to the gallows, besides ruining families every day in each year of grace! That she had administered laudanum she denied. The evidence as to the dirty condition of the children she asserted to be false. She wished to avoid all bitterness; but those who had so deposed had sworn falsely. "I feel sure their consciences will condemn them to-night," she wrote, "for having caused the death of a fellow-creature." In the face of the evidence, she felt the jury could not find any other verdict, or the judge pass any other sentence than had been done. The case had been got up, she argued, to expose a system which was wrong.

Parents wished to get rid of their ill-gotten offspring. Their one thought was to hide their own shame. "They," she concluded, "are the real sinners. If it were not for their sin, we should not be sought after."

There must surely be some whose consciences these words will prick. However this woman deserved the bitter penalty she has now paid, there is indeed a tremendous truth in her assertion that she, and such as she, are but the supply which answers their demand.

And so we filed away as the autumnal sun shone down upon that gloomy spectacle, leaving her to the "crowner's 'quest," and the dishonoured grave in the prison precincts. Up to the previous night strong hopes of a commutation of the sentence were entertained. Her brothers had memorialized the Home Secretary, and were only on the previous day informed that the law must take its course. Let us hope that this stern example will put a stop, not only to "baby-farming," which, as the dead woman truly said, is but a consequence of previous crime—but also to those "pleasant vices" which are its antecedents and encouragements.

CHAPTER XXVIII.

BREAKING UP FOR THE HOLIDAYS.

Unromantic as it sounds to say it, I know of few things more disgusting than to revisit one's old school after some twenty or thirty years. Let that dubious decade still remain as to the number of years that have elapsed since I left school. In fact, it matters to nobody when I left it; I revisited it lately. I went to see the boys break up, as I once broke up, and I felt disgusted—not with the school, or the breaking up, but with myself. I felt disgracefully old. In fact, I went home, and began a poem with these words:—

My years, I feel, are getting on:

Yet, ere the trembling balance kicks, I

Will imitate the dying swan,

And sing an ode threnodic—vixi.

I never got any farther than that. By the way, I shall have to mention eventually that the school was King's College, in the Strand. I am not going to unbosom beyond this, or to add anything in the way of an autobiography; but the locale would have to come out anon, and there is no possible reason for concealment.

Well, I went to see them break up for the holidays, and only got over my antediluvian feelings by seeing one of the masters still on the staff who was there when I was a boy.

It was a comfort to think what a Methuselah he must be; and yet, if he will excuse the personality, he looked as rosy and smooth-faced as when he used to stand me outside his door with my coat-sleeves turned inside out. It was a way he had. Well, the presence of that particular master made me feel an Adonis forthwith.

I will not go into the prizes. There were lots of them, and they were very nice, and the boys looked very happy, and their mammas legitimately proud. What I want to speak of is the school speeches or recitations, as they are termed. King's College School speeches are, to my thinking, a model of what such things ought to be.

Some schools—I name no names—go in for mere scholastic recitations which nobody understands, and the boys hate. Others burst out in full-blown theatricals. King's College acts on the motto, Medio tutissimus ibis. It keeps the old scholastic recitations, but gilds the pill by adding the accessory of costume. I can quote Latin as well as Dr. Pangloss, and certain lines were running in my mind all the time I was in King's College Hall. They were

Pueris olim dant crustula blandi

Doctores, elementa velint ut discere prima.

First we had a bit of German in the shape of an extract from Kotzebue's "Die Schlaue Wittwe," or "Temperaments." I wish I had my programme, I would compliment by name the lad who played the charming young Frau. Suffice it to say the whole thing went off sparkling like a firework. It was short, and made you wish for more—a great virtue in speeches and sermons. The dancing-master was perfect. Then came a bit of Colman's "Heir at Law." Dr. Pangloss—again I regret the absence of the programme—was a creation, and—notwithstanding the proximity of King's College to the Strand Theatre—the youth wisely abstained from copying even so excellent a model as Mr. Clarke. Of course, the bits of Latinity came out with a genuine scholastic ring. Then a bit of a Greek play, at which—mirabile dictu!—everybody laughed, and with which everybody was pleased. And why? Because the adjuncts of costume and properties added to the correct enunciation of the text, prevented even those, who knew little Latin and less Greek, from being one moment in the dark as to what was going on. The passage was one from the "Birds" of Aristophanes; and the fact of a treaty being concluded between the Olympians and terrestrials, led to the introduction of some interpolations as to the Washington Treaty, which, when interpreted by the production of the American flag and English Union Jack, brought down thunders of applause. The final chorus was sung to "Yankee Doodle," and accompanied by a fiddle. The acting and accessories were perfect; and what poor Robson used to term the "horgan" of Triballos, was wonderful. That youth would be a nice young man for a small tea party. It is to be hoped that, like Bottom the weaver, he can modulate his voice, and roar as gently as any sucking-dove.

Most wonderful, however, of all the marvels—that met me at my old school—was a scene from the "Critic," played by the most Lilliputian boys. Puff—played by Powell (I don't forget that name)—was simply marvellous. And yet Powell, if he will forgive me for saying so, was the merest whipper-snapper. Sir Christopher Hatton could scarcely have emerged from the nursery; and yet the idea of utter stolidity never found a better exponent than that same homœopathic boy.

Last of all came the conventional scene from Molière's "L'Avare." Maître Jacques was good; Harpagon more than good. I came away well satisfied, only regretting I had not brought my eldest boy to see it. My eldest boy! Egad, and I was just such as he is now, when I used to creep like a snail unwillingly to those scholastic shades. The spirit of Pangloss came upon me again as I thought of all I had seen that day,—there was nothing like it in my day. King's College keeps pace with the times. "Tempora mutantur!" I mentally exclaimed; and added, not without a pleasant scepticism, as I gazed once more on the pippin-faced master, "I wonder whether—nos mutamur in illis?"

CHAPTER XXIX.

PSYCHOLOGICAL LADIES.

There is no doubt that the "Woman's Rights" question is going ahead with gigantic strides, not only in social and political, but also in intellectual matters. Boys and girls— or rather we ought to say young ladies and young gentlemen—are grouped together on the class list of the Oxford Local Examination, irrespective of sex. A glance at the daily papers will show us that women are being lectured to on all subjects down from physical sciences, through English literature and art, to the construction of the clavecin. We had fancied, however, that what are technically termed "the Humanities," or, in University diction, "Science"—meaning thereby ethics and logic— were still our own. Now, we are undeceived. We are reminded that woman can say, without a solecism, "Homo sum," and may therefore claim to embrace even the humanities among her subjects of study. Henceforth the realm of woman is not merely what may be called "pianofortecultural," as was once the case. It has soared even above art, literature, and science itself into what might at first sight appear the uncongenial spheres of dialectics and metaphysics.

Professor G. Croom Robertson recently commenced a course of thirty lectures to ladies on Psychology and Logic, at the Hall, 15, Lower Seymour Street, Portman Square. Urged, it may be, rather by a desire to see whether ladies would be attracted by such a subject, and, if so, what psychological ladies were like, than by any direct interest in the matters themselves, I applied to the hon. secretary, inquiring whether the inferior sex were admissible; and was answered by a ticket admitting one's single male self and a party of ladies à discrétion. The very entrance to the hall—nay, the populous street itself—removed my doubts as to whether ladies would be attracted by the subjects; and on entering I discovered that the audience consisted of several hundred ladies, and two unfortunate—or shall it not rather be said privileged?—members of the male sex. The ladies were of all ages, evidently matrons as well as spinsters, with really nothing at all approaching a "blue stocking" element; but all evidently bent on business. All were taking vigorous notes, and seemed to follow the Professor's somewhat difficult Scotch diction at least as well as our two selves, who appeared to represent not only the male sex in general, but the London press in particular.

Professor Robertson commenced by a brief and well-timed reference to the accomplished Hypatia, familiar to ladies from Kingsley's novel—in the days when ladies used to read novels—and also the Royal ladies whom Descartes and Leibnitz found apter disciples than the savants. It was, however, he remarked, an impertinence to suppose that any apology was needed for introducing such subjects before ladies. He plunged therefore at once in medias res, and made his first lecture not a mere isolated or introductory one, but the actual commencement of his series. Unreasoned facts, he said, formed but a mere fraction of our knowledge—even the simplest processes resolving themselves into a chain of inference. Truth is the result of logical reasoning; and not only truth, but truth for all. The sciences deal with special aspects of truth. These sciences may be arranged in the order—1. Mathematics; 2. Physics; 3. Chemistry; 4. Biology—each gradually narrowing its sphere; the one enclosed, so to say, in the other, and each presupposing those above it. Logic was presupposed in all. Each might be expressed by a word ending in "logy," therefore logic might be termed the "science of sciences." The sciences were special applications of logic. Scientific men speak lightly of logic, and say truth can be discovered without it. This is true, but trivial. We may as well object to physiology because we can digest without a knowledge of it; or to arithmetic, because it is possible to reckon without it. Scientific progress has been great; but its course might have been strewn with fewer wrecks had its professors been more generally logicians. But then logic presupposes something else. We have to investigate the origin and growth of knowledge—the laws under which knowledge comes to be. Under one aspect this science—

psychology—should be placed highest up in the scale; but under another it would rank later in point of development than even biology itself, because it is not every being that thinks. This twofold aspect is accounted for by the peculiarity of its subject-matter—viz., mind.

The sciences are comparatively modern. Mathematics but some 3000 or 4000 years old; physics, three centuries; chemistry, a thing of the last, biology only of the present century. But men philosophized before the sciences. The ancient Greeks had but one science—mathematics. Now men know a little of many sciences; but what we want is men to connect—to knit together—the sciences; to have their knowledge all of a piece. The knowledge of the ancient Greek directed his actions, and entered far more into his daily life than ours does. This, he observed, was philosophy. This is what we want now; and this is what is to be got from psychology. There is not a single thing between heaven and earth that does not admit of a mental expression; or, in other words, possess a subjective aspect, and therefore come under psychology.

This, in briefest outline, is a sketch of the "strong meat" offered to the psychological ladies. A single branch of psychology—that, namely, of the intellect, excluding that of feeling and action—is to occupy ten lectures, the above being number one. The other twenty will be devoted to logic.

The next lecture was devoted to an examination of the brain and nervous system, and their office in mental processes. Alas, however, how different was now the audience! Only some thirty ladies—scarcely more than one-tenth of those who were present at the opening lecture—have permanently entered for the course. It is no disrespect to the ladies to hazard the conjecture whether the subject be not a little out of range for the present. We are moving ahead rapidly, and many foolish ideas as to the intellectual differences of the sexes are becoming obsolete. We have literary and artistic ladies by thousands. Scientific ladies, in the ordinary acceptation of the term, are coming well to the front. Possibly we may have to "wait a little longer" before we get, on anything like a large scale, psychological or even logical ladies.

CHAPTER XXX.

SECULARISM ON BUNYAN.

It is very marvellous to observe the number of strange and unexpected combinations that are continually occurring in that moral kaleidoscope we call society. I do not suppose that I am exceptional in coming across these; nor do I use any particular industry in seeking them out. They come to me; all I do is to keep my eyes open, and note the impressions they make on me. I was humbly pursuing my way one Tuesday evening towards the abode of a phrenologist with the honest intention of discovering my craniological condition, when, in passing down Castle Street, Oxford Market, I was made aware that Mr. G. J. Holyoake was there and then to deliver himself on the "Literary Genius of Bunyan." This was one of the incongruous combinations I spoke of; and forthwith I passed into the Co-operative Hall, resolving to defer my visit to the phrenologist. There are some facts of which it is better to remain contentedly ignorant; and I have no doubt my own mental condition belongs to that category.

I found the Co-operative Hall a handsome and commodious building; and a very fair audience had gathered to listen to Mr. Holyoake, who is an elderly thin-voiced man, and his delivery was much impeded on the occasion in question by the circumstance of his having a bad cold and cough. After a brief extempore allusion to the fact of the Duke of Bedford having erected a statue to Bunyan, which he regarded as a sort of compensation for his Grace ceasing to subscribe to the races, Mr. Holyoake proceeded to read his treatise, which he had written on several slips of paper—apparently backs of circulars—and laid one by one on a chair as he finished them.

The world, he said, is a big place; but people are always forgetting what a variety of humanity it contains. Two hundred years ago, the authorities of Bedford made it very unpleasant for one John Bunyan, because they thought they knew everything, and could not imagine that a common street workman might know more. The trade of a tinker seems an unpromising preparation for a literary career. A tinker in Bedford to-day would not find himself much flattered by the attentions paid him, especially if he happened to be an old gaol-bird as well. So much the more creditable to Bunyan the ascendancy he gained. If he mended pots as well as he made sentences he was the best tinker that ever travelled.

Bunyan had no worldly notions. His doctrine was that men were not saved by any good they might do—a doctrine that would ruin the morals of any commercial establishment in a month! He declared himself the "chief of sinners;" but judged by his townsmen he was a stout-hearted, stout-minded, scrupulous man.

He was not a pleasant man to know. He had an unrelenting sincerity which often turned into severity. Yet he had much tenderness. He had a soul like a Red Indian's—all tomahawk and truth, until the literary passion came and added humour to it. He demands in his vigorous doggerel:—

May I not write in such a style as this,

In such a method, too, and yet not miss

My end, thy good? Why may it not be done?

Dark clouds bring waters, when the bright bring none.

Like all men of original genius, this stout-minded pot-mender had unbounded confidence in himself. He was under no delusion as to his own powers. No man knew better what he was about. He could take the measure of all the justices about him, and he knew it. Every shallow-headed gentleman in Bedfordshire towns and villages was made to wince under his picturesque and satiric tongue. To clergymen, bishops, lawyers, and judges he gave names which all his neighbours knew. Mr. Pitiless, Mr. Hardheart, Mr. Forget-good, Mr. No-truth, Mr. Haughty—thus he named the disagreeable dignitaries of the town of Mansoul.

At first he was regarded by his "pastors and masters" as a mere wilful, noisy, praying sectary. Very soon they discovered that he was a fighting preacher. As tinker or Christian he always had his sleeves turned up. When he had to try his own cause he put in the jury-box Mr. True-Heart, Mr. Upright, Mr. Hate-Bad, Mr. See-Truth, and other amiable persons. His witnesses were Mr. Know-All, Mr. Tell-True, Mr. Hate-Lies, Mr. Vouch-Truth, Mr. Did-See. His Town Clerk was Mr. Do-Right, the Recorder was Mr. Conscience, the gaoler was Mr. True-Man, Lord Understanding was on the bench, and the Judge bears the dainty name of the "Golden-headed Prince."

Bunyan's adversaries are always a bad set. They live in Villain's Lane, in Blackmouth Street, or Blasphemer's Row, or Drunkard's Alley, or Rascal's Corner. They are the sons of one Beastly, whose mother bore them in Flesh Square: they live at the house of one Shameless, at the sign of the Reprobate, next door to the Descent into the Pit, whose retainers are Mr. Flatter, Mr. Impiety, Mr. False-Peace, Mr. Covetousness, who are housed by one Mr. Simple, in Folly's Yard.

Bunyan had a perfect wealth of sectarian scurrility at his command. His epithets are at times unquotable and ferocious. When, however, his friends are at the bar, the witnesses against them comprise the choicest scoundrels of all time—Mr. Envy, Mr. Pick-thank, and others, whose friends are Lord Carnal-Delight, Lord Luxurious, Lord Lechery, Sir Having Greedy, and similar villanous people of quality. The Judge's name is now Lord Hate-Good. The Jury consist of Mr. No-Good, Mr. Malice, Mr. Love-Lust, Mr. Live-Loose, Mr. Heady, Mr. Hate-Light, Mr. Enmity, Mr. Liar, Mr. Cruelty, and Mr. Implacable, with Mr. Blindman for Foreman.

Never was such an infamous gang impanelled. Rancour
and rage and vindictiveness, and every passion awakened
in the breasts of the strong by local insolence and legal
injustice, is supplied by Bunyan with epithets of immense
retaliative force. He is the greatest name-maker among
authors. He was a spiritual Comanche. He prayed like a
savage. He said himself, when describing the art of the
religious rhetorician—an art of which he was the greatest
master of his time:—

You see the ways the fisherman doth take

To catch the fish; what engines doth he make!

Behold! how he engageth all his wits,

Also his snares, lines, angles, hooks, and nets;

Yet fish there be that neither hook nor line,

Nor snare, nor net, nor engine can make thine;

They must be grop'd for, and be tickled too,

Or they will not be catch'd, whate'er you do.

Bunyan never tickled the sinner. It was not his way. He
carried a prong. He pricked the erring. He published a
pamphlet to suggest what ought to be done to holy
pedestrians, whose difficulties lay rearward. He put
detonating balls under their feet which exploded as they
stepped and alarmed them along. He lined the celestial
road with horrors. If they turned their heads they saw a
fiend worse than Lot's wife who was merely changed into a

pillar of sweet all-preserving salt. Bunyan's unfortunate
converts who looked back fell into a pit filled with fire,
where they howled and burnt for evermore.

Ah! with what pleasure must the great Bedfordshire artist
have contemplated his masterly pages as day by day he
added to them the portrait of some new scoundrel, or
painted with dexterous and loving hand the wholesome
outlines of some honest man, or devised some new phrase
which like a new note or new colour would delight singer
or painter for generations yet to come. He must have strode
proudly along his cell as he put his praise and his scorn
into imperishable similes.

But Bunyan had never been great had he been merely
disagreeable. He had infinite wit in him. It was his carnal
genius that saved him. He wrote sixty books, and two of
them—the "Siege of the Town of Mansoul" and the
"Pilgrim's Progress"—exceed all ever written for creative
swiftness of imagination, racy English speech, sentences of
literary art, cunningness in dialogue, satire, ridicule, and
surpassing knowledge of the picturesque ways of the
obscure minds of common men. In his pages men rise out
of the ground—they always come up on an open space so
that they can be seen. They talk naturally, so that you know
them at once; and they act without delay, so that you never
forget them. They surprise you, delight you, they interest
you, they instruct you, and disappear. They never linger,
they never weary you. Incidents new and strange arise at
every step in his story. The scene changes like the men and
their adventures. Now it is field or morass, plain or bypath,
bog or volcano, castle or cottage, sandy scorching desert or
cold river; the smoke of the bottomless pit or bright,
verdant, delectable mountains and enchanted lands where
there are no bishops, no gaols, and no tinkers; where

aboundeth grapes, calico, brides, eternal conversation, and trumpets. The great magician's genius forsakes him when he comes to the unknown regions, and he knoweth no more than the rest of us. But while his foot is on the earth he steps like a king among writers. His Christian is no fool. He is cunning of fence, suspicious, sagacious, witty, satirical, abounding in invective, and broad, bold, delicious insolence. Bye-Ends is a subtle, evasive knave drawn with infinite skill.

Had Bunyan merely preached the Gospel he had no more been remembered than thousands of his day who are gratefully forgotten—had he prayed to this time he had won no statue; but his literary genius lives when the preacher is very dead.

He saw with such vividness that the very passions and wayward moods of men stood apart and distinct in his sight, and he gave names to them and endowed them with their natural speech. He created new men out of characteristics of mind, and sent them into the world in shapes so defined and palpable that men know them for evermore. It was the way of his age for writers to give names to their adversaries. Bunyan imitated this in his life of Mr. Badman. Others did this, but Bunyan did it better than any man. His invention was marvellous, and he had besides the faculty of the dramatist.

If any man wrote the adventures of a Co-operator, he would have to tell of his meeting with Mr. Obstinate, who will not listen to him, and wants to pull him back. We all get the company of Mr. Pliable, who is persuaded without being convinced, who at the first splash into difficulty crawls out and turns back with a cowardly adroitness. We have all encountered the stupidity of Mr. Ignorance, which nothing can enlighten. We know Mr. Turnaway, who comes from the town of Apostacy, whose face we cannot perfectly see. Others merely gave names, he drew characters, he made the qualities of his men speak; you knew them by their minds better than by their dress. That is why succeeding ages have read the "Pilgrim's Progress," because the same people who met that extraordinary traveller are always turning up in the way of every man who has a separate and a high purpose, and is bent upon carrying it out. Manners change, but humanity has still its old ways. It is because Bunyan painted these that his writing lasts like a picture by one of the old masters who painted for all time.

Such is an outline of the paper, which was interesting from its associations, and only spoilt by the cough. We had had Bunyan in pretty well every shape possible during the last few weeks. Certainly one of the most original is this which presents the man of unbounded faith in the light of utter scepticism.

CHAPTER XXXI.

AL FRESCO INFIDELITY.

In a series of papers like the present it is necessary, every now and then, to pause and apologize, either for the nature of the work in general, or for certain particulars in its execution calculated to shock good people whose feelings one would wish to respect. Having so long been engaged in the study of infidelity in London, I may, perhaps, be permitted to speak with something like authority in the matter; and I have no hesitation in saying that I believe the policy of shirking the subject is the most fatal and foolish one that could be adopted. Not only does such a course inspire people, especially young people, with the idea that there is something very fascinating in infidelity— something which, if allowed to meet their gaze, would be sure to attract and convince them—than which nothing is farther from the truth—not only so, however, but many of the statements and most of the arguments which sound plausibly enough on the glib tongue of a popular speaker read very differently indeed, when put down in cold-blooded letter-press, and published in the pages of a book. I protest strongly against making a mystery of London infidelity. It has spread and is spreading, I know, and it is well the public should know; but I believe there would be no such antidote to it as for people to be fully made aware how and where it is spreading. That is the rôle I have all along proposed to myself: not to declaim against any man or any system, not to depreciate or disguise the truth, but simply to describe. I cannot imagine a more legitimate method of doing my work.

I suppose no one will regard it in any way as an indulgence or a luxury on the part of a clergyman, who be it remembered, is, during a portion of the Sunday, engaged in ministering to Christian people, that he should devote another portion of that day to hearing Christ vilified, and having his own creed torn to pieces. I myself feel that my own belief is not shaken, but in a tenfold degree confirmed by all I have heard and seen and written of infidelity; and therefore I cannot concede the principle that to convey my experiences to others is in any way dangerous. Take away the halo of mystery that surrounds this subject, and it would possess very slender attractions indeed.

It was, for instance, on what has always appeared to me among the most affecting epochs of our Christian year, the Fifth Sunday after Easter—Christ's last Sunday upon earth—that, by one of those violent antitheses, I went to Gibraltar Walk, Bethnal Green Road, to hear Mr. Ramsey there demolish the very system which, for many years, it has been my mission to preach. I did not find, and I hope my congregation did not find, that I faltered in my message that evening. I even venture to think that Mr. Ramsey's statements, which I shall repeat as faithfully as possible, will scarcely seem as convincing here as they did when he poured them forth so fluently to the costermongers and navvies of the Bethnal Green Road; and if this be true of Mr. Ramsey it is certainly so of the smaller men; for he is a master in his craft, and certainly a creditable antagonist for a Christian to meet with the mild defensive weapons we have elected to use.

When the weather proves fine, as it ought to have done in May, 1874, infidelity adjourns from its generally slummy halls to the street corners, and to fields which are often the reverse of green; thus adopting, let me remark in passing, one of the oldest instrumentalities of Christianity itself, one, too, in which we shall do well to follow its example. Fas est ab hoste doceri—I cannot repeat too often. Scorning the attractions of the railway arches in the St. Pancras Road, where I hope soon to be a listener, I sped viâ the Metropolitan Railway and tram to Shoreditch Church, not far from which, past the Columbia Market and palatial Model Lodging Houses, is the unpicturesque corner called Gibraltar Walk, debouching from the main road, with a triangular scrap of very scrubby ground, flanked by a low wall, which young Bethnal Green is rapidly erasing from the face of the earth. When I got here, I found an unclerical-looking gentleman in a blue great-coat and sandy moustache erecting his rostrum in the shape of a small deal stool, from whence I could see he was preparing to pour forth the floods of his rhetoric by diligent study of some exceedingly greasy notes which he held in his hand and perused at what I feel sure must have been the windiest street corner procurable outside the cave of Æolus. I fell back into the small but very far from select crowd which had already begun to gather, and an old man, who was unmistakably a cobbler, having ascertained that I had come to hear the lecture, told me he had "listened to a good many of 'em, but did not feel much for'arder." Undismayed by this intelligence I still elected to tarry, despite the cruel nor'-easter that was whistling round the corner of the Bethnal Green Road. In a few minutes I perceived a slight excitement in the small gathering due to the fact that the Christians had put in an appearance, so that there would be some opposition. Mr. Harrington, a young man whom I had heard once speak fluently enough on the theistic side at an infidel meeting, was unpacking his rostrum, which was a patent folding one, made of deal, like that of his adversary, but neatly folded along with a large Bible, inside a green baize case. Both gentlemen commenced proceedings at the same time; and as they had pitched their stools very close to one another, the result was very much like that of two grinding organs in the same street. Of the two, Mr. Harrington's voice was louder than Mr. Ramsey's. The latter gentleman had a sore throat, and had to be kept lubricated by means of a jug of water, which a brother heretic held ready at his elbow. Mr. Harrington was in prime condition, but his congregation was smaller than ours; for l kept at first—I was going to say religiously, I suppose I ought to say ir-religiously—to the infidels.

Mr. Ramsey, who had a rooted aversion to the letter "h," except where a smooth breathing is usual, began by saying that Christianity differed from other religions in the fact of its having an eternal 'Ell. The Mahometans had their beautiful ladies; the North American Indian looked for his 'Appy 'Unting Grounds; but 'Ell was a speciality of the Christian system. On the other side was the fact that you continually had salvation inundated upon you. Tracts were put into your hand, asking—"What must I do to be saved?" We had to pay for this salvation about 11,000,000l. a year to the Church of England, and something like an equal amount to the Dissenters. In fact every tub-thumper went about preaching and ruining servant girls, and for this we paid over twenty millions a year—more than the interest on the whole National Debt. After this elegant exordium, Mr. Ramsey said he proposed to divide his remarks under four heads. 1. Is Salvation necessary? 2. What are we to be saved from? 3. What for? 4. How?

1. According to the Christian theory, God, after an eternity of "doin' nothin'," created the world. He made Adam sin by making sin for him to commit; and then damned him for doing what He knew he would do. He predestined you— the audience—to be damned because of Adam's sin; but after a time God "got sick and tired of damning people," and sent His Son to redeem mankind.

This flower of rhetoric tickled Bethnal Green immensely; but Mr. Harrington was equal to the occasion, and thundered out his orthodoxy so successfully that Mr. Ramsey took a longer drink than usual, and complained that he was not having "a free platform"—it was so he dignified the rickety stool on which he was perched. He then meandered into a long dissection of Genesis i., appearing to feel particularly aggrieved by the fact of the moon being said to "rule the night," though I could not see how this was relevant to the Christian scheme of salvation; and a superb policeman, who had listened for a moment to Mr. Ramsey's astronomical lucubrations, evidently shared my feelings and passed on superciliously. I devoutly wished my duty had permitted me to do the same.

The speaker then went into a long dissertation on the primal sin; the gist of which was that though the woman had never been warned not to eat of the Forbidden Fruit, she had to bear the brunt of the punishment. Then—though one is almost ashamed to chronicle such a triviality—he waxed very wroth because the serpent was spoken of as being cursed above all "cattle." Who ever heard of snakes being called cattle? He was condemned to go on his belly. How did he go before? Did he go on his back or "'op" along on the tip of his tail? These pleasantries drew all Mr. Harrington's audience away except a few little dirty boys on the wall. Mr. Ramsey clearly knew his audience, and "acted to the gallery."

2. But what were we to be saved from? Eternal 'Ell-fire. This 'Ell-fire was favourite sauce for sermons, and served to keep people awake. Where was 'Ell? It was said to be a bottomless pit; if so, he should be all right, because he could get out at the other end! Then, again, 'Ell was said to be a very 'ot place. When the missionaries told the Greenlanders that, everybody wanted to go to 'Ell; so they had to change their tune and say it was very cold. Mr. Ramsey omitted to mention his authority for this statement.

Into his pleasantries on the monotony of life in 'Eaven, I do not feel inclined to follow this gentleman. The Atonement, he went on to remark, if necessary at all, came 4000 years too late. It should have been—so we were to believe on his ipse dixit—contemporaneous with the Fall. This atonement we were to avail ourselves of by means of faith. Idiots could not have faith, but were allowed to be saved. Consequently, argued Mr. Ramsey, in conclusion, the best thing for all of us would have been to have been born idiots, and, consistently enough, Christianity tried to turn us all into idiots.

Such were some of the statements. I refrain from quoting the most offensive, which were deliberately put forward at this al fresco infidels' meeting; and with what result? Though a vast population kept moving to and fro along that great highway there were never, I am sure, more than a hundred people gathered at the shrine of Mr. Ramsey. They laughed at his profanities, yes; but directly he dropped these, and grew argumentative, they talked, and had to be vigorously reduced to order. Gallio-like they cared for none of these things, and I am quite sure a good staff of working clergy, men like Mr. Body or Mr. Steele of St. Thomas's, who could talk to the people, would annihilate Mr. Ramsey's prestige. As for Mr. Harrington, he meant well, and had splendid lung-power, but his theology was too sectarian to suit a mixed body of listeners embracing all shades of thought and no-thought.

Supposing Mr. Ramsey to have put forth all his power that morning—and I have no reason to doubt that he did so—I deliberately say that I should not hesitate to take my own boy down to hear him, because I feel that even his

immature mind would be able to realize how little there
was to be said against Christianity, if that were all.

CHAPTER XXXII.

AN "INDESCRIBABLE PHENOMENON."

When the bulk of the London Press elects to gush over
anything or anybody, there are at all events, primâ facie
grounds for believing that there is something to justify
such a consensus. When, moreover, the object of such gush
is a young lady claiming to be a spirit-medium, the
unanimity is so unusual as certainly to make the matter
worth the most careful inquiry, for hitherto the London
Press has either denounced spiritualism altogether, or
gushed singly over individual mediums, presumably
according to the several proclivities of the correspondents.
Of Miss Annie Eva Fay, however—is not the very name
fairy-like and fascinating?—I read in one usually sober-
minded journal that "there is something not of this earth
about the young lady's powers." Another averred that she
was "a spirit medium of remarkable and extraordinary
power." Others, more cautious, described the "mystery" as
"bewildering," the "entertainment" as "extraordinary and
incomprehensible," while yet another seemed to me to
afford an index to the cause of this gush by saying that
"Miss Fay is a pretty young lady of about twenty, with a

delicate spirituelle face, and a profusion of light hair, frizzled on the forehead."

I made a point of attending Miss Annie Eva Fay's opening performance at the Hanover Square Rooms, and found all true enough as to the pretty face and the frizzled hair. Of the "indescribable" nature of the "phenomenon" (for by that title is Miss Fay announced, à la Vincent Crummles) there may be two opinions, according as we regard the young lady as a kind of Delphic Priestess and Cumæan Sibyl rolled into one, or simply a clever conjuror— conjuress, if there be such a word.

Let me, then, with that delightful inconsistency so often brought to bear on the so-called or self-styled "supernatural," first describe the "indescribable," and then, in the language of the unspiritual Dr. Lynn, tell how it is all done; for, of course, I found it all out, like a great many others of the enlightened and select audience which gathered at Miss Annie Eva Fay's first drawing-room reception in the Queen's Concert Rooms.

Arriving at the door half an hour too early, as I had misread the time of commencement, I found at the portal Mr. Burns, of the Progressive Library, and a gentleman with a diamond brooch in his shirt-front, whom I guessed at once, from that adornment, to be the proprietor of the indescribable phenomenon, and I was, in fact, immediately introduced to him as Colonel Fay.

Passing in due course within the cavernous room which might have suited well a Cumæan Sibyl on a small scale, I found the platform occupied by a tiny cabinet, unlike that of the Davenports in that it was open in front, with a green curtain, which I could see was destined to be let down during the performance of the phenomenal manifestations. There was a camp-stool inside the cabinet; a number of cane-bottomed chairs on the platform, and also the various properties of a spirit séance, familiar to me from long experience, guitar, fiddle, handbells, tambourine, &c. One adjunct alone was new; and that was a green stable bucket, destined, I could not doubt, to figure in what my Rimmel-scented programme promised as the climax of Part I.—the "Great Pail Sensation." Presently Colonel Fay, in a brief speech, nasal but fluent, introduced the subject, and asked two gentlemen to act as a Committee of Inspection. Two stepped forward immediately—indeed too immediately, as the result proved; one a "citizen of this city," as Colonel Fay had requested; but the other a Hindoo young gentleman, who, I believe, lost the confidence of the audience at once from his foreign face and Oriental garb. However, they were first to the front, and so were elected, and proceeded at once to "examine" the cabinet in that obviously helpless and imperfect way common to novices who work with the gaze of an audience upon them. Then, from a side door, stage left, enter the Indescribable Phenomenon. A pretty young lady, yes, and with light frizzled hair to any extent. There was perhaps "a spirit look within her eyes;" but then I have often found this to be the case with young ladies of twenty. Her dress of light silk was beyond reproach. I had seen Florence Cook and Miss Showers lately; and,—well, I thought those two, with the assistance of Miss Annie Eva Fay, would have made a very pretty model for a statuette of the Three Graces.

Miss Fay, after being described by the Colonel vaguely enough as "of the United States," was bound on both wrists with strips of calico; the knots were sewn by the European gentleman—as distinguished from the Asiatic youth. He was not quite au fait at the needle, but got through it in time. Miss Fay was then placed on the camp-stool, her wrists fastened behind her, and her neck also secured to a ring screwed into the back of the cabinet. A rope was tied round her ankles, and passed right to the front of the stage, where the Hindoo youth was located and bidden hold it taut, which he did conscientiously, his attitude being what Colman describes "like some fat gentleman who bobbed for eels."

First of all, another strip of calico was placed loosely round Miss Fay's neck; the curtain descended. Hey, presto! it was up again, sooner than it takes to write, and this strip was knotted doubly and trebly round her neck. A tambourine hoop was put in her lap, and this, in like manner, was found encircling her neck, as far as the effervescent hair would allow it.

The audience at this point grew a little fidgety; and though they did not say anything against the Oriental young gentleman, the 'cute American colonel understood it, adding two others from the audience to the committee on the stage, and leaving the young gentleman to "bob" down below as if to keep him out of mischief.

The other "manifestations" were really only different in detail from the first. The guitar was placed on the lap, the curtain fell and it played; so did the fiddle—out of tune, as usual—and also a little glass harmonicon with actually a soupçon of melody. A mouth-organ tootle-tooed, and what Colonel Fay described as a "shingle nail" was driven with a hammer into a piece of wood. A third of a tumbler of water laid on the lap of the Indescribable Phenomenon was drunk, and the great Pail Sensation consisted in the bucket being put on her lap and then discovered slung by the handle around her neck. The last "manifestation" is the one

to which I would draw attention; for it was by this I
discovered how it was all done. A knife was put on Miss
Fay's lap; the curtain lowered, the knife pitched on to the
platform, and behold the Indescribable Phenomenon
stepped from the cabinet with the ligature that had bound
her wrists and neck severed.

Now, all through this portion of the entertainment the
audience, instead of sitting quiet, amused themselves with
proposing idiotic tests, or suggesting audibly how it was all
done. One man behind me pertinaciously clung to the
theory of a concealed boy, and trotted him to the front after
every phase of the exhibition. He must have been
infinitesimally small; but that did not matter. It was "that
boy again" after every trick. One manifestation consisted
in putting a piece of paper and pair of scissors on Miss
Fay's lap, and having several "tender little infants" cut out,
as the Colonel phrased it.

Hereupon sprang up a 'cute individual in the room, and
produced a sheet of paper he had marked. Would Miss Fay
cut out a tender little infant from that? Miss Fay consented,
and of course did it, the 'cute individual retiring into
private life for the rest of the evening. Another wanted
Miss Fay's mouth to be bound with a handkerchief, and
there was no objection raised, until the common-sense and
humanity of the audience protested against such a needless
cruelty on a broiling night and in that Cumæan cave. An
excited gentleman in front of me, too, whose mission I
fancy was simply to protest against the spiritual character
of the phenomena (which was never asserted) would
interrupt us all from time to time by declaring his intense
satisfaction with it all. It was a splendid trick. We tried to
convince him that his individual satisfaction was irrelevant
to us, but it was, as Wordsworth says, "Throwing words

away." It was a beautiful trick; and he was satisfied, quite satisfied.

The Dark Séance, which formed the second part of the performance, was a dreadful mistake. It was not only unsatisfactory in result, but—and no doubt this was the reason—it was so mismanaged as to threaten more than once to eventuate in a riot. Twelve or fourteen persons were to form a committee representing the audience, and to sit in a circle, with the Indescribable Phenomenon in their centre, while we remained below in Egyptian darkness and received their report. Of course we all felt that we—if not on the committee—might just as well be sitting at home or in the next parish as in the cave of Cumæ. The method of electing the committee was briefly stated by Colonel Fay to be "first come first served," and the consequence was a rush of some fifty excited people on to the platform, with earnest requests on the part of the proprietary to be "still." There was no more stillness for the rest of the evening. The fifty were pruned down to about fifteen of the most pertinacious, who would not move at any price; in fact, the others only descended on being promised that the dark sitting should be divided into two, and another committee appointed. The Indescribable Phenomenon took her seat on the camp-stool in the centre, where she was to remain clapping her hands, to show she was not producing the manifestations. The gas was put out and darkness prevailed—darkness, but not silence. The disappointed and rejected committee men—and women—first began to grumble in the freedom which the darkness secured. The committee was a packed one. They were Spiritualists. This was vigorously denied by somebody, who said he saw a Press man in the circle, and therefore (such was his logic) he could not be a Spiritualist. All this time the Indescribable Phenomenon was clapping her hands, and now some of the more restless of the audience clapped theirs in concert. The guitar and fiddle began to thump and twang, and the bells to ring, and then again the more refractory lunatics amongst us began to beat accompaniment on our hats. The whole affair was worthy of Bedlam or Hanwell, or, let us add, an Indescribable Phenomenon.

The committee was changed with another rush, and those who were finally exiled from the hope of sitting took it out in the subsequent darkness by advising us to "beware of our pockets." When Colonel Fay asked for quietude he was rudely requested "not to talk through his nose." It was not to be wondered at that the séance was very brief, and the meeting adjourned.

Now to describe the indescribable. If it be a spiritual manifestation, of course there is an end of the matter; but if a mere conjuring trick, I would call attention to the following facts. The fastening of Miss Fay's neck to the back of the cabinet at first is utterly gratuitous. It offers no additional difficulty to any manifestations, and appears only intended to prevent the scrutineers seeing behind her. A very simple exercise of sleight of hand would enable the gallant Colonel to cut the one ligature that binds the two wrists, when, for instance, he goes into the cabinet with scissors to trim off the ends of the piece of calico in the opening trick. The hands being once free all else is easy. The hands are never once seen during the performance. The committee can feel them, and feel the knots at the wrists; but they cannot discover whether the ligature connecting the wrists is entire.

The last trick, be it recollected, consists in the ligature being cut and Miss Fay's coming free to the front. If my

theory is incorrect—and no doubt it is ruinously wrong—
will she consent to omit the last trick and come to the front
with wrists bound as she entered the cabinet? Of course, if
I had suggested it, she would have done it as easily as she
cut out the tender infants for the 'cute gentleman behind
me; so, to adopt the language of Miss Fay's fellow-citizen,
I "bit in my breath and swallered it down." I adopted the
course Mr. Maskelyne told me he did with the Davenports,
sat with my eyes open and my mouth shut. It is marvellous
to see how excited we phlegmatic islanders grow when
either spirits are brought to the front, or we think we have
found out a conjuring trick. I am not going to follow the
example of my gushing brethren, but I can safely say that
if anybody has an afternoon or evening to spare, he may do
worse than go to the Crystal Palace or the Hanover Square
Rooms, to see a very pretty and indescribable
phenomenon, and to return as I did, a wiser, though
perhaps a sadder man, in the proud consciousness of
having "found out how it is all done."

CHAPTER XXXIII.

A LADY MESMERIST.

When a man's whole existence has resolved itself into
hunting up strange people and poking his nose into queer
nooks and corners, he has a sorry time of it in London
during August; for, as a rule, all the funny folks have gone

out of town, and the queer nooks and corners are howling wildernesses. There is always, of course, a sort of borderland, if he can only find it out, some peculiar people who never go out of town, some strange localities which are still haunted by them; only he has to find them out—people and places—for it is so universally allowed now-a-days that all genteel people must be out of London in August, and all respectable places must be covered up in old newspapers, that it is difficult to get them to own the soft impeachment.

However, there is one queer place that is never shut up, the Progressive Library in Southampton Row; and Mr. Burns and the Spiritualists, as a rule, do not shut up shop even in August. Their Summerland lies elsewhere than Margate or the Moors; and a valse with a pirouetting table or a little gentle levitation or elongation delights them more than all the revels of the countryside. I was getting a little blasé, I own, on the subject of Spiritualism after my protracted experiences during the Conference, and I do not think I should have turned my steps in the direction of the Progressive Institution that week had not the following announcement caught my eye as I scanned the ghostly pages of the Medium and Daybreak:—

"a mesmeric séance.

"We have been authorized to announce that Miss Chandos, whose advertisement appears in another part of this paper, will give a mesmeric séance at the Spiritual Institution, 15, Southampton Row, on Wednesday evening, August 19th, at eight o'clock. Admission will be free by ticket, which may be obtained at the Institution. The object which Miss Chandos has in view is to interest a few truth-seekers who could aid her in promoting a knowledge of psychological phenomena. As a crowded meeting is not desired, an early application should be made for tickets."

I do not know that I said "Eureka!" Indeed I have considerable historic doubts as to whether anybody ever did, but I felt it. I was a truth-seeker forthwith. I resolved to sit at the feet of Miss Chandos, and, should her mesmeric efforts prove satisfactory, "aid her in promoting a knowledge of psychological phenomena." I did not go through the prescribed process of getting a ticket beforehand, because I thought in my innocence that everybody would be out of town, or that the Hall of the Progressive Institute would certainly accommodate those who remained. Never was a more fatal mistake. The psychological folks were all in London, and the capacities of the Progressive Library are not palatial. Miss Chandos had a crowded meeting whether she desired it or not. Genius will not be concealed; and Miss Chandos was learning that lesson in a very satisfactory way. It was a sultry evening when a small boy opened the back door of the little first floor apartment in Southampton Row, and squeezed me in like the thirteenth in an omnibus, and I found myself walking on people's toes, and sitting down on their hats in the most reckless manner. At length, however, I struggled to a vacant corner, and deposited myself perspiring and expectant.

Mr. Burns was "orating" on the revival mesmerism was destined to make, and telling us how, like the Plumstead Peculiars, we should be able to do without doctors as soon as the healing powers of animal magnetism were properly recognised and diffused. I did not listen very carefully, I fear, for I was nervously looking about for Miss Chandos. Nervously, I say, because lady mediums and mesmerizers are so apt to run to eighteen stone, or be old and frumpish, that I had terrible fears lest I should be scared when I met Miss Chandos in the flesh. I was very agreeably surprised, however, for when Mr. Burns resumed—not his chair but his table, since he sat on that article of furniture, a very pretty young lady indeed, of not more than eighteen or twenty years of age, took his place, and, in a few well-chosen words, said this was her first appearance as a public mesmerist, and claimed indulgence should any failure in the phenomena result. She also drew attention to the fact that the apartment was "pernicious snug" (she put it, of course, in more scientific language), and straightway proceeded to business.

When Miss Chandos invited patients to put themselves in her hands I thought the room had risen en masse. Everybody wanted to be mesmerized. I had no chance in my retired position; but she soon got a front row of likely people, and I sat down once more disappointed and exuding.

She was a tall active young lady was Miss Chandos, and had a mystic crop of long black curls, which waved about like the locks of a sibyl when she made a lunge at an innocent looking young man who sat No. 1—and whom, with the other patients, I shall designate thus numerically. He seemed to like it immensely, and smiled a fatuous smile as those taper fingers lighted on his head, while the other hand rested on the frontal portion of his face, as though Miss Chandos were going to pull his nose. He was off in a moment, and sat facing the audience in his magnetic trance, looking like a figure at a waxwork show. Miss Chandos then passed on to a gentleman, No. 2, who never succumbed during the entire evening, though she made several onslaughts upon him. Consequently I dismiss No. 2

as incorrigible forthwith. No. 3 was a lady who only gave way after a lengthened attack, and did not seem to appreciate the effect of Miss Chandos' lustrous eyes so much as No. 1 did. He gave signs of "coming to," but Miss Chandos kept looking round at him and No. 2, while she was attending to No. 3, and directly she did this No. 1 closed his eyes, and slept the sleep of innocence again.

Having reduced No. 3 to a comatose condition Miss Chandos reverted to No. 1, and by attractive passes got him on his legs and made him follow her up and down the limited space at her disposal. She looked then like a pretty Vivien manipulating a youthful Merlin; and I was not at all surprised at the effect of her "woven paces and her waving hands." She asked him his name, and he told her. It was W——. "No," she said, "it's Jones. Mary Jones. What's your name?" But the youth was not quite so far gone as to rebaptize himself with a female cognomen just yet. He stuck to his W., and Miss Chandos put him into his waxwork position again, and got No. 3 on her legs at last, but did nothing more with her than make her walk up and down. Presently No. 3 woke up, and was put to air at the window.

No. 4 was now selected, in the person of a big burly man; and I could not help thinking, as she manipulated him, what a capital pose it would have been for Hercules and Omphale. He seemed to like it exceedingly, and I thought was dropping comfortably off when he whispered something to his operator (I have no notion what the feminine of that word is), who fixed her brilliant eyes on somebody near me—I feared it was actually on me—and said, "Somebody at the back of the room is exercising control. I shall be glad if they will refrain." I was quite innocent of exercising conscious control, and did not quite know what the phrase meant. I certainly had once or twice thought it must be much pleasanter to be operated upon by so pretty a young lady than by some bull-necked male mesmerist or aged spinster above-mentioned, but I could scarcely believe that such a mild sentiment could affect that colossal man. However, I recollected the delicacy of these psychological relations, and sat down conscience-stricken and warmer than ever.

Miss Chandos selected No. 5 in the person of a young man with a nascent moustache, who had successfully struggled into the front row at the outset. He promised well at first; but, like other young men with incipient moustaches, disappointed us afterwards. Then came No. 6 upon the scene.

No. 6 was a lady who came late, and at once pushed to the front with the air of a person who was not doing so for the first time. She went off in a moment—far too suddenly, in fact, and then did everything she was told in a very obedient way. Being told that she was in a beautiful garden, she stooped down on the floral carpet and proceeded to gather materials for a bouquet. I confess I did not care about No. 6, and was proceeding to read Professor Tyndall's Belfast Address, which I had in my pocket, when Miss Chandos looked up No. 1 again.

Reduced to a proper frame of mind, either by Miss Chandos' continued attentions or the contagion of No. 6's docility, the youth was now all submission. He walked up and down any number of times like a tame animal at the Zoological Gardens, and now quite agreed that his name was Mary Jones. He sang "Tom Bowling" at command, and No. 6, not to be outdone, warbled a ditty called, I think, "The Slave Girl's Love," the refrain of which, according to her version, was, "I cannot love, because I ham a slave." She broke down in the middle of this aspiring ditty, and then personated a Jew old clo' man, a woman selling "ornaments for your firestoves," and various other characters, all of which she overacted considerably. I may be wrong, of course, but I fancied the fair lecturess was as dissatisfied with No. 6 as I was. The audience was an indulgent one, and thought it splendid. Mr. Burns sat on the table and yawned. I relapsed into Tyndall, and wondered what he would have said about it all; or, at least, I did not wonder, for I knew he would have consigned us all to the nearest lunatic asylum as exceptions to the rule that the European has so many more cubic inches of cerebral development than the Papuan.

When it was drawing near ten, Miss Chandos brought the proceedings to a close by animating—like Pygmalion—her waxwork statues. She apologized once more, in a few well-chosen sentences, for what she was pleased to call her "failure," but the audience would not hear of the term, and applauded to the echo, only there was no room for an echo in the Progressive Institute. The young man, No. 1, who I found was a spirit medium, wound up by an address from his Indian guide on the subject of "control."

I confess I failed to gather from the perambulating youth and maidens No. 1 and 3, or the impersonations of No. 6, any signs of the revival alluded to by Mr. Burns at the outset; and there was not the remotest connexion with the healing art. In fact, nobody seemed suffering from anything except heat.

Miss Chandos said to me, however, in a sensible conversation with which she favoured me in private, that all she had attempted to show was but the lowest manifestation of a power which had far higher ends in view. She doubted almost whether it was not something like sacrilege to use such a power for playing tricks and gratifying curiosity.

She was thoroughly in earnest; and laboured both physically during the evening and logically in her after-discourse, with an energy which some persons would have said was worthy of a better cause.

It was nearly eleven when I left the miniature hall of the Progressive Institute, and as I passed along the streets, digesting what I had seen and heard during the evening, I took myself to task severely—as it is always well to do, if only to prevent somebody else doing it for me—and asked whether, if the lecturess had not been a lecturess but a lecturer—if being a lecturess she weighed eighteen stone, or was old and wizen, or dropped her h's—whether I should have stayed three mortal hours in that stuffy room, and I frankly own I came to the conclusion I should not.

CHAPTER XXXIV.

A PSYCHOPATHIC INSTITUTION.

Reading my Figaro the other day—as I hope I need not state it is my custom devoutly to do—I came upon the following passage in the review of a book called "Psychopathy; or, the True Healing Art. By Joseph Ashman. London: Burns, Southampton Row. We have not the pleasure of being personally acquainted with Joseph Ashman, and we fear that the loss is ours. Judging him through the medium of his book, he must, indeed, be a rara avis.... The one great thing," it went on to say, "that Joseph Ashman wants the world to know is, that he cures disease by very simple means. And all that the world wants to know from Joseph Ashman is, Are these cures real—are his statements facts? Why, then, does not Joseph content himself with his facts? He has plenty of them. Here is one:—'Seeing one day a cabman with a swollen face standing by a police-court ready to prosecute a man who had assaulted him, I asked if, on condition I healed him, he would forgive his adversary. He replied that he would, and we accordingly got into his cab together. Bringing out the magnetized carte, I told him to look at it, and at the same time made a few motions over the swelling with my hand. I then left him feeling much better, and returned in an hour's time, when I found him taking a glass of beer with his antagonist, whom he had forgiven.'"

Now as the one pursuit and end of my present existence is the discovery of raræ aves, I need not say I at once took up the clue herein afforded, and went in pursuit of Joseph Ashman. I found not only him but his institution, for Mr. Ashman does not work single-handed. It is in the Marylebone Road, almost opposite the Yorkshire Stingo; and is most modest and unpretending in its outward semblance, being situated in one of those semi-rustic houses so indicative of suburban London, down an overstocked garden, into which you enter by means of a blistered iron gate, painted violently green, and swinging heavily on its hinges. Down a vista of decrepit dahlias one sped to the portal, alongside which was a trio of bell-handles, one above the other, showing that the Psychopathic Institution did not occupy the whole even of that modest domicile. I always approach these manifold bells with considerable diffidence, conscious that I must inevitably ring the wrong one; so, on this occasion, I rang none at all, but knocked a faint double knock on the knocker by way of compromise—very faint, indeed, lest I should disturb any patients who were being "psychopathized." While I waited I had leisure to observe that hidden among the dahlias, and thatched over as it were with a superannuated costermonger's barrow, was a double perambulator, which set me calculating the probabilities of Mr. Ashman being a family man.

The door was opened before I had settled the point to my own mental satisfaction, by a short, cheery-looking man, with long, straight flaxen hair flowing down over the shoulders of his black frock-coat, a beard a few shades lighter, and a merry twinkling eye, which looked more sympathetic than psychopathic, and I should think was calculated to do patients good directly it lighted on them. He looked as much as to ask whether I was psychopathically wrong, when I informed him that I had not come as a patient, but simply to inspect his institution if he would permit me. The permission was at once accorded. "We are hard at work," he said, as he ushered me into the front parlour; "but come in and see what we are about."

A man who looked like a respectable artisan was sitting at the table; and a second, in his shirt sleeves, was astride of a chair in what appeared to be rather an idiotic ride-a-cock-horse-to-Banbury-Cross fashion, and Mr. Ashman was pinching him and prodding him as butchers do fat animals at the Smithfield Show.

"That there gentleman," said Mr. Ashman, in a broad provincial dialect, "couldn't get astride that chair when he come here half-an-hour ago. How d'ye feel now, sir?"

"Feel as though I should like to race somebody twenty rods for five pound a-side," answered the patient, getting up and walking about the room as if it were a new sensation. He had been brought, it appeared, to Mr. Ashman by his friend, who was sitting at the table, and who was an old psychopathic patient. He assured me he had suffered from rheumatism for twenty years, and was completely disabled without his stick until he came into that room half-an-hour since. He walked up and down stickless and incessantly as the carnivora at the Zoo all the time he was telling me.

"Would you mind putting your ear to this man's back, sir?" said Mr. Ashman to me. I did so; and when he bent, his backbone seemed to go off with a lot of little cracks like the fog-signals of a railway. "That there old rusty hinge we mean to grease." And away he went psychopathizing him again. When he was done, Mr. Ashman explained to me learnedly, and with copious illustrations from anatomical plates, his theory of this disease, which was his favourite one for treatment, because it yielded rapidly. Paralysis and that class of disease are much slower. He had succeeded in acute rheumatism, and also in calculus. "I like fat men— fighting men to heal," he said. "I leave the delicate ones to others." The sturdy little psychopathist looked healthy enough to heal a sick rhinoceros.

While he was lecturing me his hands were not idle. I should think they seldom were. He was pouring salad oil

from a flask on to flannel to give to the other man who was
sitting at the table, and had approached convalescence
from a chronic disease after one or two visits, and who
used this oiled flannel to keep up the influence. Both the
men seemed perfectly genuine; and the rheumatic
gentleman, when he left, pronounced the effect of his
psychopathizing miraculous. The fee was five shillings. "I
shan't charge you nothin' for the flannel," he said to No. 2.
I began to take quite a fancy to Joseph Ashman, and
thanked Figaro inwardly for directing me to the institution.

A working woman who was next in the little row of
patients assembled in the back room, came in with her
wrists bound up in bits of flannel, and her hands looking
puffed and glazy. She, too, had lost the use of them for six
years, she told me, and had been pronounced incurable by
the doctors. This was her fourth visit to Mr. Ashman.
"Take up the chair, ma'am," he said to his patient; and she
did carry it in rather a wobbly fashion across the room.
"Now the other hand," and she did it with the other hand.
"Now show the gentleman how you did it when you came
to me. She's rather hard o' hearin'," he explained to me; but
after one or two repetitions the poor old body
comprehended, and carried it in her crooked elbow. "Now
I'll call my assistant," he said, and summoned a ruddy, red-
bearded man, who looked as though he might have just
come in from a brisk country walk. "When these cases
require a good deal of rubbing I let my assistants do the
preliminary work, and then come in as the Healing
Medium myself." The rubbers, he informed me, like the
Medium, must be qualified, not only physically, but
morally. Benevolence was the great requisite; and certainly
both these men seemed running over with it, if looks meant
anything. When Joseph Ashman took his turn, working the
poor old patient's stiff wrists, and pulling her fingers till

they cracked, like children playing "sweethearts," she never winced, but actually seemed to like it, and trotted off well satisfied with her fourth instalment of good health.

The next rubber who was introduced to me was not such a ruddy man, being, in fact, somewhat saturnine in appearance; but I could quite understand that he was, as he described himself, brimful of electricity. His chevelure was like that on the little man we stick on the conductor of an electrical machine and make each particular hair stand on end like quills upon the fretful porcupine.

I could not for the life of me see the difference between this treatment and simple mesmerism, except that it was much more rapid in its effects than any magnetic treatment I have ever witnessed. Indeed, I frankly confess I do not understand it now, though Mr. Ashman made me accept one of his little books on Psychopathic healing, and told me I should see the distinction when I had read it. I must be very dense, for I have read it diligently through, and still fail to trace the distinction.

The man made a great impression on me. I felt he was just one of those who would carry life into a sick room, and communicate vital power—supposing it to be communicable—from the dumpy fingers of his fat soft hand. The perambulator did not belie him. Numbers of pretty black-eyed children were running about, and there was a Mrs. Ashman somewhere among the poor patients in the back room. All the children came to me except the eldest boy, who, his father told me in a mysterious tone, had suffered some indignity at the hands of my cloth, and dreaded a parson ever after. I believe my injudicious brother had set him a long task (perhaps his Duty to his Neighbour), and the poor lad was always afraid he should be dropped down upon to "say it." Mr. Ashman's book is a little bewildering to an outsider who fails to distinguish the two vital forces. He says: "It is much rarer to find a high development of a temperament in which the psychical element prevails, than in which it is well blended with the vital-magnetic, or than in which the latter excels. In nearly all popular public men there is a blending of the two. We see it well exemplified in John Bright, Spurgeon, and others. This is the secret of their drawing, magnetic power. It is the secret, too, of many a physician's success: his genial magnetism cures when his medicine is useless, although, of course, he does not know it. As is the difference between these two forces, so is the difference in the method of their employment for the purpose of cure." However, when I left I promised—and I mean to keep my vow—that if ever I am unfortunate enough to find my vertebræ creaking like "an old hinge," I will come to Mr. Ashman and have it greased. The remark in his book as to the success of medicine depending on the qualities of him who administered it was, we may recollect, confirmed at the 1874 meeting of the British Association in Belfast.

Joseph Ashman has had a chequered history. He has dwelt in the tents of the Mormonites; has been one of the Peculiar People. In early life he was in service in the country, where his master used to flog him until, to use his own expression, he nearly cut him in two. His earliest patients were cattle. "For a healer," he said, "give me a man as can clean a window or scrub a floor. Christ himself, when He chose those who were to be healers as well as preachers, chose fishermen, fine, deep chested men, depend upon it, sir," and he rapped upon his own sonorous lungs until they reverberated. He was certainly blessed with a superabundance of good health, and looked

benevolent enough to impart all his surplus stock to
anybody who wanted it.

CHAPTER XXXV.

A PHRENOLOGICAL EVENING.

The experience I am about to chronicle occurred when the
Beecher-Tilton scandal was at its height; and I was
attracted by the somewhat ambiguous title "Burns upon
Beecher."

Mr. James Burns, the spirited proprietor of the Progressive
Library, Southampton Row, having devoted himself to the
study of phrenology, has for some time past held a series
of craniological séances on Tuesday evenings, at which he
"takes off" the head of some well-known person, or your
own, if you like, whether you are well-known or born to
blush unseen, not in the way of physical decapitation, but
by the method of phrenological diagnosis. I greatly
regretted having, on a previous occasion, missed the
analysis of Dr. Kenealy's cerebral developments. I believe
the Claimant himself was once the object of Mr. Burns'
remarks; but when Mr. Beecher's cranium was laid down
for dissection at the height of the Beecher-Tilton sensation,
I could resist no longer, but, despite all obstacles, repaired
to the Institute of Progress.

About a score of people were gathered in that first-floor front where I had seen so many strange things. Of these persons some formed the regular phrenological class conducted there weekly by Mr. Burns. The others were, generally speaking, of the ordinary lecture-audience type. One stout lady occupied an easy-chair in a corner, and slept from first to last.

The first part of the lecture was a little discursive, I fancy for my especial benefit, and summarized Mr. Burns' system, which is to a great extent original. Beginning by a disavowal of all dogmas, he began by advancing what was to me the entirely novel doctrine, that the brain was not the sole organ of the mind, but that the whole organism of man had to be taken into account in the diagnosis of character, since the entire body was permeated with the mind. The bones, fluids, and viscera were all related to mental phenomena. The lecturer even questioned whether the science he promulgated was properly termed phrenology. It certainly did not answer to the conventional idea of that craft. Referring to a calico diagram which was pinned to the curtains of the first-floor front, and at which he pointed with a walking-stick, Mr. Burns notified four divisions of the animal frame—1, the vital organs; 2, the mechanical; 3, the nervous (which in the lower orders were ganglionic only); 4, the cerebral apparatus. He defended the animal powers from the debased idea usually attached to them, and pointed out their close connexion with the spirit, nearer to which they were placed than any portion of the economy.

He then proceeded to apply his preliminary remarks to preachers in general. Theodore Parker, for instance, was a man of spare body and large brain. He was surrounded by intellectual people, and his disciples were quite sui generis. On the other hand, Spurgeon was a man of strong animal and perceptive powers, and so able to send the Walworth shopkeepers into ecstasies. His ganglions were big, as was the case in all great preachers. Emotion, he said, was more a matter of bowels than of brain. The ganglionic power carried the brain; but there were, of course, combinations of all grades.

In the case of Henry Ward Beecher, two of whose photographs he held in his hand, he dwelt on the disadvantage of having only the shadow instead of the substance of his head to deal with. Here, he said, we had all the elements on a large scale. The brain, thoracic system, osseous structure, and abdominal development were all in excess. The face was, as it were, the picture of all. Henry Ward Beecher was emphatically a large man. The blood was positive; the circulation good. The digestion was perfect, and the man enjoyed good food. Especially the length from the ear to the front of the eyebrows denoted intellectual grasp. There was not much will power. Whatever he had done (and Mr. Burns emphatically disclaimed passing any judgment on the "scandal") he had not done of determination, but had rather "slid into it." He was no planner. He gathered people round him by the "solar" force of his mind. If he had been a designing man—if largely developed behind the ears—he would have gone to work in a different way. There was good development in the intellectual, sympathetic, and emotional part of his nature; and this combination made him a popular preacher. There was more than mere animal magnetism needed to account for this; there was intellectual power, but not much firmness or conscientiousness. If he were present, he would probably acknowledge that something had led him on to do whatever he had done in spite of himself. What was very peculiar in the man was his youthfulness. He had been before the world for forty years. Mr. Fowler, the phrenologist, of Ludgate Circus, had been a fellow student of Beecher, and had measured his head, which he ascertained to have grown an inch in ten years. Beecher was essentially a growing man—growing like a boy. The ganglionic power was that which kept people always growing, and was the great means of their getting a hold over other people.

Mr. Burns then passed in review the three portraits of Beecher, Tilton, and Mrs. Tilton respectively, in the Pictorial World. Mrs. Tilton he described as a negative person, inclined to be hysterical and "clinging." There was in her a high type of brain, morally, intellectually, and spiritually. Still the brain, he said, did not make us good or bad. Again repudiating all judgment as to the scandal, he dwelt upon the close social relationships between Beecher and Mrs. Tilton, and recurred to the strong vital influence of the former, comparing it to that of Brigham Young upon his "spiritual affinities." In all probability, taking into account the different natures of Beecher and Mrs. Tilton, whatever had occurred "the people couldn't help themselves."

Then as to Theodore Tilton. Mr. Burns had read the Golden Age, and pronounced it a smart publication. There was, however, in Tilton a want of ganglionic power; he was all brain. He was a man who might be read, but he could not lecture or preach. His was a higher mind than Beecher's, but not one that would command much human sympathy.

Suppose Mrs. Tilton were not the wife of either, her relations to each might be conscientious, but still violate the laws of monogamic life. The influence of Beecher over her would be ganglionic as well as intellectual; that of Tilton purely intellectual: when lo, a gust of ganglionic power would supervene on the latter, and carry all before it.

Concluding his analysis of Mr. Beecher thus, Mr. Burns discovered that he had two clerics among his audience, and asked us—for I was one of them—if we would be examined. I readily consented, and handed my notes to Miss Chandos (the young lady mesmerist, whose séance I reported a few pages back) to report progress. She, therefore, is responsible for the diagnosis that follows.

Handling me from head to foot, much as a fancier does a prize ox at Smithfield, Mr. Burns found the life power good, and the muscles well nourished, the working faculties being in a high state of activity. The head—I blushed to hear—measured one inch beyond the average of a man of my size, and the cerebral faculties were harmoniously organized. I had large perceptive powers; and my human nature (wherever that may be located) was full, as was also firmness. The thinking sphere was good. I should have made, Mr. Burns informed me, a good sculptor or artist.

Omitting one or two complimentary remarks which Miss Chandos has faithfully, if not flatteringly, reported, and the enunciation of which quite confused me as I sat the centre and cynosure of that wondering group, I was glad to learn that I was an open man, though possessed of sufficient caution and not defective in moral courage. In fact "pluck" was large. I really wished Mr. Burns would relieve me by finding some bad bumps; but no—the worst he could say of me was that I was restless. What chiefly seemed to strike him, though, were my vital powers, and he really covered me with confusion when he began to calculate my Beecher powers on a possible Mrs. Tilton. However, he toned down this remark by noticing that my domestic faculties were well developed. My faith and hope were small. I was a "doubting" man. The positive and negative were well blent in me, and I was also "mediumistic."

The diagnosis of two ladies concluded the evening's exercises, but neither of these personages displayed any very remarkable traits; Mr. Burns declaring he felt some difficulty in discovering the bumps under the "back hair."

CHAPTER XXXVI.

A SPIRITUAL PICNIC.

In a volume bearing the title of Mystic London it would seem perchance that Spiritualism, as par excellence the modern mystery, should stand first. I have thought it better, however, to defer its treatment somewhat, working up to it as to a climax, and then gently descending to mundane matters once more ere I close my present work.

Of London at this hour, just as of Rome in the later Republic and Empire, it may be safely affirmed that there is in its midst an element of the mysterious and occult utterly undreamed of by the practical people. Many phases of this element have already been treated of in my different works; and I add some of the more exceptional as properly belonging to my present subject.

Now I candidly confess that, up to a recent date, I had not given Spiritualists—quâ spiritualists—credit for being a cheerful or convivial people. Though there exist upon the tablets of my memory recollections of certain enjoyable dinners, cosy teas, and charming petits soupers, eaten at the mahogany of believers in the modern mystery, yet these were purely exceptional events, oases in the desert of spiritualistic experiences. Generally speaking, the table, instead of groaning under its accumulated bounties, leapt about as if from the absence thereof; and the only adjuncts of the inhospitable mahogany were paper tubes for the spirit voices, handbells for the spirit hands, and occasional accordions and musical boxes for the delectation of harmonious ghosts. It was a "flow of soul" if not always a "feast of reason;" but, as regarded creature comforts, or any of the ordinary delights of mundane existence, a very Siberian desert. A grave subject of discussion (I am not, I assure you, indulging in a sepulchral pun) at the recent Liverpool Conference was how to feed mediums, and I fancy the preponderating opinion was that fasting was a cardinal virtue in their case—a regimen that had come to be in my mind, perhaps unfairly, associated with séances in general. I was glad, therefore, when I read in the columns of the Medium the announcement of the spiritual picnic or "demonstration," at the People's Garden, Willesden. Still I wanted to see Spiritualists enjoy themselves in the "normal condition." I sympathized with the avowed object of the gathering, that the followers of the new creed should know one another, as surely the disciples of a common school ought to do. Armed, therefore, with a ticket, I proceeded, viâ the North London Railway, to the scene of action. It was not what we materialistic people should call a fine August day. It was cold and dull, and tried hard to rain; but it was far more in keeping with the character of the meeting than what Father Newman calls the "garish day" one looks for in mid-August. In the words of the circle the "conditions were excellent;" and as I journeyed on, reading my Medium like a true believer, I marvelled to see, by the evidence of its advertisements, how the new creed had taken hold of a certain section, at all events, of society. Besides a dozen public mediums who paraded their varied attractions at terms ranging from 2s. 6d. to 21s., there were spiritualistic young men who put forward their creed as a qualification for clerkships—perhaps they had no other claim—spiritual lodging-house keepers, and even spiritual undertakers, all pervaded by what we may literally call a common esprit de corps.

In due course we reached the People's Garden, the popular title whereof seemed to have been given on the lucus a non principle, for the London folk have not, as yet, affected it largely. Why this should be so one cannot guess, for it is the very ideal of a Cockney Paradise, and is admirably worked by a body of shareholders, most of whom belong to the artisan class, though under very distinguished patronage indeed. When I got to the grounds the Spiritualists were indulging in a merry-go-round during a refreshing drizzle. A temporary rush under cover ensued, and then the weather became more favourable, though the skies preserved their neutral tint. Mrs. Bullock, a suburban medium, who had become entranced, had located herself in a bower, and beckoned people from the audience to receive her "benediction," which was given in a remarkable dialect. I thought it was Yorkshire, but a spiritualistic gentleman explained to me that it was "partly North American Indian." The Osborne Bellringers next gave a campanological concert, which was exceedingly good of its kind, the small gentleman who played the bass bell working so actively as to suggest the idea that he could not long survive such hard labour in his fleshly condition. These campanologists are said to be big mediums, and occasionally to be floated or otherwise spirited during their performances; but nothing abnormal occurred at the People's Garden. Then there was dancing on the monster platform, which is, I should think, correctly described as "the largest in the world." This was indeed a new phase of Spiritualism: the terpsichorean spiritualists generally let their tables do the dancing for them, as Eastern potentates hire their dancing-girls. Donkey-races, croquet, and other unspiritual diversions varied the order of proceedings; and as for the one-and-ninepenny teas, I can only say I should think the Garden Committee did not get much profit out of them, for the Spiritualists regaled themselves in the most material fashion. During the afternoon the arrivals were fast and frequent. All the medium-power of London seemed present; and the only wonder was that we were not all floated bodily away. There was Mrs. Guppy, who, in answer to my demand whether she had been "floated" from Highbury, informed me that she had come far less romantically—"nine in a cab!" There was Dr. Monk, too, a Nonconformist clergyman, who had lately been taking aërial journeys of the Guppy order about Bristol. In fact, the élite of the sect were well represented; and during the whole afternoon, despite the dirty-looking day, the fun was fast and furious, and all went merry as the proverbial marriage-bell.

Part of the programme was an entertainment by a
gentleman bearing the delightfully sepulchral name of Dr.
Sexton, whose mission in life it is to "expose" the tricks of
Dr. Lynn and Messrs. Maskelyne and Cooke. How those
gentlemen are to be "exposed," seeing they only claim to
deceive you by legerdemain, I cannot comprehend; but
they made the Spiritualists very angry by taking their
names in vain on the handbills of the Egyptian Hall, and
more than insinuating that there was a family likeness
between their performances; and, consequently, the
conjurors were to be "exposed;" that is, the public were to
have their visit to the Temple of Magic spoilt by being
shown beforehand how the tricks were done. Aided by an
expert assistant named Organ, Dr. Sexton soon let us into
the mysteries of the cabinet business, which seemed just as
easy as making the egg stand on end—when you know
how. It is perfectly true that, after hearing Dr. Sexton's
exposition—rather than exposé—it is quite easy for any
one to frustrate the designs of these clever conjurors, if he
wishes to do so. I am not sure that the exposé is wise.
Illogical people will not see the force of Dr. Sexton's
argument, and will possibly think it "proves too much." If
so much can be done by sleight of hand and ingenious
machinery, they will argue, perhaps, that the Davenports
and other mediums are only cleverer conjurors still, or
have better machinery. Alas! all my fairyland is pasteboard
now. I know how the man gets out of the corded box—I
could do it myself. I know where the gorilla goes when he
seems lost in the magic cabinet. It is all a clever
combination of mirrors. The blood-red letters of some dear
departed friend are only made with red ink and a quill pen,
and the name of the "dear departed" forged. Well, I
suppose I am illogical, too. If one set of things is so simple
when it is shown to you, why may not all be? I fear the

Willesden outing has unscttlcd my convictions, and shaken my faith in most sublunary things.

The gathering clearly proved the growth of Spiritualism in London. That such numbers could be got together in the dead season bespeaks a very extensive ramification indeed.

CHAPTER XXXVII.

A GHOSTLY CONFERENCE.

A distinct and well-marked epoch is reached in the history of any particular set of opinions when its adherents begin to organize and confer, and the individual tenets become the doctrines of a party. Such a culmination has been attained by the believers in Modern Spiritualism. For a long while after the date of the now historical Rochester Rappings, the manifestations were mostly individual, and in a great degree limited to such exercises as Mr. Home's elongation, Mrs. Guppy's flight from Highbury to Lamb's Conduit Street, or, more recently still, the voices and manipulations of John and Katie King, the orations of Mrs. Hardinge, Mr. Morse, and Mrs. Tappan. But all this was spasmodic, and not likely to take the world by storm, while Spiritualists had adopted the time-honoured maxim— "Magna est veritas et prevalebit." Therefore they must organize. They have done so, not without protest on the part of some of the most noted of their adherents; but the majority carried the day, and the result is the British National Association of Spiritualists, which has recently been sitting in solemn conclave at its first Annual Conference in Lawson's Rooms, Gower Street.

Now I plead guilty to being greatly interested in this subject of Spiritualism generally, and in the doings of the Conference in particular. I cannot help thinking that clergymen and scientists ought to look into any set of opinions whose professors have attained the dimensions of this body. Their doctrines have spread and are spreading. Already the Spiritualists number among them such men as Mr. Alfred Wallace, Mr. Varley, Mr. Crookes, Mr. S. C. Hall, &c., and are extending their operations amongst all classes of society, notably among the higher. I could even name clergymen of all denominations who hold Spiritualistic views, but refrain, lest it should seem invidious, though I cannot see why it should be incongruous for the clergy to examine doctrines which profess to amplify rather than supplant those of revelation, any more than I can why scientists stand aloof from what professes to be a purely positive philosophy, based upon the inductive method. So it is, however; Spiritualism is heterodox at once in its religious and philosophical aspects. I suppose that is why it had such special attraction for me. Certain it is, I have been following the ghostly conference like a devotee.

We began on Monday evening with a musical soirée at the Beethoven Rooms, in Harley Street; and there was certainly nothing ghostly or sepulchral in our opening day; only then there was nothing very spiritualistic either. For a long time I thought it was going to be all tea and muffins and pianoforte. By-and-by, however, Mr. Algernon Joy read a report of the organization, which was rather more interesting than reports generally are, and Mr. Benjamin Coleman, a venerable gentleman, the father of London Spiritualists, delivered a Presidential address. Still there were no ghosts—not even a spirit rap to augment the applause which followed the speakers. Once my hopes revived when two new physical mediums, with letters of recommendation from Chicago, were introduced, and I expected to see the young gentlemen elongate or float round the room; but nothing of the kind occurred; and a young lady dashed my hopes to the ground by singing "The Nightingale's Trill." Mr. Morse gave an address in the trance state—as I was afterwards informed; but he looked and spoke so like an ordinary mortal that I should not have found out that he was in an abnormal condition.

I fear I went home from Harley Street not quite in so harmonious a frame of mind as could have been wished.

The next morning (Wednesday) Dr. Gully presided at the opening of the Conference proper in Gower Street, where the rooms were more like vaults and smelt earthy. The President ably enough summarized the objections which had been raised to the Association, and also the objects it proposed to itself. He said:—"If the Association keeps clear of dogmatic intrusion, then will there be no fear of its becoming sectarian. Already, however, there is a signal of dogmatism among Spiritualists—and already the dogmatizers call themselves by another name. But the Association has nothing to do with this. It knows its function to be the investigation of facts, and of facts only; and, as was said, no sect was ever yet framed on undoubted facts. Now what are the facts of Spiritualism up to this date? They are reducible to two:—1st. The continued life and individuality of the spirit body of man after it has quitted its body of flesh; and, 2nd. Its communion with spirits still in the flesh, under certain conditions, by physical exhibition and mental impression. Spirit identity cannot be regarded yet as an established fact—at all events, not so as to warrant us in building upon it."

I was agreeably surprised with the moderate tone of this address; and after a brief theological discussion, Mr. W. H. Harrison, the editor of the Spiritualist, followed with a paper on Organization. I do not know what Mr. Harrison was not for organizing. Libraries, reading-rooms, colleges, everything was to be spiritualized. Later in the day there was a paper on Physical Manifestations. I should have preferred the manifestations without the paper, for I fear I am a poor believer at second hand. The reader told some "stumping" stories. Here is one as a specimen—spiritual in more senses than one:—

"One evening I accompanied the Davenports to Mr. Guppy's residence in Great Marlborough Street. After supper Ira, the eldest of the brothers, Mr. Guppy, and myself, adjourned to a dark room, which Mr. Guppy had had prepared for experimental purposes. To get to this room we had to pass through a room that served the combined purposes of a sculptor's studio and a billiard room. Emerging from this room we came into a yard, in one corner of which the dark cabinet in question was constructed. Taking our seats, we extinguished the light. Mr. Guppy was at the time smoking a cigar. This was at once taken from his hand, and carried in the air, where it could be seen by the light given out by its combustion. Some whisky and water was standing on the table. This was handed to us to drink. When it came to my turn, I found there was but little left in the glass. This I pointed out. The glass was forthwith taken from my mouth, and replenished and brought back again."

On Thursday Mr. Everitt read a paper on Direct Writing by Spirits, telling us that on one occasion nine hundred and thirty-six words were written in six seconds. Mr. Everitt must be a bold man—I don't mean altogether for asking us to believe that, but for saying what he did about the medium, who was his wife:—"There are many considerations why it would be impossible for the medium to have produced these writings. For instance, we have sixteen papers upon the same subject, and in those papers there are a great many ancient authors referred to. Mrs. Everitt has never read or seen a single book of any of these authors, and, with a few exceptions, their names had never been heard by her before, much less did she know the age they lived in, the country they belonged to, the works they had written, or the arguments made use of for the defence of their doctrines and teachings. Besides the above reasons there are physical and mental difficulties which preclude the possibility of their being produced by the medium. The physical impossibility is the marvellous rapidity of their production, as many as 936 words having been written in six seconds. The mental difficulty is that the medium has not a logical mind. Like most females, she takes a short cut by jumping to conclusions. She does not, indeed cannot, argue out any proposition by the ordinary rules of logic. Now the papers referred to show that the author or authors are not only well acquainted with ancient lore and the classics, but also possessed very high ability as logicians. For the above reasons we conclude that the medium, from sheer incapacity, both mentally and physically, could not have written these papers, nor any other human being under the same circumstances. We are therefore absolutely driven, after looking at the subject from every conceivable point of view, to conclude respecting their production that they came from a supernatural source, and were produced by supernatural means."

In the afternoon of this day a clergyman, whose name it would be highly indecorous in me to mention, descanted on the aspect of Spiritualism from his point of view in the Church of England. I understood the purport of the paper to be (1) that he claimed the right of members of the Church of England to investigate the phenomena; (2) that, if convinced of their spiritual origin, such conviction need not shake the investigator's previous faith. If the clergyman in question really said no more than the printed reports of the Conference represent him to have done, he rather reversed the conduct of Balaam, and cursed those he came to bless. This is the curt résumé that went forth:—

"The Rev. —— read a paper, in which he defined his position with regard to Spiritualism as that of a mere inquirer, adding that even if he became convinced of its truth, he saw no reason why he should alter the opinions he at present held as a clergyman of the Church of England. After eighteen months' inquiry into the subject, however, he was, perhaps, more of a sceptic than before." If that was all the clergyman in question had to say for the Association, they must rather regret they ever "organized" him, and might well pray to be saved from their friends; but I heard it whispered—presumably by a spirit voice— that there had been a passage at arms between the lady secretary and the clergyman in question, and that Miss— but no, I must not mention names—the fair official punished the delinquent that most awful penalty—silence.

Friday finished the Conference with a trance paper—I did not know there were such things—dictated to Mrs. Cora

Tappan by invisible guides, and was read by Miss—I mean by the fair incognita above-mentioned. Not a manifestation—literally not the ghost of one—only this very glowing peroration:—"But it is in a larger sense of social, mental, political, and even religious renovation, that Spiritualism is destined to work its chief results. The abrogation of the primal terror of mankind, the most ancient spectre in the world of thought, grim and shadowy Death, is, in itself, so vital a change that it constitutes a revolution in the world of mind. Chemistry has already revealed the wonderful fact that no ultimate atom can perish. The subtle chemistry of Spiritualism steps in where science ceases, gathering up the ultimate atoms of thought into a spiritual entity and proving them imperishable. Already has this thought pervaded the popular mind, tinged the decaying forms of theology and external science with its glow, and made the life of man a heritage of immortal glory. More than this, taking spirit as the primal basis of life, each individual, and all members of society and humanity in the aggregate, must for ever strive to express its highest life (i.e. the life of the spirit). The child will be taught from within, external methods being employed only as aids, but never as dictators of thought. Society will be the flowing out of spiritual truths, taking shape and substance as the expression of the soul. Governments will be the protecting power of a parent over loving children, instead of the dictates of force or tyranny. Religion will wear its native garb of simplicity and truth, the offspring of the love and faith that gave it birth. Modern Spiritualism is as great a solvent of creeds, dogmas, codes, scientific sophisms, as is the sunlight of the substances contained in earth and air, revealing by the stages of intermediate life, from man, through spirits, angels, archangels, seraphim, and cherubim, to God, the glorious destiny of every soul. There is a vine growing in the islands of the tropic seas that thrives best upon the ancient ruins or crumbling walls of some edifice built by man; yet ever as it thrives, the tiny tendrils penetrate between the fibres of the stone, cutting and cutting till the whole fabric disappears, leaving only the verdant mass of the foliage of the living vine. Spiritualism is to the future humanity what this vine is to the ancient ruin."

There was another paper coming on "Compound Consciousness," but the title did not attract me. After my four days' patient waiting for ghosts who never came and spirits that would not manifest, I felt, perhaps, a little impatient, put on my hat and left abruptly—the fair secretary, of whom I shall evermore stand in supreme awe, scowling at me when I did so. As I passed into Gower Street—sweet, serene Gower Street, sacred from the wheels of profane cabmen, I was almost surprised to see the "materialized" forms around me; and it really was not until I got well within sound—and smell—of the Underground Railway that I quite realized my abased position, or got out of the spheres whither the lofty periods of Mrs. Tappan's paper, so mellifluously delivered, had wafted me!

CHAPTER XXXVIII.

AN EVENING'S DIABLERIE.

Mr. Spurgeon a short time since oracularly placed it on
record that, having hitherto deemed Spiritualism humbug,
he now believes it to be the devil. This sudden conversion
is, of course, final; and I proceed to narrate a somewhat
exceptional endorsement of the opinion which has recently
occurred within my own experience. There was a time,
how long ago it boots not to say, when I considered
Spiritualism humbug; and a good deal came in my way
which might have led me to the same conclusion as Mr.
Spurgeon, if I had been disposed—which I am not—to go
with a hop, skip, and jump.

The investigator who first presented the "diabolical" theory
to my notice was a French Roman Catholic priest, who had
broken discipline so far as to enter the married state, but
retained all the doctrines of his former faith intact. He had,
in fact, anticipated to some extent the position of Père
Hyacinthe; for it was several years ago I first became
acquainted with him. Individually as well as nationally this
gentleman, too, was prone to jump at conclusions. He lost
a dear friend, and immediately proceeded to communicate
with the departed by means of table-turning and rapping.
For a few days he was quite convinced of the identity of
the communicating spirit; but then, and all within the
compass of a single week, he pronounced the exorcism of
the Catholic Church on the intelligence, I suppose
experimentally in the first instance; found his challenge not
satisfactorily answered, and immediately jumped to the
conclusion that it was the foul fiend himself. I sat very

frequently with this gentleman afterwards, prior to the experience I am about to narrate; and certainly the intelligence always gave itself out to be the spirit unmentionable to ears polite, whose presence my friend had taken for granted.

I once went with this gentleman to the Marshalls, when they were at their zenith. We arranged previously that he should not sit at the table, but on one side, and give me a secret signal when he was silently pronouncing the exorcism. He did so; and certainly all manifestations at once ceased, though we had been in full converse with the invisibles a moment before. Old Mrs. M. had to announce with much chagrin, "The sperrits is gone!"

My other partner in diablerie was a barrister whom I must not mention by name, but who possessed considerable power as a writing medium. The presiding intelligence in his case was, however, of a low character, and given to very bad language. He avowed himself to have been a bargee in the earth-plane—should one say the water-plane?—and certainly swore like one.

As for myself, I am destitute of all "medium-power," whatever that may be, though enthusiastic spirituelle ladies tell me I am "mediumistic"—a qualification which is still more occult to me. I own to being greatly interested in spiritualistic inquiries, except as regards dark séances, which have a tendency to send me to sleep; and I believe that my presence does not "stop manifestations:" so that I suppose I am not a hopeless sceptic.

On the occasion of which I am about to speak we met in my study, where I am in the habit of rearing a few pet snakes. I had just got a fine new specimen; and having no proper habitation for it, had turned my waste-basket upside-down on a small chess table, and left him to tabernacle under it for the night. This was the table we generally used for séances; and my legal friend, who was writing, immediately began to use most foul language, on the subject of the snake, exhorting me to "put him anywhere, put him in the cupboard, old boy." Such was the edifying style of communication we always got through this worthy limb of the law, but it was so much worse than usual on the present occasion as to fairly make us roar at its insane abuse. The gentleman himself, I ought to add, is by no means prone to profane swearing. My priestly friend was making a wide-awake hat reply by tilts; and still got his old reply that his Satanic Majesty was personally present. I did not in the least credit this assertion, any more than I accepted as proven the identity of the bargee, though I hold the impersonation in either case to be a strange psychological fact. That I did not do so is best evidenced by the circumstance that I said, "This spirit asserts himself to be his Satanic Majesty. Have you either of you any objection to communicate with him supposing such to be the case?"

Neither one nor the other had the slightest. My Catholic friend, I knew, always carried a bottle of holy water in his pocket, and at my entreaty forbore for the moment to exorcise. The legal gentleman, though a "writer" himself, was not at all convinced about the phenomena, as was perhaps natural, seeing the exceedingly bad company to which it professed to relegate him. As for me, my scepticism was to me robur et æs triplex. I disposed of the snake, put out the gas; and down we three sat, amid profound darkness, like three male witches in "Macbeth," having previously locked the door to prevent any one disturbing our hocus-pocus.

Any one who has sat at an ordinary dark séance will recollect the number of false starts the table makes, the exclamations, "Was that a rap?" when the wood simply cracks, or, "Did you feel a cold air?" when somebody breathes a little more heavily than usual. I have myself made the experiment, though not without adding an open confession immediately afterwards. I have blown on the fingers of the sitters, and made them feel sure it was a "spirit aura," have done the neatest of raps with my index-finger when my little finger has been securely hooked in that of my next neighbour. In fact, for test purposes, dark séances are a mistake, though they are admirable for a flirtation.

On this occasion, however, we were very much in earnest, and there was no waiting—I hope no collusion. I am quite sure I did not myself consciously produce any manifestation. I can answer for my legal friend, as far as any one person can answer for another; and we neither of us suspected—or suspect—the priest of the order of St. Benedict; only we would rather he had not pronounced such decided opinions; because the wish might have been father to the thought, or rather the thought might, in some utterly unaccountable way, have produced the effects that followed. I have an idea that if Mr. Spurgeon in his present frame of mind were to sit at a table for manifestations, he would obtain the clearest assurance that it was "all the devil," just as it is well known Roman Catholic sitters get communications from Roman Catholic spirits, theists from theistic, and Mormons from the denizens of some spiritualistic Utah.

We had not, on this occasion, a moment to wait. The table forthwith began to plunge and career about the room as though the bargee—or the other personage himself—had actually been "in possession." It required all our agility to follow it in its rapid motion about the room. At last it became comparatively quiet; and I received in reply to a question as to who was present the exceedingly objectionable name which Mr. Spurgeon has coupled with the whole subject. Some persons I know entertain a certain amount of respect, or at all events awe, for the intelligence in question. For myself I feel nothing of the kind, and therefore I added, "If you are what you profess to be, give us some proof." We were sitting with only the tips of our fingers on the table; but it forthwith rose up quite perpendicularly, and came down with a crash that completely shivered it in pieces. I have not the slightest idea how it was done—but it certainly was done. A large portion of the table was reduced to a condition that fitted it for Messrs. Bryant and May's manufactory. When we lighted the gas and looked at our watches we found we had only been sitting a very few minutes.

Of course the obvious explanation will be that the gentleman with the diabolical theory and the evidently strong will-power (as evidenced in the dénouement at Mrs. Marshall's) produced the diabolical effects consciously or unconsciously. I do not think the former was the case; and if it is possible to get such results unconsciously, that phenomenon is quite as curious as the spiritualistic explanation. In fact I am not sure that the psychological is not more difficult than the pneumatological theory. My own notion is that the "Psychic Force" people are clearly on the right track, though their cause, as at present elaborated, is not yet equal to cover all the effects.

Mr. Spurgeon and the "diabolists" concede the whole of the spiritualistic position. They not only say that the effects are due to spiritual causes, but they also identify the producing spirit. I have never been able to get as far as that. I did not feel on the occasion in question at all as though I had been in communication with his sable Majesty. If I was, certainly my respect for that potentate is not increased, for I should have fancied he would have done something much "bigger" in reply to my challenge than smash up a small chess-table. However, there was a sort of uncanny feeling about the experience, and it seemed to me so far illustrative of Mr. Spurgeon's position as to be worth committing to paper. If that gentleman, however, lends such a doctrine the sanction of his approval, he will, let him be assured, do more to confirm the claims of Spiritualism than all the sneers of Professors Huxley and Tyndall, and the scorn of Mr. George Henry Lewes can undo.

CHAPTER XXXIX.

SPIRITUAL ATHLETES.

I am about for once to depart from my usual custom of narrating only personal experiences, and in this and the two following chapters print the communications of a friend who shares my interest in these matters, and has frequently accompanied me in my investigations into this mysterious Borderland. In these cases, however, he investigated on his own account, and I am not responsible for the conclusions at which he arrives:—

"Attracted," he says, "by an article in a popular journal on the subject of 'Spirit Faces,' I determined, if possible, to 'assist' at a séance. I had not hitherto taken much interest in spiritualistic matters, because in the first place, the cui bono question remained persistently unanswered; and, secondly, because most of the 'doings' were in the dark; and it appears to me that, given darkness, there are few things in the way of conjuring and ventriloquism that could not be done. Terpsichorean tables and talking hats never had any particular charm for me, because I could always make a table dance, or a hat say anything I wanted it to say. I saw the Davenports, and preferred Professor Anderson. I even went to a dark séance at the Marshalls', and noticed that when Mr. and Mrs. Marshall had perceptibly partaken of beefsteak and onions, or some equally fragrant food, for dinner, the breath which accompanied the spirit-voices was unmistakably impregnated with onions too; and hence I drew my own conclusions. I am not saying I know how Mr. and Mrs. Marshall do John King and Katie King. I don't know how Professor Anderson or Professor Pepper do their tricks. I confess Mr. Home and the Marshalls have the pull of the professors in one way—that is, they don't perform on a platform but in a private room, and they let you examine everything beforehand. Theirs is the ars celare artem. Again, I don't know how men in the street get out of the very curious knots in which I have tied them, but I know they do it; and therefore I am sure the Davenports could do it without calling in the ghost of one's deceased grandmamma as a sort of Deus—or rather Dea—ex machinâ. I have never seen Mr. Home handle fire or elongate. I have seen him 'levitate,' or float, and I candidly confess I don't know how he does it, any more than I can solve Sir David Brewster's trick by which four young ladies can lift a heavy man on the points of their fingers. It's very mysterious, and very nice for the man.

"So it happened that I had shelved spiritualism for some time, when the article on 'Spirit Faces' came under my notice. I did not care so much about the face part of the matter (at least not the spirit face), but I wanted to test it as a matter of athletics. In one respect the physiognomy did interest me, for I read that the medium was pretty— mediums, according to my experience, being generally very much the reverse—and I found that report had certainly not misrepresented the young lady in this respect. Her name is now public property, so I need not veil it under the pseudonyms of Miss Blank, or Asterisk, or anything of that sort. Miss Florence Cook, then, is a trim little lady of sweet sixteen, and dwells beneath the parental roof in an eastern suburb of London. It is quite true she does not accept payment for séances, which I strove to impress upon her was very foolish indeed, for she works almost as hard as Lulu twice in the week. However, she, or rather her parents, take high ground in the matter, which of course is very praiseworthy on their parts, and convenient for their guests if they happen to be impecunious.

"Now, I do not purpose going through the details of the séance, which was considerably irksome, being protracted by endless psalm singing. What I want to do—with Miss Cook's permission—is to calculate the chances of her being sufficiently athletic to perform the tricks herself, without the aid of spirits. Does she not underrate her unaided powers in assigning a supernatural cause for the effects produced?

"Well, then, this lithe little lady is arrayed in the ordinary garb of the nineteenth century with what is technically

termed a 'pannier,' and large open sleeves, each of which, I
fear, she must have found considerably in the way, as also
the sundry lockets and other nick-nacks suspended from
her neck. However, there they were. We put her in a
cupboard, which had a single Windsor chair in it, and laid
a stoutish new cord on her lap. Then came singing, which
may or may not have been intended to drown any noise in
the cupboard; but, after some delay, she was found tied
around the waist, neck, and two wrists, and the ends of the
cord fastened to the back of the chair. These knots we
sealed, and consigned her to the cupboard again. Shortly
after there appeared at an aperture in the upper portion of
the cupboard a face which looked utterly unspiritual and
precisely like that of the medium, only with some white
drapery thrown over the head. The aperture was just the
height that would have allowed Miss Cook to stand on the
chair and peep out. I do not say she did; I am only
calculating the height. The face remained some minutes in
a strong light; then descended. We opened the cupboard,
and found the little lady tied as before with the seals
unbroken. Spiritual, or material, it was clever.

"After a pause, the same process was gone through again;
only this time stout tape was substituted for rope. The cord
cut the girl's wrists; and tape was almost more satisfactory.
Again she was bound, and we sealed the knots; and again a
face appeared—this time quite black, and not like the
medium at all. I noticed that the drapery ran right round the
face, and cut it off at a straight line on the lower part. This
gave the idea of a mask. I am not saying it was a mask. I
am only throwing out a hint that, if the 'spirits' wish to
convince people they should let the neck be well seen. I am
bound to say it bore a strong light for several minutes; and
some people say they saw eyelids. I did not. I do not say

they were not there. I know how impossible it is to prove a negative, and only say I did not see them.

"What followed possessed no special interest for any but the professed spiritualist, as it was done without any tying; Miss Cook arguing logically enough that, if the previous manifestations were clearly proved to have taken place by other agency than that of the medium herself, mere multiplication of proofs was unnecessary. I had only gone to study the matter from an athletic point of view; and I certainly came away impressed with the idea that, if Miss Florence Cook first got into and then got out of those knots, she was even more nimble and lithesome than she looked, and ought to start an Amateur Ladies' Athletic Society forthwith. As to her making faces at us through the window, I did not care sufficiently about the matter to inquire whether she did or not, because, if she got out of the ropes, it was easy enough to get on the chair and make faces.

"Of course the cui bono remains. The professors make money by it; and Miss Cook can make at most, only a little mild and scarcely enviable notoriety. A satirical old friend of mine, when I told him the above facts, chuckled, and said, 'That's quite enough for a girl of sixteen; and anything that's do-able, a girl of those years will do.' It was no use talking to him of panniers and loose sleeves, and lockets. He was an old bachelor, and knew nothing about such things. At least, he had no business to, if he did.

"I cannot forbear adding a domestic episode, though it is perhaps scarcely relevant to the subject. Certain young imps in my house, hearing what I had seen, got up an exhibition of spirit faces for my benefit. They rigged up a kind of Punch-and-Judy erection, and the cleanest of them did the spirit face, with a white pocket-handkerchief over his head. He looked as stolid and unwinking as the genuine spirit-physiognomy itself. The gas was lowered to a 'dim religious light,' and then a black coal-scuttle, with features chalked on it, deceived some of the circle into the idea that it was a nigger. But the one element which interested me was wanting; there was no rope-tying which could at all entitle the juvenile performance to be categorized under 'Spiritual Athletics.'"

CHAPTER XL.

"SPOTTING" SPIRIT MEDIUMS.

"Among the recent utterances of spiritualistic organs is one to the effect that 'manifestations' come in cycles—in 'great waves,' I believe was the actual expression; and of the many fluctuations to which spiritualistic society has been exposed of late is a very prominent irruption of young lady mediums. The time seems to have gone by for portly matrons to be wafted aërially from the northern suburbs to the W.C. district, or elderly spinsters to exhibit spirit drawings which gave one the idea of a water-colour palette having been overturned, and the resulting 'mess' sat upon for the purposes of concealment. Even inspirational speakers have so far 'gone out' as to subside from aristocratic halls to decidedly second-rate institutions down back streets. In fact, the 'wave' that has come over the spirit world seems to resemble that which has also supervened upon the purely mundane arrangements of Messrs. Spiers and Pond; and we anxious investigators can scarcely complain of the change which brings us face to face with fair young maidens in their teens to the exclusion of the matrons and spinsters aforesaid, or the male medium who was once irreverently termed by a narrator a 'bull-necked young man.'

"The names of these interesting young denizens of two worlds are so well known that it is perhaps unnecessary caution or superfluous gallantry to conceal them; but I will err, if error it be, on the safe side, and call No. 1 Miss C. and No. 2 Miss S., premising only that each is decidedly attractive, with the unquestioned advantage of having seen only some sixteen or seventeen summers apiece. Miss C. has been 'out' some time; her familiar being 'Katie King;' while Miss S. has made her debut more recently, having for her attendant sprites one 'Florence Maple,' a young lady spirit who has given a wrong terrestrial address in Aberdeen, and Peter, a defunct market gardener, who sings through the young lady's organism in a clear baritone voice. It was to me personally a source of great satisfaction when I learnt that Miss C. had been taken in hand by a F.R.S.—whom I will call henceforth the Professor—and Miss S. by a Serjeant learned in the law. Now, if ever, I thought, we have a chance of hearing what science and evidential acumen have to say on the subject of 'Face Manifestations.' Each of these gentlemen, I ought to mention, had written voluminously on the subject of Spiritualism, and both seemed inclined to contest its claims in favour of some occult physical—or, as they named it, psychic—force. This would make their verdict the more valuable to outsiders, as it was clear they had not

approached the subject with a foregone conclusion in its
favour. True, the Spiritualists claimed both the Professor
and the Serjeant persistently as their own; but Spiritualists
have a way of thinking everybody 'converted' who simply
sits still in a decorous manner, and keeps his eyes open
without loudly proclaiming scepticism.

"Personally I had been, up to the date of present
occurrences, accustomed to summarize my convictions on
the subject by the conveniently elastic formula that there
might be 'something in it.' I still think so; but perhaps with
a difference.

"For the former of the two exposés—if such they shall be
deemed—I am compelled to rely on documentary
evidence; but I have 'sat' so many times with Miss S., have
been requested so often by the inspirational Peter to 'listen
to the whip-poor-will, a-singin' on the tree,' have shaken
the spirit hand, gazed on the spirit face, and even cut off
portions of the spirit veil of the fair Florence, that I can
follow the order of events just as though I had been
present. I must confess the wonderful similarity existing
between Miss S. and Florence had exercised me
considerably, and perhaps prepared me to accept with
calmness what followed. Why delay the result? Miss S.
and her mamma were invited to the country house of the
learned Serjeant. A 'cabinet' was extemporized in the bay
of the window, over which the curtains were drawn and a
shawl pinned. With a confidence which is really charming
to contemplate, no 'tests' were asked of the medium, no
'conditions' imposed on the sitter. Miss S. was put in the
cabinet with only a chair, and the expectant circle waited
with patience. In due time the curtains were drawn aside,
and the spirit-face appeared at the opening. It was still the
facsimile of Miss S., with the eyes piously turned up and a

ghostly head-dress covering the hair. One by one the assembled were summoned to look more closely. The initiated gazed and passed on, knowing they must not peep; but, alas, one lady who was not initiated, and therefore unaware of the tacitly imposed conditions, imitated the example of Mother Eve, drew aside the curtains and exposed the unspiritual form of Miss S. standing on the chair; the 'spirit-hands' at the same time struggling so convulsively to close the aperture that the head-gear fell off, and betrayed the somewhat voluminous chignon of Miss S. herself. Hereupon ensued a row, it being declared that the medium was killed, though eventually order was restored by the rather incongruous process of a gentleman present singing a comic song. The learned Serjeant still clings to the belief that Miss S. was in a condition of 'unconscious somnambulism.' I only hope, if ever I am arraigned before him in his judicial capacity, he will extend his benevolent credulity to me in an equal degree, and give me the benefit of the doubt.

"It may be in the recollection of those who follow the fluctuations of the Spiritual 'wave' that some months ago a Dialectical gentleman seized rudely on the spirit form of Katie, which struggled violently with him, scratching his face and pulling out his whiskers, eventually making good its retreat into the cupboard, where Miss C. was presumably bound hand and foot. I must confess the fact of that escape rather prejudiced me in favour of Katie, though I would rather she had evaporated into thin air, and left the dialectical whiskers intact. Still it scored a point on Katie's side, and I eagerly availed myself of the opportunity to pay my devoirs at the shrine of Miss C.; the more so as the Professor had asserted twice that he had seen and handled the form of the medium while looking on and conversing with that of the spirit at the same time. If I could retain my former faith in the Professor, of course this would be final and my conversion an accomplished fact.

"We sat no longer in the subterranean breakfast room of Miss C.'s parental abode; but moved up to the parlour floor, where two rooms communicated through folding doors, the front apartment being that in which we assembled, and the back used as a bedroom, where the ladies took off their 'things.' This latter room, be it remembered, had a second room communicating with the passage, and so with the universe of space in general. One leaf of the folding doors was closed, and a curtain hung over the other. Pillows were placed on the floor, just inside the curtain, and the little medium, who was nattily arrayed in a blue dress, was laid upon them. We were requested to sing and talk during 'materialization,' and there was as much putting up and lowering of the light as in a modern sensation drama. The Professor acted all the time as Master of the Ceremonies, retaining his place at the aperture; and I fear, from the very first, exciting suspicion by his marked attentions, not to the medium, but to the ghost. When it did come it was arrayed according to orthodox ghost fashion, in loose white garments, and I must confess with no resemblance to Miss C. We were at the same time shown the recumbent form of the pillowed medium, and there certainly was something blue, which might have been Miss C., or only her gown going to the wash. By-and-by, however, with 'lights down,' a bottle of phosphorized oil was produced, and by this weird and uncanny radiance one or two privileged individuals were led by the 'ghost' into the back bedroom, and allowed to put their hands on the entranced form of the medium. I was not of the 'elect,' but I talked to those who were, and their opinion was that the 'ghost' was a much stouter, bigger woman than the medium; and I must confess that certain unhallowed ideas of the bedroom door and the adjacent kitchen stairs connected themselves in my mind with recollections of a brawny servant girl who used to sit sentry over the cupboard in the breakfast room. Where was she?

"As a final bonne bouche the spirit made its exit from the side of the folding door covered by the curtain, and immediately Miss C. rose up with dishevelled locks in a way that must have been satisfactory to anybody who knew nothing of the back door and the brawny servant, or who had never seen the late Mr. Charles Kean act in the 'Corsican Brothers' or the 'Courier of Lyons.'

"I am free to confess the final death-blow to my belief that there might be 'something in' the Face Manifestations was given by the effusive Professor who has 'gone in' for the Double with a pertinacity altogether opposed to the calm judicial examination of his brother learned in the law, and with prejudice scarcely becoming a F.R.S.

"I am quite aware that all this proves nothing. Miss S. and Miss C. may each justify Longfellow's adjuration—

'Trust her not, she is fooling thee;'

and yet ghosts be as genuine as guano. Only I fancy the 'wave' of young ladies will have to ebb for a little while; and I am exceedingly interested in speculating as to what will be the next 'cycle.' From 'information I have received,' emanating from Brighton, I am strongly of opinion that babies are looking up in the ghost market, and that our next manifestations may come through an infant phenomenon."

CHAPTER XLI.

A SÉANCE FOR SCEPTICS.

"Attracted by the prominence recently given to the subject of Spiritualism in the Times, and undeterred by that journal's subsequent recantation, or the inevitable scorn of the Saturday Review, I determined to test for myself the value of the testimony so copiously quoted by believers in the modern marvel. Clearly if certain published letters of the period were to be put in evidence, Spiritualism had very much the better, and Science exceedingly little to say for itself. But we all know that this is a subject on which scientific men are apt to be reticent. 'Tacere tutum est' seems the Fabian policy adopted by those who find this new Hannibal suddenly come from across sea into their midst. It is moreover a subject about which the public will not be convinced by any amount of writing or talking, but simply by what it can see and handle for itself. It may be of service, then, if I put on record the result of an examination made below the surface of this matter.

"Like most other miracles this particular one evidently has its phases and comes about in cycles. For a generation past, or nearly so, Modern Spiritualism has been so far allied with Table-turning and mysterious rappings as to have appropriated to itself in consequence certain ludicrous titles, against which it vainly protests. Then cropped up 'levitations' and 'elongations' of the person, and Mr. Home delighted to put red-hot coals on the heads of his friends. None of these manifestations, however, were sufficient to make the spiritualistic theory any other than a huge petitio principii. The Davenports were the first to inaugurate on anything like an extended scale the alleged appearance of the human body, or rather of certain members of the human body, principally arms and hands, through the peep-hole of their cabinet. Then came 'spirit-voices' with Mrs. Marshall, and aërial transits on the part of Mrs. Guppy; then the entire 'form of the departed' was said to be visible chez Messrs. Herne and Williams in Lamb's Conduit Street, whose abode formed Mrs. Guppy's terminus on the occasion of her nocturnal voyage. Then came Miss Florence Cook's spirit faces at Hackney, which were produced under a strong light, which submitted to be touched and tested in what seemed a very complete manner, and even held conversations with persons in the circle. Finally, I heard it whispered that these faces were being recognised on a somewhat extensive scale at the séances of Mrs. Holmes, in Old Quebec Street, where certain other marvels were also to be witnessed, which decided me on paying that lady a visit.

"Even these, however, were not the principal attractions which drew me to the tripod of the seeress in Quebec Street. It had been continually urged as an argument against the claims of Modern Spiritualism, first, that it shunned the light and clave to 'dark' circles; secondly, that it was over-sensitive on the subject of 'sceptics.' Surely, we are all sceptics in the sense of investigators. The most pretentious disciple of Spiritualism does not claim to have exhausted the subject. On the contrary, they all tell us we are now only learning the alphabet of the craft. Perhaps the recognised Spirit-faces may have landed us in words of one syllable, but scarcely more. However, the great advantage which Mrs. Holmes possessed in my eyes over all professors of the new art was that she did not object to sceptics. Accordingly to Quebec Street I went, for the distinct purpose of testing the question of recognition. If I myself, or any person on whose testimony I could rely, established a single case of undoubted recognition, that, I felt, would go farther than anything else towards solving the spiritualistic problem.

"I devoted two Monday evenings to this business; that being the day on which Mrs. Holmes, as she phrases it, 'sits for faces.' On the former of the two occasions twenty-seven persons assembled, and the first portion of the evening was devoted to the Dark Séance, which presented some novel features in itself, but was not the special object for which I was present. Mrs. Holmes, who is a self-possessed American lady, evidently equal to tackling any number of sceptics, was securely tied in a chair. All the circle joined hands; and certainly, as soon as the light was out, fiddles, guitars, tambourines and bells did fly about the room in a very unaccountable manner, and when the candle was lighted, I found a fiddle-bow down my back, a guitar on my lap, and a tambourine ring round my neck. But there was nothing spiritual in this, and the voice which addressed us familiarly during the operation may or may not have been a spirit voice.

"Mrs. Holmes having been released from some very perplexing knots, avowedly by Spirit power, proceeded to what is called the 'Ring Test,' and I was honoured by being selected to make the experiment. I sat in the centre of the room and held both her hands firmly in mine. I passed my hands over her arms, without relaxing my grasp, so as to feel that she had nothing secreted there; when suddenly a tambourine ring, jinglers and all, was passed on to my arm. Very remarkable; but still not necessarily spiritual. Certain clairvoyants present said they could witness the 'disintegration' of the ring. I only felt it pass on to my arm. On the occasion of my second visit this same feat was performed on an elderly gentleman, a very confirmed sceptic indeed. This second circle consisted of twenty persons, many of them very pronounced disbelievers, and not a little inclined to be 'chaffy.' However all went on swimmingly.

"After about an hour of rather riotous dark séance, lights were rekindled and circles re-arranged for the Face Séance which takes place in subdued light. In the space occupied by the folding doors between the front and back room a large black screen is placed, with an aperture, or peep-hole, about eighteen inches square, cut in it. The most minute examination of this back room is allowed, and I took care to lock both doors, leaving the keys crosswise in the key-hole, so that they could not be opened from the outside. We then took our seats in the front room in three or four lines. I myself occupied the centre of the first row, about four feet from the screen, Mr. and Mrs. Holmes sitting at a small table in front of the screen; the theory being that the spirits behind collect from their 'emanations' material to form the faces. Soon after we were in position a most ghostly-looking child's face appeared at the aperture, but was not recognised. Several other corpse-like visages followed with like absence of recognition. Then came a very old lady's face, quite life-like, and Mrs. Holmes informed us that the cadaverous people were those only recently deceased. The old lady looked anxiously round as if expecting to be recognised, but nobody claimed acquaintance. In fact no face was recognised at my first visit. The next was a jovial Joe Bagstock kind of face which peered quite merrily round our circle, and lastly came a most life-like countenance of an elderly man. This face, which had a strange leaden look about the eyes, came so close to the orifice that it actually lifted its grey beard outside. On the occasion of my second visit a lady present

distinctly recognised this as the face of her husband, and
asked the form to show its hand as an additional mark of
identity. This request was complied with, the figure lifting
a thin, white and—as the widow expressed it—'aristocratic'
hand, and kissing it most politely. I am bound to say there
was less emotion manifested on the part of the lady than I
should have expected under the circumstances; and a
young man who accompanied her, and who from the
likeness to her must have been her son, surveyed his
resuscitated papa calmly through a double-barrelled opera
glass. I am not sure that I am at liberty to give this lady's
name; but, at this second visit, Mrs. Makdougall Gregory,
of 21, Green Street, Grosvenor Square, positively
identified the old lady above-mentioned as a Scotch lady of
title well known to her.

"I myself was promised that a relation of my own would
appear on a future occasion; but on neither of those when I
attended did I see anything that would enable me to test the
value of the identifications. The faces, however, were so
perfectly life-like, with the solitary exception of a dull
leaden expression in the eye, that I cannot imagine the
possibility of a doubt existing as to whether they belonged
to persons one knew or not. At all events here is the
opportunity of making the test. No amount of scepticism is
a bar to being present. The appearances are not limited to a
privileged few. All see alike: so that the matter is removed
out of the sphere of 'hallucinations.' Everything is done in
the light, too, as far as the faces are concerned. So that
several not unreasonable test-conditions are fulfilled in this
case, and so far a step made in advance of previous
manifestations.

"We may well indeed pause—at least I know I did—to
shake ourselves, and ask whereabouts we are. Is this a

gigantic imposture? or are the Witch of Endor and the
Cumæan Sibyl revived in the unromantic neighbourhood
of the Marble Arch, and under circumstances that
altogether remove them from the category of the
miraculous? England will take a good deal of convincing
on this subject, which is evidently one that no amount of
'involuntary muscular action,' or 'unconscious cerebration,'
will cover. What if the good old-fashioned ghost be a
reality after all, and Cock Lane no region of the
supernatural?

"What then? Why, one may expect to meet one's deceased
ancestors at any hour of the day or night, provided only
there be a screen for them to 'form' behind, and a light
sufficiently subdued to prevent disintegration; with, of
course, the necessary pigeon-hole for the display of their
venerable physiognomies. On their side of the question, it
will be idle to say, 'No rest but the grave!' for there may
not be rest even there, if Delphic priestesses and Cumæan
Sibyls come into vogue again; and we may as well omit the
letters R. I. P. from our obituary notices as a purely
superfluous form of speech."

Speaking now in my own proper person as author, I may
mention—as I have purposely deferred doing up to this
point—that a light was subsequently struck at one of Mrs.
Holmes's Dark Séances, and that the discoveries thus made
rendered the séance a final one. Mr. and Mrs. Holmes
retired, first to Brighton, and then to America.

They were, at the time of my writing, holding successful
séances in the latter place; and public (Spiritualistic)

opinion still clings to the belief that Mrs. Holmes is a genuine medium.

CHAPTER XLII.

AN EVENING WITH THE HIGHER SPIRITS.

At the head of social heresies, and rapidly beginning to take rank as a religious heresy as well, I have no hesitation in placing modern Spiritualism. Those who associate this latest mystery only with gyrating articles of furniture, rapping tables, or simpering planchettes, are simply in the abyss of ignorance, and dangerously underrate the gravity of the subject. The later development of Spirit Faces and Spirit Forms, each of which I have examined thoroughly, and made the results of my observations public, fail to afford any adequate idea of the pitch to which the mania— if mania it be—has attained. To many persons Spiritualism forms the ultimatum, not only in science, but also in religion. Whatever the Spirits tell them they believe and do as devoutly as the Protestant obeys his Bible, the Catholic his Church, or the scientific man follows up the results of his demonstrations. That is, in fact, the position they assume. They claim to have attained in matters of religion to demonstration as clear and infallible as the philosopher does in pure science. They say no longer "We believe," but "We know." These people care little for the vagaries of Dark Circles, or even the doings of young ladies with "doubles." The flight of Mrs. Guppy through the air, the elongation of Mr. Home's braces, the insertion of live coals among the intricacies of Mr. S. C. Hall's exuberant locks, are but the A B C which have led them to their present advanced position. These physical "manifestations" may do for the neophytes. They are the initiated. I am the initiated; or I ought to be, if patience and perseverance constitute serving an apprenticeship. I have devoted a good portion of my late life to the study. I have given up valuable evenings through several consecutive winters to dark séances; have had my hair pulled, my head thumped with paper tubes, and suffered other indignities at the hands of the "Invisibles;" and, worse than all, my friends have looked upon me as a lunatic for my pains, and if my enemies could have wrought their will they would have incarcerated me as non compos, or made an auto-da-fe of me as a heretic years ago.

Through sheer length of service, then, if on no other account, I had grown somewhat blasé with the ordinary run of manifestations. Spirit Faces no longer interest me; for I seek among them in vain the lineaments of my departed friends. Spirit Hands I shake as unconcernedly as I do those of my familiar acquaintances at the club or in the street. I have even cut off a portion of the veil of Miss Florence Maple, the Aberdeen Spirit, and gone away with it in my pocket: so that it was, at all events, a new sensation when I received an invitation to be present at a trance séance, where one of the Higher Spirits communicated to the assembled things undreamed of in mundane philosophy. The sitting was a strictly private one; so I must not mention names or localities; but this does not matter, as I have no marvels in the vulgar sense of the word to relate: only Higher Teachings, which will do just as well with asterisks or initials as with the names in full.

The scene, then, was an artist's studio at the West End of London, and the medium a magnetic lady with whom I had frequently sat before, though not for the "Higher" teachings. Her instruction had so far come in the shape of very vigorous raps, which ruined my knuckles to imitate them, and in levitation of a small and volatile chess table, which resisted all my efforts to keep it to the paths of propriety. This lady was not young; and I confess frankly this was, to my thinking, an advantage. When I once told a sceptical friend about Miss Florence Cook's séance, and added, triumphantly, "Why, she's a pretty little simple girl of sixteen," that clenched the doubts of this Thomas at once, for he rejoined, "What is there that a pretty little simple girl of sixteen won't do?" Miss Showers is sweet sixteen, too; and when "Peter" sings through her in a clear baritone voice, I cannot, despite myself, help the thought occasionally flitting across my mind, "Would that you were six-and-twenty, or, better still, six-and-thirty, instead of sixteen!" Without specifying to which of the two latter classes our present medium belonged, one might venture to say she had safely passed the former. She was of that ripe and Rubens-like beauty to which we could well imagine some "Higher" spirit offering the golden apple of its approval, however the skittish Paris of the spheres might incline to sweet sixteen. I had a short time before sat infructuously with this lady, when a distressing contretemps occurred. We were going in for a dark séance then, and just as we fancied the revenants were about to justify the title, we were startled by a crash, and on my lighting up, all of the medium I could see were two ankles protruding from beneath the table. She had fainted "right off," as the ladies say, and it required something strong to bring her to. In fact, we all had a "refresher," I recollect, for sitting is generally found to be exhausting to the circle as well as to the medium. On the present occasion, however, everything was, if not en plein jour, en plein gaz. There was a good deal of preliminary difficulty as to the choice of a chair for the medium. Our artist-friend had a lot of antique affairs in his studio, no two being alike, and I was glad to see the lady select a capacious one with arms to it, from which she would not be likely to topple off when the spirits took possession. The rest of us sat in a sort of irregular circle round the room, myself alone being accommodated with a small table, not for the purposes of turning (I am set down as "too physical") but in order to report the utterances of the Higher Spirits. We were five "assistants" in all—our host, a young lady residing with him, another lady well known as a musical artiste, with her mamma and my unworthy self. Installed in her comfortable chair, the medium went through a series of facial contortions, most of which looked the reverse of pleasing, though occasionally she smiled benignantly par parenthèse. I was told—or I understood it so—that this represented her upward passage through different spheres. She was performing, in fact, a sort of spiritualistic "Excelsior." By way of assimilating our minds to the matter in hand, we discussed the Apocryphal Gospels, which happened to be lying on the table; and very soon, without any other process than the facial contortions having been gone through, the medium broke silence, and, in measured tones of considerable benignity, said:— "Friends, we greet you in the name of our Lord and Master. Let us say the Lord's Prayer."

She then repeated the Lord's Prayer, with considerable alterations from the Authorized Version, especially, I noticed, inserting the Swedenborgian expressions, "the Heavens," "on earth;" but also altering the order of the clauses, and omitting one altogether. She then informed us

that she was ready to answer questions on any subject, but
that we were not bound to accept any teaching which she—
or let us say they, for it was the spirits now speaking—
might give us. "What did we wish to know?" I always
notice that when this question is asked at a spirit circle
everybody simultaneously shuts up, as though the desire
for knowledge were dried at its source. Nobody spoke, and
I myself was not prepared with a subject, but I had just
been reviewing a Swedenborgian book, and I softly
insinuated "Spiritual Marriage." It was graciously
accepted; and our Sibyl thus delivered herself:—Mankind,
the higher Spirit or Spirits, said was originally created in
pairs, and the soul was still dual. Somehow or other—my
notes are not quite clear how—the parts had got mixed up,
separated, or wrongly sorted. There were, however, some
advantages in this wrong sorting, which was so frequent an
accident of terrestrial marriage, since it was possible for
people to be too much alike—an observation I fancied I
had heard before, or at least not so profound a one as to
need a ghost "Come from the dead to tell us that, Horatio!"
When the right halves did get together on earth the good
developed for good, the evil for evil, until they got to the
heavens or the other places—they were all plurals.
Swedenborgianism has an objection to the singular
number; and I could not fail to identify the teaching of the
Higher Spirit at once with that of the New Jerusalem
Church. Two preliminary facts were brought before us; the
Higher Spirits were in theology Swedenborgian, and in
medical practice homœopaths. So was the Medium.
Although there was no marriage in the spiritual world, in
our sense of the term, there was not only this re-sorting and
junction of the disunited bivalves, but there were actual
"nuptials" celebrated. We were to be careful and
understand that what terrestrials called marriage celestials
named nuptials—it seemed to me rather a distinction

without a difference. There was no need of any ceremony, but still a ceremony was pleasing and also significant. I asked if it was true, as I had read in the Swedenborgian book, that all adult angels were married. She replied, "Yes; they married from the age of 18 to 24, and the male was always a few years older than the female."

There was a tendency, which I continually had to check, on the part of the Medium to wander off from matrimonial to theological subjects; and the latter, though trite, were scarcely so heterodox as I expected. I had found most "spiritualistic" teaching to be purely Theistic. Love to God and man were declared to be the great essentials, and creeds to matter little. If a man loved truth, it was no matter how wild or absurd his ideas might be. The love of God might seem a merely abstract idea, but it was not so. To love goodness was to love God. The love of the neighbour, in the sense of loving all one's kind, might seem hard, too; but it was not really so. There were in the sphere where this Intelligence dwelt millions of angels, or good spirits, working for the salvation of men.

I ought to mention that this lady, in her normal condition, is singularly reticent, and that the "communications" I chronicle were delivered fluently in one unbroken chain of what often rose into real eloquence.

So Christ came for the good of man, and Christ was not the only Messiah who had appeared on earth. In the millions of ages that had passed over our globe, and in the other planets of our solar system, there had risen up "other men filled with the spirit of good, and so Sons of God." I here tried to get at the views of the Higher Spirits on the Divinity of Christ, but found considerable haziness; at one time it was roundly asserted, at another it seemed to me explained away by such expressions as I have quoted above.

Our planet, I was informed, had been made the subject of special care because we were more material, more "solid" than the inhabitants of any other orb. There was an essential difference between Christ and all other great teachers, such as Buddha; and there were no historical records of any other manifestation of the Messiah than that we possessed; but such manifestations had taken place.

The Spirit then gave us an account of its surroundings, which is, I believe, purely Swedenborgian. The "celestial" angels were devoted to truth, the "spiritual" angels to goodness; and so, too, there were the Homes of the Satans, where falsehoods prevailed, and of the Devils, where evils predominated. Spirits from each of these came to man and held him in equilibrio; but gained power as his will inclined towards them. The will was not altogether free, because affected by inherited tendencies; but the "determination" was. I have no idea what the Higher Spirit meant by this; and I rather fancy the Higher Spirit was in some doubt itself. It rather put me in mind of the definition of metaphysics: "If you are talking to me of what you know nothing about, and I don't understand a word of what you are saying—that's metaphysics."

All can do good, continued the Sibyl. Evil cannot compel you. Utter only such an aspiration as, "God help me," and it brings a crowd of angels round you. From those who came to them from this world, however, they (the Higher Spirits) found that teachers taught more about what we were to think than what we were to do. Goodness was so easy. A right belief made us happier; but right action was essential.

Pushed by our host, who was rather inclined to "badger" the Higher Spirit, as to irresistible tendencies, the Intelligence said they were not irresistible. When we arrived in the Spirit World we should find everything that had occurred in our lives photographed. You will condemn yourselves, it was added. You will not be "had up" before an angry God. You will decide, in reference to any wrong action, whether you could help it. Even in the act of doing it a man condemns himself; much more so there. The doctrine of the Atonement was summarily disposed of as a "damnable heresy." "Does the Great Spirit want one man to die? It hurts us even to think of it!"

I then questioned the Medium with regard to the resurrection of the body; and was told that man, as originally created, was a spiritual being, but had "superinduced" his present body of flesh—how he managed it I did not quite gather. As to possible sublimation of corporeal integument, the case of ghosts was mentioned. It was to no purpose I gently insinuated I had never seen a ghost, or had the existence of one properly authenticated. I was told that if I fired a pistol through a ghost only a small particle of dust would remain which could be swept up. I was not aware that even so much would remain. Fancy "sweeping up" a Higher Spirit!

I could not help once or twice pausing to look round on this strange preacher and congregation. The comfortable-looking lady propped in an arm-chair, and with an urbane smile discoursing on these tremendous topics, our little congregation of five, myself writing away for dear life, the young hostess nursing a weird-looking black cat; the other young lady continually harking back to "conjugal" subjects, which seemed to interest her; the mamma slightly flabbergastered at the rather revolutionary nature of the communications; and our host every now and then throwing in a rude or caustic remark. I dreaded to think what might have been the result of a domiciliary visit paid by a Commissioner in Lunacy to that particular studio!

Back, then, the musical young lady took us to conjugal pairs. It was very difficult to convey to us what this conjugal love was like. Was it Elective Affinity? I asked. Yes; something like that, but still not that. It was the spontaneous gravitation in the spheres, either to other, of the halves of the dual spirit dissociated on earth. Not at all—again in reply to me—like flirting in a corner. The two, when walking in the spheres, looked like one. This conjugal puzzle was too much for us. We "gave it up;" and with an eloquent peroration on the Dynamics of Prayer, the séance concluded.

The Lord's Prayer was again said, with even more varieties than before; a few extemporaneous supplications were added. The process of coming-to seemed even more disagreeable, if one may judge by facial expression, than going into the trance. Eventually, to get back quite to earth, our Sibyl had to be demesmerized by our host, and in a few minutes was partaking of a ham sandwich and a cup of coffee as though she had never been in nubibus at all.

What the psychological condition had been I leave for those more learned than myself to determine. That some exaltation of the faculties took place was clear. That the resulting intelligence was of deep practical import few, I fancy, would aver. Happily my mission is not to discuss, but to describe; and so I simply set down my experience in the same terms in which it was conveyed to me as "An Evening with the Higher Spirits."

CHAPTER XLIII.

SPIRIT FORMS.

Some years ago I contributed to the columns of a daily paper an article on Spirit Faces, which was to me the source of troubles manifold. In the first place, the inquirers into Spiritualism, whose name I found to be legion, inundated me with letters, asking me to take them to the house of pretty Miss Blank, the medium. Miss Blank might have been going on till now, holding nightly receptions, without having exhausted her list of self-invited guests; I had but one answer; the lady was a comparative stranger to me, and not a professional medium; ergo, the legion must ask some one to chaperone them elsewhere. Spirit Faces had got comparatively common and almost gone out since I wrote. We are a long way beyond faces now. Then, again, my second source of trouble was that forthwith, from the date of my writing, the Spiritualists claimed me for their own, as Melancholy did the young gentleman in Gray's elegy. Though I fancied my paper was only a calm judicial statement of things seen, and I carefully avoided saying whether I was convinced or not, I found myself nolens volens enrolled among the initiated, and expected to devote about five evenings out of the seven to séances. I did go, and do go still to a great many; so that I feel pretty well posted up in the "Latest Intelligence" of the Spiritual world. But the worst of all is that my own familiar friends, in whom I trusted, have also lifted up their heels against me—I mean metaphorically, of course. "What's the last new thing in spirits?" they ask me out loud in omnibuses or railway carriages, causing my fellow-travellers to look at me in doubt as to whether I am a licensed victualler or a necromancer. As "bigots feign belief till they believe," I really begin to have some doubts myself as to the state of my convictions.

But I wish to make this paper again a simple statement of things heard and seen—especially seen. I flatter myself the title is a nice, weird, ghostly one, calculated to make people feel uncomfortable about the small hours of the morning. Should such be the case—as they say in prefaces—the utmost hopes of the writer will be realized. When last I communicated my experiences, the ultimate end we had reached was the appearance of a white counterpart of pretty Miss Blank's face at the peep-hole of a corner cupboard. There were a good many more or less— generally less—successful imitations of this performance in various quarters, and the sensation subsided. Miss B. was still facile princeps from the fact that she stood full light—I mean her spirit-face did—whilst all the others leaned to a more or less dim religious kind of gloom. In a short time, however, "Katie"—as the familiar of Miss B. was termed—thought she would be able to "materialize" herself so far as to present the whole form, if we re-arranged the corner cupboard so as to admit of her doing so. Accordingly we opened the door, and from it suspended a rug or two opening in the centre, after the fashion of a Bedouin Arab's tent, formed a semicircle, sat and sang Longfellow's "Footsteps of Angels." Therein occurs the passage: "Then the forms of the departed enter at the open door." And, lo and behold, though we had left Miss B. tied and sealed to her chair, and clad in an ordinary black dress somewhat voluminous as to the skirts, a tall female figure draped classically in white, with bare arms and feet, did enter at the open door, or rather down the centre from between the two rugs, and stood statue-like before us, spoke a few words, and retired; after which we entered the Bedouin tent and found pretty Miss B. with her dress as before, knots and seals secure, and her boots on! This was Form No. 1, the first I had ever seen. It looked as material as myself; and on a subsequent occasion—for I have seen it several times—we took four very good photographic portraits of it by magnesium light. The difficulty I still felt, with the form as with the faces, was that it seemed so thoroughly material and flesh-and-blood like. Perhaps, I thought, the authoress of "The Gates Ajar" is right, and the next condition of things may be more material than we generally think, even to the extent of admitting, as she says, pianofortes among its adjuncts. But I was to see something much more ghostly than this.

The great fact I notice about Spiritualism is, that it is obeying the occult impetus of all great movements, and steadily going from east to west. From Hackney and Highbury it gravitates towards Belgravia and Tyburnia. I left the wilds of Hackney behind, and neared Hyde Park for my next Form. I must again conceal names and localities; I have no desire to advertise mediums, or right to betray persons who have shown me hospitality—and Spirit Forms. We arranged ourselves in a semicircle around the curtains which separated the small back drawing-room from the large front one, joined hands, sang until we were hoarse as crows, and kept our eyes steadily fixed on an aperture left between the curtains for the faces to show themselves. The room was in blank darkness, and, feeling rather tired of the incantation, I looked over my shoulder into the gloom, and lo! a shadowy form stood self-illuminated not far from me. At last I had seen it—a good orthodox ghost in white, and visible in the darkness. It was the form of the redoubtable John King himself, who was, I believe, a bold buccaneer in the flesh, but who looked more like an Arab sheikh in the spirit. He sailed about the room, talked to us, and finally disappeared. Eventually he reappeared behind the curtains, and for a brief space the portière was drawn aside, and the spirit form was seen lighting up the recumbent figure of the medium, who was stretched on a sofa, apparently in deep trance. It must be borne in mind that we were forming a cordon round the passage from one room to the other during the whole of this time. A trio of "spirits" generally puts in an appearance at these séances. In this case there were John King, whom I had now seen, as well as heard; Katie, the familiar of Miss B.; and a peculiarly lugubrious gentleman named Peter, who, I fancy, has not been seen, but who has several times done me the favour of grasping my hand and hoisting me towards the ceiling, as though he were going to carry me off bodily to spirit-land. I stand some six feet in my boots, and have stepped upon my chair, and still felt the hand coming downwards to me—where from I have no idea.

But my later experiences have still to be told. I was invited a few weeks ago to a very select séance indeed, where the same medium was to officiate. This family, who spared no expense in their investigations, had actually got a large, handsome cabinet standing in their dining-room as a recognised piece of furniture. It was only used, however, on this occasion for the imprisonment of the medium. The evolutions of John King, who soon appeared, all took place outside the cabinet door. He was only "materialized" to the middle; and, to our utter amazement, came up to the table, and apparently through the table, into the very middle of the circle, where he disported himself in various ways, keeping up an animated conversation the whole time, and frequently throwing himself into the attitude of a person swimming on his back. He also went upwards as high as the gasalier, and altogether did a good many marvellous things, considering that all this time he presented the

appearance of only half a man illuminated by his own
light.

On one occasion only have I been seated next to the
medium during the manifestation of any of these forms. At
this séance I held him firmly by one hand, and a slightly
sceptical lady had the other. We never let go for a moment,
but during the whole of the sitting, while John King, Katie,
and Peter were talking, tiny children's hands were playing
with my arm, hands, and hair. There were, of course, no
children in the room. Peter, the lugubrious, is great at light
porterage. I have known him bring a large collection of
valuable Sèvres china, and a timepiece with its glass case,
from the chimney-piece to the table—no easy task in the
light, much less in blank darkness. He also frequently takes
down the pictures from the wall and puts them on the table.
Katie winds up a large musical box, and wafts it, while
playing, all over the room. Of course we rub our eyes and
ask what on earth, if it be on earth, does this mean? I have
not—to keep up the diction of my subject—the ghost of an
idea. If it's conjuring, why don't the mediums say so, and
enter the field openly against Messrs. Maskelyne and
Cooke and Dr. Lynn? Even if I had a decided opinion
about it I should refrain from propounding it here, because,
in the first place, it would be an impertinence, and, in the
second, no conclusion can be arrived at upon testimony
alone. People must see for themselves and draw their own
inferences. In the meantime the thing, whatever it is, grows
and grows upwards. A year ago I had to journey down east
to find it. Now I must array myself gorgeously like a
Staffordshire miner, and seek the salons of the West. The
great desideratum, it still appears to me, is that some man
with a name in science should examine the matter,
honestly resolving to endorse the facts if true, but to
expose them mercilessly if there be a loophole for

suspicion. Omne ignotum pro magnifico habetur. I used to think ghosts big things, but that was before I knew them. I should think no more of meeting a ghost now than a donkey on a dark night, and would infinitely sooner tackle a spirit than a burglar. People's curiosity is roused, and the sooner somebody gets at the truth the better. It is a somewhat irksome task, it is true; but no general principle can be arrived at except by an induction of particulars. Let us be Baconian, even to our ghosts. If they are ghosts, they are a good deal more substantial than I had thought. If they are not, let somebody, in the name of nineteenth-century science, send them off as with the crow of chanticleer, and let us hear no more of Spirit Faces or Spirit Forms.

CHAPTER XLIV.

SITTING WITH A SIBYL.

The connexion of modesty with merit is proverbial, though questioned by Sydney Smith, who says their only point in common is the fact that each begins with an—m. Modesty, however—waiving the question of accompanying merit— is a trait which, in my mystic inquiries and devious wanderings, I meet with far more frequently than might be expected. I have just met with two instances which I hasten to put on record, if only to confute those who say that the age in general, and spirit mediums in particular, are not prone to be modest and retiring. My first modest person was a Spirit Photographer; my second was a Sibyl. I might have looked for bashfulness in the latter, but was certainly surprised to meet with it in the former. I suddenly learnt from the Medium the fact that a Spirit Photographer had settled down in my immediate neighbourhood, and the appearance of his ghostly advertisement brings to my recollection some previous mystic experiences I myself had in this way.

A now celebrated medium, Mrs. Guppy, née Miss Nicholl, was, in the days of her maidenhood, a practitioner of photography in Westbourne Grove; and, as far as I know, she might have been the means of opening up to the denizens of the Summer Land this new method of terrestrial operations. Ever on the qui vive for anything new in the occult line, I at once interviewed Miss Nicholl and sat for my portrait, expecting at the least to find the attendant spirit of my departed grandmamma or defunct maiden aunt standing sentinel over me, as I saw departed relations doing in many cartes de visite in the room. I confess there was a kind of made-up theatrical-property look about the attendant spirits which gave one the idea that the superior intelligences must have dressed in a hurry when they sat or stood for their portraits. They looked, in fact, if it be not irreverent to say it, rather like so many bundles of pneumatical rags than respectable domestic ghosts. However, as long as I got the ghosts I did not care about the dress. Tenue de soir point de rigueur, I would have said, as they do outside the cheap casinos in Paris, or "Evening dress not required," if one must descend to the vernacular. Well, I sat persistently and patiently through I am afraid to say how many operations, and the operator described me as being surrounded by spirits—I always am according to Mediums, but my spirits must be eminently unsociable ones, for they seldom give me a word, and on this occasion refused to be "taken" as resolutely as the bashful gentleman in the Graphic who resisted the operations of the prison officials to obtain a sun-picture of his interesting physiognomy. There was indeed a blotch on one of the negatives, which I was assured was a spirit. I could not see things in that light.

Foiled on this particular occasion my anxiety was dormant, but never died out. I still longed for a denizen of the other world to put in an appearance, and kept on being photographed over and over again until I might have been the vainest man alive, on the bare hope that the artist might be a Medium malgré lui or undeveloped. I had heard there were such beings, but they never came in my way. I was really serious in this wish, because I felt if it could be granted, the possibility of deception being prevented, the objectivity of the phenomena would be guaranteed. At this time I was heretical enough to believe that most ghosts were due to underdone pork or untimely Welsh rare-bits, and that the raps assigned to their agency were assignable to the active toes of the Medium which might be anywhere and up to anything with the opportunities of a dark séance.

A short time since, however, M. Buguet, a celebrated French Spirit Photographer came from Paris to London, and received sitters for the modest sum of 30s. each. This would have been much beyond my means; but I suppose my wish had transpired, and that gentleman sent me an invitation to sit gratis, which, I need not say, I thankfully accepted. I felt sure that M. Buguet did not know either my long-lost grandmother or lamented maiden aunt, so that any portraits I might get from him would be presumably genuine. I sat; and over my manly form, when the negative came to be cleaned, was a female figure in the act of benediction. I have no notion how she got there—for I watched every stage in the operation, and selected my plate myself; but neither, on the other hand, does she bear the faintest resemblance to anybody I ever knew.

Still M. Buguet is not my modest photographer. Elated by success so far, I called on the local gentleman who advertised in the Medium; but the local gentleman was "engaged." I wrote to the local gentleman appointing an interview; but the local gentleman replied not. Yet still his advertisement remains; and I see in every spiritualistic album dozens of "property" relations in the shape of quasi-spirits, and wonder why the local gentleman would not take me, so as to be immortalized in these pages.

Equally modest was the advertising Sibyl. I wrote to the Sibyl, and somebody replied, and "respectfully declined." But I was not to be done. There is more than one Sibyl in the world. I called on No. 2 without announcing my intention or sending in my name. This Sibyl at once admitted me, and I mounted to the first floor front of a respectable suburban lodging-house.

I waited anxiously for a long time, wondering whether Sibyl was partaking of the onions, whose presence in that modest domicile was odoriferously evidenced to my nose, though it was then scarcely half-past one o'clock. Presently a portly middle-aged man, who might have been Sibyl's youthful papa, or rather aged husband, entered, wiping his mouth. He had clearly been partaking of the fragrant condiment.

Where was Sibyl?

"She would be with us directly," the gentleman said, varying the proceedings by picking his teeth in the interim.

She was with us in a minute, and never, I suppose, did picturesque anticipations more suddenly collapse and come to grief than mine. I had pictured Sibyl a bright ethereal being, and the realization of my ideal weighed twelve stone, if an ounce. She was a big, fleshy, large-boned woman of an utterly uncertain age, not without considerable good-nature in her extensive features; but the pervading idea that you had when you looked at Sibyl was that there was too much of her. I could not help thinking of the husband who said he did not like a big wife: he preferred two small ones; and then again I fell into wonderment as to whether the man who was still engaged with his dental apparatus was Sibyl's husband or papa.

I told them I was anxious to test Sibyl's powers; and, with a few passes from his fat dumpy hands, the man soon put her to sleep. It looked to me like an after-dinner nap, but I was told it was magnetic. It might have been. By the way, I had unmistakable evidence from my olfactory organ that Sibyl had been eating onions.

I had provided myself with two locks of hair, as I had heard that "psychometry" was among Sibyl's qualifications. I handed her the first, and she immediately proceeded to describe a series of tableaux which appeared to pass through her mind. She kept handling the lock of hair, and said, "The person to whom this belongs is ill— weak," which was true enough, but might, I thought, be a shot. I should mention, however, that it was quite impossible Sibyl could know me. She had not even heard my name. She then described a bedroom, with some person—she could not see what person—lying in bed, and a lady in a blue dress bending over her. This, again, I thought might flow out as a deduction from her premises of the hair belonging to an invalid. The blue dress was correct enough, but still so little special as to be a very possible coincidence. She then, however, startled me by saying, "I notice this, that on the table by the bedside, where the bottles of medicine are standing, milk has been spilt—a large quantity—and not wiped up." This was a trivial detail, not known to me at the time, but confirmed on subsequent inquiry.

She then passed on to describe a second tableau, where the same person in the blue dress was in a room all hung over with plates, along with a gentleman whom she described very accurately. He was the occupant of the house where the patient lay, and, having a hobby for old china, had turned his dining-room into a sort of crockery shop by hanging it all over with the delf.

This was curious enough, though not very convincing. It seemed as though the influence of this person who had given me the hair was stronger than that of the hair itself. With the second lock of hair we failed utterly. She said that also came from a sick person, but a person not sick with the same disease as the other. She was quite positive they came from different people, and asked me to feel the difference of texture. I am sorry, for Sibyl's sake, to say they both came from the same person, and were cut at the same time, though from different parts of the head, which made one look silkier than the other.

As a test of Sibyl's clairvoyance, this was not very satisfactory. She read the inscription on a card when her eyes were bandaged, pressing it to her forehead; but then olden experiences in the way of blindman's buff convince me that it is very difficult to say when a person is properly blinded.

Altogether, then, I never quite got over my previous disappointment at Sibyl's bulk. Had she been pretty and frizzle-headed like Miss Annie Eva Fay, or like Miss Showers or Miss Florence Cook, I might have been disposed to make more of her coincidences and to wink at her failures. We are so liable to be led away by our feelings in these matters. Sibyl was large, had eaten onions, and would have been improved if she had brushed her hair, and so I am afraid I rather grudged the somewhat exorbitant fee which the fat-handed man—not Sibyl—took and pocketed in an interval of his dental pursuit, and I passed out from that suburban lodging, none of us, I fancy, very well satisfied with one another. I have an idea I unconsciously expressed my inner feelings of disappointment with Sibyl and something stronger in reference to her male companion.

CHAPTER XLV.

SPIRITUALISTS AND CONJURERS.

"How it's done" is the question which, in the words of Dr. Lynn, we want to settle with reference to his own or kindred performances, and, still more, in the production of the phenomena known as spiritual. I have spent some years of my existence in a hitherto vain endeavour to solve the latter problem; and the farther I go, the more the mystery seems to deepen. Of late, the two opposed parties, the

Spiritualists and the Conjurers, have definitely entered the
arena, and declared war to the knife. Each claims to be
Moses, and denounces the others as mere magicians. Mr.
Maskelyne holds a dark séance, professing to expose the
spiritualistic ones; Dr. Lynn brandishes against them his
strong right arm upon which is written in letters all of
blood the name of one's deceased grandmother, while, in
return, Dr. Sexton exposes the conjurers, and spoils one's
enjoyment of a hitherto enjoyable evening, by showing
"how it's done"—how the name of one's departed relative
is forged and painted early in the afternoon, instead of
"coming out" on the spot—and in spots—like measles or
nettle-rash (as we feel defunct relations ought to come) or
walking in and out of the corded box at pleasure, and even
going so far as to give the address of the clever mechanist
down a by-street near Notting-hill Gate, who will make the
mysterious packing case to order in return for a somewhat
heavy "consideration."

I accepted Dr. Lynn's invitation to be present on his
"opening night;" and wondered, in passing, why everybody
should not make their cards of invitation such thorough
works of art as his. Now I am going to do even-handed
justice all the way round; and I must say that Dr. Lynn's
experiment of fastening his attendant to a sort of
penitential stool with copper wire, surrounded by
scrutineers from the audience, and then making the man's
coat come off, and a ring pass over his arm, behind a
simple rug held in front of him, is quite as wonderful as
anything I have ever witnessed at a séance. It has the great
advantage of being done in the light, instead of, as in Mr.
Fay's case, in darkness, and without a cabinet. In fact, I
have no idea how it's done; though I have no doubt the first
time I see Dr. Sexton he will point to something
unsatisfactory in the bolts to which that doorkeeper is

fastened, and give me the addresses of the ironmonger who will sell me some like them, or the tailor who will manufacture me a swallow tail coat with an imperceptible slit down the back. Then again, I have, as I said, seen young Mr. Sexton go in and out of the corded box, and I know how that's done; but Dr. Lynn's man goes into three, one inside the other. Well, I can understand that if Dr. Sexton's theory be correct, it may perhaps be as easy to get into a "nest" of three as into one box; but how, in the name of nature—or art—does the nautical gentleman get out of the double sack in which he is tied? I cannot bring myself to print what Dr. Sexton's theory of the box is, because it appears to be such a wanton cruelty to "expose" things when people go to the Egyptian Hall on purpose to be mystified. I remember how the fact of having seen Dr. Sexton do the trick of reading the names in the hat spoilt my enjoyment of Dr. Lynn's experiment. He really appeared quite bungling when I knew all he was about. He did not, on this occasion, produce the letters on his arm; but I saw he could quite easily have done so, though the doing it would have been no sort of reproduction of Mr. Forster's manifestation, who showed you the name of some relative when you had looked in on him quite unexpectedly. I can quite understand how it is that the spiritualists, who hold these matters to be sacred as revelation itself—in fact, to be revelation itself, are shocked at seeing their convictions denounced as trickery and "exposed" on a public platform; but I confess I do not quite see how they can adopt the tu quoque principle, and "expose" Dr. Lynn and Messrs. Maskelyne and Cooke as tricksters, because they do not pretend to be anything else. It would have been fatal if the magicians had "found out" Moses, and they wisely refrained from trying; but it would have served no purpose for Moses to "find out" the magicians: and it strikes me Moses would have deemed it very infra dig. to make the attempt. The two things stand on quite different grounds; and I cannot help thinking that the spiritualists unwisely concede a point when they accept the challenge of the conjurers. I am quite aware that the theory of the spiritualists makes of many a conjurer a medium malgré lui, and says he ought to come out in his true colours. It was so Messrs. Maskelyne and Cooke were originally introduced to a London public at the Crystal Palace under the auspices of an eminent spiritualist; but it really appears to me that such an assertion amounts to begging the question; for I doubt whether it would not "pay" quite as well to come out boldly in Mr. Williams's or Mr. Morse's line as in that of Dr. Lynn or Mr. Maskelyne.

In a lengthened confab which I once had with Mr. Maskelyne himself after one of his performances, he told me that by constant attendance at the séances of the Davenports he found out how that was all done; and, being a working watchmaker, was able soon to get the necessary apparatus constructed. I must again be just, and state that while the cabinet séance of Messrs. Maskelyne and Cooke seems to me the exact counterpart of the Davenports', their dark séance fails to reproduce that of the spiritualists as the performances of Professor Pepper himself. True, this latter gentleman does all his exposés on a platform which is sacred against all intrusion, and Messrs. Maskelyne and Cooke assume to allow as much examination as the spiritualists. But I myself, who have seen Mr. Home float around Mr. S. C. Hall's drawing-room, and handled him above and below in transitu, quite fail to discern any reproduction of that phenomenon in the heavy, lumbering levitation of the lady by means of the scissors-like apparatus behind her, which we are only privileged to behold from the stalls. The dancing walking-stick is as palpably made terpsichorean by a string as the chairs I have seen cross Mr. Hall's drawing-room in full light were not drawn by strings, for I was able to look closely at them; and I do not know how that was done.

Fresh from Dr. Lynn's really marvellous performances of recent times, and with Messrs. Maskelyne and Cooke's equally clever tricks in my mind's eye, though not quite so recently, I still am bold to say I believe there are still six of one to half-a-dozen of the other. If the conjurers reproduce the spiritual phenomena in some instances, the spiritualists distance the conjurers in others. I speak of phenomena only. The magicians produced many of the same phenomena as Moses; but, even so, if we are orthodox we must believe the source of such manifestations to have been utterly different.

But I am, as I said, wise in my generation, and stick to phenomena. I venture to think the conjurers unwise in irritating the spiritualists, who are a growing body, by placarding their entertainment as exposés, even though such announcements may "draw" the non-spiritual public. I suppose, however, they understand the science of advertising better than I do; but I feel sure the spiritualists are unwise to follow their example, because they have got nothing to expose. Dr. Lynn or Messrs. Maskelyne and Cooke are as much pleased as conscientious mediums would be shocked at being proved clever tricksters. The only folks who are injured by being told "how it's done," are the British Public, who pay their five shillings to be mystified at the Egyptian Hall, just as the spiritualists do in Lamb's Conduit Street.

If it is to come to a race for the championship—and seriously it would seem that, having begun, the two parties are bound to continue the strife—one can scarcely imagine anything more attractive than such a combined display of talent. Dr. Lynn gets lots of people to come and see "How it's done"—the gentleman with the mandolin is well worth a visit, and I cannot guess how he does it—while Messrs. Maskelyne and Cooke must really be making a good thing of it. Mr. Williams's séances are decidedly attractive (and how he does it has puzzled me for years, as I said), nor does the Progressive Institute seem to decrease in interest; but let us only picture the fascination of a long evening where Pepper's Ghost should be pitted against John King, Mrs. Guppy and Messrs. Maskelyne and Cooke's lady float in competition round the room or even in from the suburbs, while the Davenports and Dr. Lynn's man should wriggle out of or into iron rings and their own dress coats! Until some such contest takes place, the public mind will probably gravitate towards the conjurers rather than the spiritualists, and that through the actually suicidal policy of the latter; because while the spiritualists of necessity can show no visible source of their manifestations, one of their own rank devotes himself to aiding the conjurers by showing in reference to their tricks, "How it's done." It would have been wiser, surely, to stand upon dignity, and in a truly conservative spirit (is it too late even now to reassume it?), say, "These men are mediums, but it does not suit their pockets to confess it."

Well, they are signs of the times. London loves to be mystified, and would only have one instead of manifold methods to be so if the spiritualists and conjurers were to strike hands, and reduce us all to the dead level of pure faith or relentless reason and cold common sense!

CHAPTER XLVI.

PROS AND CONS OF SPIRITUALISM.

It has been repeatedly urged upon me on previous occasions, and also during the progress of these sheets through the press, that I should make a clean breast of my own belief or disbelief in spiritualism; that besides being descriptive, I should go one step beyond a mere catalogue of phenomena, and, to some extent at least, theorize on this mysterious and generally proscribed subject.

Let me say at the outset that against the proscription of this, or indeed any topic which does not offend against morals, I would at the very outset protest as the height of unwisdom. Thus to taboo a subject is at once to lend it a factitious interest, and more than half to endorse its truth: and I believe modern spiritualism has been very generally treated in this way. Whether truth has gained by such indiscriminate condemnation and prejudgment is, I think, greatly open to question.

For myself, I have, from the first, steadily refused to look upon spiritualism in this bugbear fashion. The thing was either true or false—or, more probably still, partly true and partly false: and I must bring to bear on the discovery of its truth or falsehood, just the same critical faculties that I should employ on any other problem of common life. That, I fancy, is no transcendental view of the matter; but just the plain common sense way of going to work. It was, at all events, right or wrong, the method I adopted to get at such results as I proceed to make public. I declined to be scared from the study either by Bogey or my esteemed friend Mrs.

Grundy, but went at it just in the calm Baconian inductive method in which I should have commenced any other study or pursuit.

What I want to do is to tabulate these results in the same order as that in which they occurred to me; and here I am met by a preliminary difficulty, not incidental to this subject only, but common to any narrative where we have to take a retrospective glance over a number of years. We are apt to view the subject from our present standpoint; and I shall try to avoid this by quoting, whenever I can, what I published, or committed to writing in the course of my investigations. I shall not cull from others, because I want to make this purely a personal narrative.

Let me add, too, I do not in the least expect persons to believe what I say. Some, I think, will regard me as a harmless (if a harmless) lunatic, on account of certain statements I may have to make. Others will consider the whole thing as decidedly unorthodox and "wrong." For each of these issues I am prepared. I would not have believed any one else if they had, prior to my experience, told me what I am going to tell them here; and therefore I do not expect them to believe me. All I hope to do is to interest persons sufficiently in the subject to induce them to look into the matter on their own account; for verily I believe, as a distinguished spiritualist once said to me, that this thing is either an important truth or else one of the biggest swindles ever palmed off upon humanity.

One word more, and I proceed to my narrative. Of the three aspects under which it is possible to view spiritualism, the scientific, the theological, and the social, I shall not touch at all on the first since I am not a scientific man; shall only glance at the second, because this is not the place for a theological discussion. I shall confine myself to the third, therefore, which I call the social aspect; looking at the subject as a question of the day, the truth about which we are as much interested in solving as any other political or social question, but the investigation of which need not make us get excited and angry and call one another bad names. I venture to hope that by these means I may manage to compile a not unedifying or uninteresting narrative, though our subject be withal somewhat a ponderous one.

In order then to cover the preliminary part of my narrative, and to let my readers somewhat into the state of my own mind, when I had looked at the subject for several years, I will quote some extracts from a paper I read before a society of spiritualists at the Beethoven Rooms a few years ago under the title "Am I a Spiritualist?" I may mention that the assembly was divided, and never decided whether I was or not, and what is more, I do not think they are quite decided to the present day. I am a patient investigator still; but I really do not feel it necessary to issue perpetual bulletins as to the state of my convictions.

Taking as my thesis, then, the question, Am I a Spiritualist? it will certainly appear, at first sight, I said, that the person best qualified to answer this question is precisely the person who puts it; but a little consideration will, I think, show that the term "Spiritualist" is one of such wide and somewhat elastic meaning—in fact, that the word varies so widely according to the persons who use it—that the question may really be asked of one's self without involving an inconsistency.

When persons ask me, as they often do, with a look of unmitigated horror, "Is it possible that you, a clergyman, are a spiritualist?" I am often inclined to answer, "Yes, madam,"—(for it is generally a lady who puts the question in that particular shape)—"I am a spiritualist, and precisely because I am a clergyman. I have had to express more than once my unfeigned assent and consent to the Common Prayer Book, and the Thirty Nine Articles; and that involves belief in the inspiration of all the Bible (except the Apocrypha), and the whole of that (not excepting the Apocrypha) is spiritual, or spiritualistic (if you prefer the term) from beginning to end; and therefore it is not in spite of my being a clergyman, but because I am a clergyman that I am such a confirmed spiritualist."

I could answer thus, only I do not, simply because to do so would be dishonest. I know my questioner is using the word in an utterly different sense from what I have thought proper to suppose. Besides such an answer would only lead to argumentation, and the very form of the question shows me the person who puts it has made up her mind on this, as probably on most other subjects; and when a feminine mind is once made up (others than ladies have feminine minds on these subjects) it is very little use trying to alter it. I never do. I administer some orthodox verbal sedative, and change the subject. But even accepting the term in the way I know it is meant to be used—say, for instance, as it comes from the mouth of some conservative old gentleman, or supposed scientific authority—one's medical man to wit—"Do you believe in spiritualism?" meaning "Are you such an ass as to believe in table-turning, and rapping, and all that kind of nonsense?"—even so, the question would admit of being answered by another question; though I rarely enter so far on the matter with those whose minds are evidently quite comfortably made up on the matter. It is such a pity to interfere with cherished opinions. I have found out that there are

Athanasian creeds in science as well as in theology; and really, whilst they form recognised formulæ in the one or the other, it is positively lost labour to go running one's head against them. The question I want to ask—not the gentle apothecaries, but my readers—is, What do you mean by believing in spiritualism? Many of the phenomena of spiritualism I cannot but believe, if I am to take my five senses as my guides in this as in other matters, and quite setting aside any credence I may give to respectable testimony. When, however, I pass from facts to theories, and am asked to account for those facts, then I hesitate. There are some here, I know, who will say that the spiritualist like the lady who hesitates is lost—who think me as heterodox for doing so, as the inflexible old ladies and the omniscient apothecaries did on account of my even deigning to look into the evidence of such phenomena. I feel really that I have set myself up like an animated ninepin to be knocked down by the first thorough-going spiritualist who cares to bowl at me. But whatever else they think of me—sceptical though they deem me on subjects where perhaps you are, many of you, a little prone to dogmatize—I claim the character at least of an honest sceptic. I do not altogether disavow the title, but I understand it to mean "inquirer." I confess myself, after long years of perfectly unbiassed inquiry, still an investigator—a sceptic. It is the fashion to abuse St. Thomas because he sought sensible proofs on a subject which it was certainly most important to have satisfactorily cleared up. I never could read the words addressed to him at all in the light of a rebuke—"Because thou hast seen thou hast believed." The Church of England treats the doubt of St. Thomas as permitted by God "for the more confirmation of the faith;" and I feel sure that professed spiritualists will not be so inconsistent as to censure any man for examining long and carefully matters which they believe to admit of demonstration. I heard the most eloquent of their advocates say, when comparing spiritual with credal conviction, "Our motto no longer is 'I believe,' but 'I know.'" Belief may be instantaneous, but knowledge will be gradual; and so it is that, standing at a certain fixed point in very many years' study of spiritualism, I pause, and—so to say, empanelling a jury—ask the question it seems I ought to answer at others' asking—Am I a Spiritualist?

One word of apology further before entering on the details of the matter. It will be inevitable that the first personal pronoun shall recur frequently in the course of this paper, and that so the paper shall seem egotistical. The very question itself sounds so. I am not vain enough to suppose that it matters much to anybody here whether I am a spiritualist or not, except in so far as I may be in any sense a representative man. I believe I am. That is, I believe, nay, am sure, that a great many persons go as far as I do, and stop where I stop. There is a largish body of investigators, I believe, dangling there, like Mahomet's coffin, between heaven and earth, and it would be a charity to land them somewhere. Of the clerical mind, I do not claim to be a representative, because the clerical mind, quâ clerical, has made up itself that the phenomena in question are diabolical. Of course if I accepted this theory my question would be utterly irrelevant, and I should claim a place among the spiritualists at once. The diabolical people not only accept the phenomena, but admit their spiritual origin, and, more than this, identify the spirits. They are in point of fact the most thorough-going spiritualists of all.

In sketching their creed, I have mentioned the three stages through which most minds must go in this matter. Some few, indeed, take them by intuition, but most minds have to plod patiently along the path of inquiry, as I have done. The first stage is acceptance of the phenomena, the second the assignment of those phenomena to spirits as their source, the third is identification of these spirits.

1. On the first part of my subject I shall venture to speak with some boldness. I am not a philosopher, therefore I can afford to do so. I shall suppose my five senses to serve my purposes of observation, as they would be supposed to serve me if I were giving evidence in a court of justice. If I saw a table move, I shall say it did move, not "it appeared to move." I do this in my capacity of a commonplace instead of a philosophical investigator; and I must say, if I were, as I supposed myself just now, in the witness-box, with a good browbeating counsel cross-examining me on this point, I would rather have to defend the position of the commonplace inquirer than the philosopher, pledged to defend the philosophy of the last fifty years, and bound hand and foot by his philosophic Athanasian Creed, and I don't know how many articles, more than thirty-nine, I fancy.

In the latter part of the year 1856, or beginning of 1857, then, I was residing in Paris, that lively capital being full of Mr. Home's doings at the Tuileries. At that time I knew nothing, even of table-turning. I listened to the stories of Mr. Home and the Emperor as mere canards. I never stopped to question whether the matter were true, because I in my omniscience knew it to be impossible. It is this phase of my experience that makes me so unwilling to argue with the omniscient people now; it is such a waste of time. At this period my brother came to visit me, and he had either been present himself or knew persons who had been present at certain séances at Mr. Rymer's. He seemed staggered, if not convinced, by what he had heard or seen, and this staggered me too, for he was not exactly a gullible person and certainly by no means "spiritual." I was staggered, I own, but then I was omniscient, and so I did what is always safest, laughed at the matter. He suggested that we should try experiments instead of laughing, and, not being a philosopher, I consented. We sat at the little round table in our tiny salon, which soon began to turn, then answered questions, and finally told us that one of the three, viz., my wife, was a medium, and consequently we could receive communications. I went to a side table and wrote a question as to the source of the manifestations, keeping it concealed from those at the table, and not rejoining them myself. The answer spelt out by them was—"We, the spirits of the departed, are permitted thus to appear to men." Again I wrote—"What object is served by your doing so?" The answer was—"It may make men believe in God." I have said I am not a philosopher, therefore I do not mind confessing that I collapsed. I struck my flag at once as to the impossibility of the matter. At the same time I did not—as I know many ardent spiritualists will think I ought—at once swallow the whole thing, theory and all. I should not have believed if a man had told me this; was it to be expected that I should believe a table? Honesty is my best policy; and I had better, therefore, say I was never so utterly knocked over by anything that occurred to me in my life before or since. My visage of utter, blank astonishment is a joke against me to this hour. We pursued the inquiry almost nightly during the remainder of my stay in Paris—up to late in the summer of 1857 that is—and also on our return to England; but, strangely as it seems to me now, considering how we began, we did it more as a pastime than anything else. The only time we were serious was when my wife and I sat alone, as we often did. Of course when I came to inquire at all into the matter I was met by Faraday's theory of involuntary muscular action, and also with the doctrine of unconscious cerebration—I was quite ready to accept either. My own position, as far as I can recall it, then was that the spiritual agency was "not proven." My wife had great reluctance against admitting the spiritual theory. I was simply passive; but two circumstances seemed to me to militate against the theories I have mentioned: (1.) The table we used for communicating was a little gimcrack French affair, the top of which spun round on the slightest provocation, and no force whatever, not even a philosopher's, applied to the surface would do more than spin the top round; but when the table turned, it turned bodily, legs and all. (2.) As to that ponderously difficult theory of unconscious cerebration communicated by involuntary muscular action, whenever we asked any questions as to the future, we were instantly checked, and told it was better that the future should not be revealed to us. I was anxious about a matter in connexion with an election to an appointment in England, and we asked some questions as to what form the proceedings would take. The reply was that certain candidates would be selected from the main body, and the election made from these. I thought I had caught the table in an inconsistency, and said— "There now you have told us something about the future." It immediately replied—"No, I have not; the matter is already settled in the minds of the examiners." Whence came that answer? Certainly not from our minds, for it took us both by surprise. I could multiply a hundredfold instances of this kind, but, of course, to educated spiritualists these are mere A B C matters; whilst non-spiritualists would only accept them on the evidence of their own senses. I do not mean to say they actually question the facts to the extent of doubting one's veracity, or else nearly all testimony must go for nothing; but there is in these matters always room for doubting whether the narrator has not been deceived; and, moreover, even if accepted at secondhand, I doubt whether facts so accepted ever become, as it were, assimilated, so as to have any practical effect.

My facts at all events came at first-hand. I suppose a man need not be considered credulous for believing in his own wife, and nearly all these phenomena were produced by my wife's mediumship. It was not until late in the year 1865 or early in 1866, that I ever sat with a professional medium. My wife, moreover, from first to last, has steadily disbelieved the spirit theory, so that she has not laid herself open to suspicion of being prejudiced in favour of the subject. She has been emphatically an involuntary, nay, even unwilling agent in these matters.

During these eight or nine years the communications were generally given by automatic writing, though sometimes still by tilting of the table. I am very much tempted to quote two, which linger in my recollection, principally, I believe, because they were so destructive of the cerebration theory, besides being curious in themselves. I kept no records until a later date. At present all rests on tradition. Each of these cases occurred in presence of myself, my wife, and a pupil. In the former, he was a young Englishman, who had lived a great deal abroad, whose mother was a Catholic and father a Protestant. He had been brought up in the latter faith; and when I desired him to ask a mental question, he asked, in French—that being the language most familiar to him—"Is the Catholic or the Protestant religion the true one?" Mark you, he never articulated this, or gave the least hint that he was asking in French. He did it in fact, spontaneously. My wife immediately wrote "Ta mère est Catholique"—so far, in

French, with difficulty, and then breaking off into English, "Respect her faith."

In the second instance, my pupil was a French youth, a Catholic, who was living in my house, but used to go to his priest frequently to be prepared for his first communion. One day when we were writing, this youth asked who the communicating spirit was, and received in reply the name of Louis D——. The name was totally unknown to us; but to our surprise when the youth came back from his visit to the priest that day he informed us that his reverend instructor had dwelt strongly on the virtues of Louis D——. Seeing the boy look amazed as the name which had just been given at our séance was pronounced, the priest inquired the reason; and, on being informed, of course directed his catechumen never to join in such diablerie again.

The impression, then, left on my mind by these years of desultory dabbling with—rather than study of—the subject, was decidedly that the phenomena of spiritualism were genuine. Looking at the matter from my present standpoint and frame of mind, it seems to me incredible that I should have thought so little of the source of the phenomena. It was, as I said, that I was then dabbling with, not studying, the subject.

But even without advancing beyond this rudimentary stage, I saw a very serious result produced. I saw men who literally believed in nothing, and who entered on this pursuit in a spirit of levity, suddenly staggered with what appeared to afford even possibility of demonstration of another world, and the continued existence of the spirit after bodily death. I believe a great many persons who have never felt doubt themselves are unaware of the extent

to which doubt prevails amongst young men especially;
and I have seen many instances of this doubt being—if not
removed—shaken to its very foundation by their
witnessing the phenomena of spiritualism. "Yes, but did it
make good consistent Christians of them?" asks one of my
excellent simple-minded objectors. Alas! my experience
does not tell me that good consistent Christians are so
readily made. Does our faith—I might have asked—make
us the good consistent Christians it ought to do, and would
do perhaps, if we gave it fair play?

So, then, my study of spiritualism had been purely
phenomenal. It was a very sad and serious event which
drove me to look deeper. Some people will, I daresay,
think it strange that I allude to this cause here. The fact that
I do so shows, at all events, that I have looked seriously at
spiritualism since. It was none other than the loss, under
painful circumstances, of one of my children. Now I had
always determined that, in the event of my losing one near
and dear to me, I would put spiritualism to the test, by
trying to communicate with that one. This will, I think,
show that, even then, if I did not accept the spiritualistic
theory, I did not by any means consider the position
untenable. The very day after my boy's death, I got his
mother to sit, and found she was writing a little loving
message purporting to come from him. This, a sceptic
would say, was natural enough under the circumstances. I
said no word, but sat apart, and kept writing "Who is it that
communicates? write your name." Suddenly the sentence
was broken off, and the child's name written, though I had
not expressed my wish aloud. This was strange; but what
followed was stranger still. Of course, so far all might have
been fairly attributed to cerebration—if such a process
exists. It was natural enough, it might be urged, that the
mother, previously schooled in the belief of the probability

of communication, should write in her lost child's name. For years the same thing never occurred again, though we sat night after night for the purpose of renewing such communications. I can certainly say of myself that, at this time, I was a spiritualist—as thorough and devout a one as any existing; and the fact that I was so, when carried away by my feelings, makes me the more cautious to test and try myself as to whether my feelings may not sometimes sway my judgment even now; whether the wish be not often father of the thought, at all events in the identification of spiritual communications, and so, possibly, of the spiritual nature of such communications altogether.

However, from this time—the autumn of 1865—my spiritual studies underwent an entire change—they were studies—serious studies. I now kept a careful journal of all communications, which journal I continued for three years, so that I can trace all my fluctuations of opinion—for I did fluctuate—during that period. Now, too, it was necessary for me to consult those who had already gone deeply into the subject; and the record of my experiences would be both imperfect and ungracious if I did not here acknowledge the prompt kindness of the two gentlemen to whom I applied—Mr. Benjamin Coleman and Mr. Samuel Carter Hall. I was comparatively a stranger to each of them, but they replied to my inquiries with the most ready courtesy, and I am happy to date my present friendship with each of them from this time. At Mr. Hall's I met Mr. Home, and on the second occasion of my doing so, not only saw him float, but handled him above and below during the whole of the time he floated round Mr. Hall's drawing-room. I am unphilosophical enough to say that I entirely credit the evidence of my senses on that occasion, and am as certain that Mr. Home was in space for five minutes as I am of my own existence. The ordinary solution of cranes and other cumbrous machinery in Mr. Hall's drawing-room I cannot credit, for I think we should have seen them, and I am sure I should have felt ropes round Mr. Home's body. Chairs went from one end of the room to the other in full light; and nobody had previously tumbled over strings and wires, so that I don't think there could have been any there.

I fancy, as far as any order is traceable in the somewhat erratic course of spiritualistic experiences, that most people arrive at spiritualism viâ mesmerism. It so happened that this order was exactly inverted in my case. It was not until 1866 that I found I possessed the power of magnetism, and moreover, had in my house a subject whom Alphonse Didier (with whom I afterwards put myself in communication) declared to be "one in a thousand." Some of the details of this lady's case are very curious, but this is scarcely the place to dilate upon them further than as they affected my spiritualistic studies. She passed with extraordinary ease into the condition of lucidity, when she was conscious only of basking in light, anxious to be magnetized more deeply so as to get more thoroughly into the light, and, moreover, aware only of the existence of those who had passed away from earth. She knew they were with her: said I must know it, as I was there too, and that it was I only who would not "let her" see them. The fact that "our life is twofold" was to me most marvellously brought out by my magnetic treatment of this lady; and, moreover, the power of influencing action could not fail to be suggestive of the truth of one of the cardinal doctrines of spiritualism—that we are thus influenced by disembodied spirits, as I, an embodied spirit, could influence another spirit in the body. Some of the likes and dislikes which I, so to say, produced then in 1866 have remained to the present hour. For instance, one particular article of food (I will not mention what, or it would be fatal to my reader's gravity), for which she previously had a penchant, I rendered so distasteful to her that the very smell of it now makes her uncomfortable. I must plead guilty to having experimented somewhat in this way; but what a wonderful light it sheds upon the great problem of the motives of human action! By the simple exercise of my will I could make my patient perform actions the most abhorrent to her. For instance—the ladies will appreciate this power—at a time when crinolines were extensive, I made that poor creature draggle about in a costume conspicuous by the absence of crinoline, and making her look like some of the ladies out of a Noah's ark.

During this period my wife and I constantly sat alone, and she wrote. It is no disrespect to her to say that writing is not her forte, but the communications she made in this way were exceedingly voluminous, and couched in a particularly happy style, though on subjects far above the range of ordinary compositions. We never obtained a single communication purporting to come from our child, but the position claimed by the communicating intelligence was that of his spirit-guardian.

Having now probably said enough in these confessions to convince every non-spiritualist that I am insane, because I believed the evidence of my senses, and even ventured to look into matters so unorthodox and unscientific as mesmerism and spiritualism, I go on to "make a clean breast," and set myself wrong with the other moiety of my readers. I must candidly confess that the experiences of this year (1866) did not confirm my sudden conviction of the spiritual agency in these phenomena. I drifted back, in fact, to my previous position, accepting the phenomena, but holding the cause an open question. The preface to the book, "From Matter to Spirit," exactly expressed—shall I say expresses?—my state of mind. There is one passage in that preface which appears to me to clinch the difficulty— "I am perfectly convinced that I have both seen and heard, in a manner which should make unbelief impossible, things called spiritual, which cannot be taken by a reasonable being to be capable of explanation by imposture, coincidence, or mistake. So far I feel the ground firm under me. But when it comes to what is the cause of these phenomena I find I cannot adopt any explanation which has yet been suggested. If I were bound to choose among things which I can conceive, I should say that there is some sort of action—some sort of combination of will, intellect, and physical power, which is not that of any of the human beings present. But thinking it very likely that the universe may contain a few agencies, say half a million, about which no man knows anything, I cannot but suspect that a small proportion of these agencies, say five thousand, may be severally competent to the production of all the phenomena, or may be quite up to the task among them. The physical explanations which I have seen are easy, but miserably insufficient: the spiritual hypothesis is sufficient but ponderously difficult." This statement is natural enough from the scientific side of the question. Perhaps the theological inquirer, taking the fact into consideration that Scripture certainly concedes the spiritual origin of kindred phenomena, would rather reverse the statement, and say (what I individually feel) that the psychological explanation is the ponderously difficult—the pneumatological, the comparatively easy one.

It is now no secret that the author of this excellent treatise, is Professor De Morgan; and I can only say that if I am accused of heterodoxy, either from the spiritualist or anti-spiritualist side of the discussion, I am not ashamed to be a heretic in such company. Let me put the matter in the present tense, indicative mood—that is the state of my opinion on the cause of the phenomena. Admitting the facts, I hold the spiritual theory to be "not proven," but still to be a hypothesis deserving our most serious consideration, not only as being the only one that will cover all the facts, but as the one I believe invariably given in explanation by the intelligence that produces the phenomena, even when, as in our case, all those present are sceptical of or opposed to such a theory.

3. It may perhaps sound illogical if, after stating that I hold the spiritual origin of these phenomena unproven, I go on to speak of the identification of the communicating spirit; but I hope I have made it clear that, even if I do not consider the spiritualistic explanation demonstrated, it is still a hypothesis which has much in its favour.

I have already mentioned the subject of identification in the case of the first communication purporting to come from our little child, and how no such communications were received for a period of some years after. In December, 1866, I went to the Marshalls', entering as an entire stranger, and sitting down at the table. I saw some strong physical manifestations—a large table being poised in space, in full light, for some seconds. It was signified there was a spirit present who wished to communicate, and the message given by raps to me was—"Will you try to think of us more than you have done?" I asked the name, and my child's was correctly given, though I had not been announced, and I have no reason to believe my name was known. The place where he passed away from earth was also correctly specified. I then asked for my father, and his name was correctly given, and a message added, which I cannot say was equally suggestive of individuality. It was—"Bright inspiration will dawn upon your soul, and do not hide your light under a bushel."

Another case in which I tested individuality strongly, with utter absence of success, was also brought before me somewhat earlier in this year. I was sent for by a lady who had been a member of my congregation, and who had taken great interest in these questions. She was suddenly smitten down with mortal disease, and I remained with her almost to the last—indeed, I believe her last words were addressed to me, and referred to this very subject of identification—she consulting me as to the great problem she was then on the very point of solving! As soon as she had gone from us, I went home, and tried to communicate with her. I was informed that her spirit was present, and yet every detail as to names, &c., was utterly wrong.

In the spring of the following year I went again to the Marshalls', in company with one or two other persons, my own object being to see if I could obtain communication from the spirit of a highly-gifted lady who had recently died—and also, I may mention—had been the medium of my previous slight acquaintance with Mr. Coleman. She was very much interested in these matters, and, when in this world, her great forte had been writing. She published a volume of poems, which won the special commendation of the late Charles Dickens, and her letters were most characteristic ones. I mentioned that I wished to communicate with the spirit I was thinking of, and said I should be quite satisfied if the initials were correctly given. Not so—the whole three names were immediately given in full. I do not feel at liberty to mention the names; but the surname was one that nine out of ten people always spelt wrongly (just as they do my name), but on this occasion it was correctly spelt. I asked for a characteristic message, and received the words, "I am saved, and will now save others;"—about as unlike my friend's ordinary style as possible. It may be said her nature had undergone revolution, but that was not the question. The test was that something should be given, identifying the spirit, by the style of its former writing while embodied on earth.

With one more case, bearing on this subject of identity, and bringing the matter up to the present date, I feel I may advantageously close this portion of my experiences— though as I do so, I am thoroughly dissatisfied with myself to find how much I have left unsaid. It is so difficult to put these things on paper, or in any way to convey them to another;—most difficult of all for one unblessed with leisure, and combining in his single self the pursuits of some three laborious callings.

Last year, whilst sitting at Mrs. B——'s, I was touched by a hand which seemed to me that of a small girl, and which attracted my attention by the way it lingered in mine—this would amuse Professor Pepper—and the pertinacity with which it took off my ring. However, I never took any steps to identify the owner of the hand.

Some few months ago, my wife and I were sitting, and a communication came ostensibly from our child. It was quite unexpected; and I said, "I thought you could not communicate." "I could not before," was the reply. "But you have not tried me for two years." This we found was true; but we actually had to look into dates to ascertain it. He added, that he always was present at séances where I went, and especially at Mrs. B——'s. It will, I daresay, sound strange to non-spiritualists, but the initiated can understand the conversational tone we adopt. I said, "But, Johnny, that was not your hand that touched me at Mrs.

B——'s. It was too large." The answer was, "No! it was Charlie's turn." I said, "What do you mean by Charlie's turn?" The word was rewritten with almost petulant haste and remarkable plainness, "Charlie's twin." Charlie is my eldest boy, and his twin-brother was still-born. He would be between thirteen and fourteen years of age, and that was precisely the sized hand I felt. This was curious; as the event had occurred a year before, and such an explanation had never even crossed my mind. I was promised that, if I would go to Mrs. B——'s again, each of the children would come and place a hand in mine. I went to the ordinary séance some time before Christmas, and was then told that the test I wished—which I had not then specified—should be given to me at a private séance. We had the private séance, but nothing occurred.

Such is my case. To one section of my readers I shall appear credulous, to another hard of belief. I believe that I represent the candid inquirer. As for being scared off from the inquiry by those who call it unorthodox, or cry out "fire and brimstone," I should as little think of heeding them as the omniscient apothecaries who smile at my believing in mesmerism. If a man's opinions are worth anything—if he has fought his way to those opinions at the bayonet's point—he will not be scared off from them by the whole bench of Bishops on the one side, or the College of Surgeons on the other. Not that I for one moment plead guilty to heterodoxy, either scientific or theological. I am not, as I have said several times, a philosopher, but I believe it is scientific to hold as established what you can prove by experiment. I don't think my creed contains a jot or tittle beyond this. And as for theological orthodoxy, I simply take my stand upon the Canons of the Church of England. If all this spiritual business is delusion, how comes it that No. 72 of the Constitutions and Canons

Ecclesiastical says: "Neither shall any minister, not licensed, attempt, upon any pretence whatever, either of possession or obsession, by fasting or prayer, to cast out any devil or devils?"

The question, however, is not of this kind of orthodoxy. It rather refers to the creed of spiritualism. The question, in fact, to which I and the many who think with me pause for a reply, is:—Allowing, as we do, some of the phenomena—but considering the pneumatological explanation hypothetical only—and therefore any identification of communicating intelligence impossible— are we (for I am sincerely tired of that first person singular, and glad to take refuge in a community), are we, or are we not, spiritualists?

So far was I able to commit myself in my address to the spiritualists of Harley Street. I was, I confess, greatly pleased when, in 1869, the Dialectical Society took up this matter, because I felt they were just the people to look into it dispassionately. They were bound to no set of opinions, but regarded everything as an open question, accepting nothing save as the conclusion of a logical argument. I joined the Society—straining my clerical conscience somewhat to do so—and eventually formed one of the committee appointed by the Society to inquire into the matter, and having a sub-committee sitting at my own house. This, however, broke up suddenly, for I found even philosophers were not calm in their examination of unpalatable facts. One gentleman who approached the subject with his mind fully made up, accused the lady medium of playing tricks, and me of acting showman on the occasion. As there was no method of shunting this person, I was obliged to break up my sub-committee. To mention spiritualism to these omniscient gentlemen is like shaking a red rag at a bull. As a case in point (though, of course, I do not credit these gentlemen with the assumption of omniscience), I may quote the replies of Professor Huxley and Mr. G. H. Lewes to the Society's invitation to sit on their committee:—

"Sir,—I regret that I am unable to accept the invitation of the Council of the Dialectical Society to co-operate with a committee for the investigation of 'spiritualism;' and for two reasons. In the first place, I have no time for such an inquiry, which would involve much trouble and (unless it were unlike all inquiries of that kind I have known) much annoyance. In the second place, I take no interest in the subject. The only case of 'spiritualism' I have had the opportunity of examining into for myself, was as gross an imposture as ever came under my notice. But supposing the phenomena to be genuine—they do not interest me. If anybody would endow me with the faculty of listening to the chatter of old women and curates in the nearest cathedral town, I should decline the privilege, having better things to do.

"And if the folk in the spiritual world do not talk more wisely and sensibly than their friends report them to do, I put them in the same category.

"The only good that I can see in a demonstration of the truth of 'spiritualism' is to furnish an additional argument against suicide. Better live a crossing-sweeper than die and be made to talk twaddle by a 'medium' hired at a guinea a séance.

"I am, Sir, &c.,

"T. H. Huxley.

"29th January, 1869."

Confessedly Professor Huxley only tried one experiment. I cannot help thinking if he had not approached the subject with a certain amount of prejudice he would have been content to "Try again." The side-hit at curates of course I appreciate!

"Dear Sir,—I shall not be able to attend the investigation of 'spiritualism;' and in reference to your question about suggestions would only say that the one hint needful is that all present should distinguish between facts and inferences from facts. When any man says that phenomena are produced by no known physical laws, he declares that he knows the laws by which they are produced.

"Yours, &c.,

"G. H. Lewes.

"Tuesday, 2nd February, 1869."

I am not, as I have said, a scientific man, nor do I advance the slightest pretensions to genius; therefore I have no doubt it is some mental defect on my part which prevents my seeing the force of Mr. G. H. Lewes's concluding sentence. I have worked at it for years and am compelled to say I cannot understand it.

I sat, however, through the two years' examination which the Society gave to the subject; and it is not anticipating the conclusion of this chapter to say I was fully able to concur in the report they subsequently issued, the gist of which is continued in the final paragraph:—

"In presenting their report, your committee taking into consideration the high character and great intelligence of many of the witnesses to the more extraordinary facts, the extent to which their testimony is supported by the reports of the sub-committees, and the absence of any proof of imposture or delusion as regards a large portion of the phenomena; and further, having regard to the exceptional character of the phenomena, the large number of persons in every grade of society and over the whole civilized world who are more or less influenced by a belief in their supernatural origin, and to the fact that no philosophical explanation of them has yet been arrived at, deem it incumbent upon them to state their conviction that the subject is worthy of more serious attention and careful investigation than it has hitherto received."

With those cautiously guarded words I venture to think that any one who even reads the body of evidence contained in the Dialectical Society's report will be able to coincide.

To return to my more personal narrative.

As far as I can trace any order in this somewhat erratic subject, I think I may venture to say that the manifestations of the last few years have assumed a more material form than before. It sounds a little Hibernian to say so, I know; but I still retain the expression. Supposing, for the moment, that the effects were produced by spirits, the control of the medium for the production of trance, spirit-voice, automatic writing, or even communications through raps and tilts of the table was much more intellectual—less physical than those of which I now have to speak— namely, the production of the materialized Spirit Faces and Spirit Forms.

Two phases of manifestation, I may mention in passing, I have not seen—namely, the elongation of the body, and the fire test—both as far as I know peculiar to Mr. Home: nor again have I had personal experience of Mrs. Guppy's aërial transit, or Dr. Monk's nocturnal flight from Bristol to Swindon. Nothing of the kind has ever come at all within the sphere of my observation: therefore I forbear to speak about it.

I shall never forget the delight with which I received a letter from a gentleman connected with the literature of spiritualism, informing me that materialized Spirit Faces had at last been produced in full light, and inviting me to come and see. I was wearied of dark séances, of fruit and flowers brought to order. John King's talk wearied me; and Katie's whispers had become fatally familiar: so I went in eagerly for the new sensation, and communicated my results to the world in the two papers called Spirit Faces and Spirit Forms, the former published in Unorthodox London, the latter in Chapter 43 of the present volume. This class of manifestation has since become very common. I cannot say I ever considered it very satisfactory. I have never discovered any trickery—and I assure my readers I have kept my eyes and ears very wide open—but there are in such manifestations facilities for charlatanism which it is not pleasant to contemplate. This, let me continually repeat, is a purely personal narrative, and I have never seen any Spirit Face or Form that I could in the faintest way recognise. Others, I know, claim to have done so; but I speak strictly of what has occurred to myself. The same has been the case with Spirit Photographs. I have sat, after selecting my own plate and watching every stage in the process; and certainly over my form there has been a shadowy female figure apparently in the act of benediction; [2] but I cannot trace resemblance to any one I ever saw in the flesh. Perhaps I have been unfortunate in this respect.

Very similar to Miss Cook's mediumship was that of Miss Showers; a young lady whom I have met frequently at the house of a lady at the West-end of London, both the medium and her hostess being quite above suspicion. In this case, besides the face and full form we have singing in a clear baritone voice presumably by a spirit called Peter— who gives himself out as having been in earth-life, I believe, a not very estimable specimen of a market-gardener. I am exceedingly puzzled how to account for these things. I dare not suspect the medium; but even granting the truth of the manifestations, they seem to me to be of a low class which one would only come into contact with under protest and for the sake of evidence.

Mr. Crookes used to explain, and Serjeant Cox still explains these manifestations as being the products of a so-called Psychic Force—a term which I below define. Although I am as little inclined to hero-worship, and care as little for large names as any man living, yet it is quite impossible not to attach importance to the testimony of these gentlemen; one so eminent in the scientific world, and privileged to write himself F.R.S., the other trained to weigh evidence and decide between balanced probabilities. But it would seem that while Psychic Force might cover the ground of my earlier experiences, it singularly fails to account for the materializations, and obliges us to relegate them to the category of fraud, unless we accept them as being what they profess to be. This I believe Serjeant Cox ruthlessly does. He claims as we have seen to have "caught" Miss Showers, and was not, I believe, convinced by Miss Cook. Mr. Crookes was: and, when we remember that Mr. Wallace, the eminent naturalist, and Mr. Cromwell

Varley, the electrician, both accept the spiritual theory, it really looks as though the scientific mind was more open to receive—perhaps driven to receive—this which I frankly concede to be the only adequate cause for the effects, while the legal mind still remains hair-splitting upon conflicting evidence. Whereabouts the theological mind is I do not quite know—perhaps still dangling between the opposite poles of Faith and Reason, and dubiously debating with me "Am I a Spiritualist or not?"

In a recent pamphlet reprinted from the Quarterly Journal of Science, Mr. Crookes thus compendiously sums up the various theories which have been invented to account for spiritualistic phenomena, and, in so doing, incidentally defines his now discarded theory of Psychic Force which owns Mr. Serjeant Cox for its patron:—

First Theory.—The phenomena are all the results of tricks, clever mechanical arrangements, or legerdemain; the mediums are impostors, and the rest of the company fools.

It is obvious that this theory can only account for a very small proportion of the facts observed. I am willing to admit that some so-called mediums of whom the public have heard much are arrant impostors who have taken advantage of the public demand for spiritualistic excitement to fill their purses with easily earned guineas; whilst others who have no pecuniary motive for imposture are tempted to cheat, it would seem, solely by a desire for notoriety.

Second Theory.—The persons at a séance are the victims of a sort of mania or delusion, and imagine phenomena to occur which have no real objective existence.

Third Theory.—The whole is the result of conscious or unconscious cerebral action.

These two theories are evidently incapable of embracing more than a small portion of the phenomena, and they are improbable explanations for even those. They may be dismissed very briefly.

I now approach the "spiritual" theories. It must be remembered that the word "spirits" is used in a very vague sense by the generality of people.

Fourth Theory.—The result of the spirit of the medium, perhaps in association with the spirits of some or all of the people present.

Fifth Theory.—The actions of evil spirits or devils, personifying who or what they please, in order to undermine Christianity and ruin men's souls.

Sixth Theory.—The actions of a separate order of beings, living on this earth, but invisible and immaterial to us. Able, however, occasionally to manifest their presence; known in almost all countries and ages as demons not necessarily bad, gnomes, fairies, kobolds, elves, goblins, Puck, &c.

Seventh Theory.—The actions of departed human beings—the spiritual theory par excellence.

Eighth Theory.—(The Psychic Force Theory).—This is a necessary adjunct to the 4th, 5th, 6th, and 7th theories, rather than a theory by itself.

According to this theory the "medium," or the circle of people associated together as a whole, is supposed to possess a force, power, influence, virtue, or gift, by means of which intelligent beings are enabled to produce the phenomena observed. What these intelligent beings are is a subject for other theories.

It is obvious that a "medium" possesses a something which is not possessed by an ordinary being. Give this something a name. Call it "x" if you like. Mr. Serjeant Cox calls it Psychic Force. There has been so much misunderstanding on this subject that I think it best to give the following explanation in Mr. Serjeant Cox's own words:—

"The Theory of Psychic Force is in itself merely the recognition of the now almost undisputed fact that under certain conditions, as yet but imperfectly ascertained, and within a limited, but as yet undefined, distance from the bodies of certain persons having a special nerve organization, a Force operates by which, without muscular contact or connexion, action at a distance is caused, and visible motions and audible sounds are produced in solid substances. As the presence of such an organization is necessary to the phenomenon, it is reasonably concluded that the Force does, in some manner as yet unknown, proceed from that organization. As the organism is itself moved and directed within its structure by a Force which either is, or is controlled by, the Soul, Spirit, or Mind (call it what we may) which constitutes the individual being we term 'the Man,' it is an equally reasonable conclusion that the Force which causes the motions beyond the limits of the body is the same Force that produces motion within the limits of the body. And, inasmuch as the external force is seen to be often directed by Intelligence, it is an equally reasonable conclusion that the directing Intelligence of the external force is the same Intelligence that directs the Force internally. This is the force to which the name of Psychic Force has been given by me as properly designating a force which I thus contend to be traced back to the Soul or Mind of the Man as its source. But I, and all who adopt this theory of Psychic Force, as being the agent through which the phenomena are produced, do not thereby intend to assert that this Psychic Force may not be sometimes seized and directed by some other Intelligence than the Mind of the Psychic. The most ardent spiritualists practically admit the existence of Psychic Force under the very inappropriate name of Magnetism (to which it has no affinity whatever), for they assert that the Spirits of the Dead can only do the acts attributed to them by using the Magnetism (that is, the Psychic Force) of the Medium. The difference between the advocates of Psychic Force and the spiritualists consists in this—that we contend that there is as yet insufficient proof of any other directing agent than the Intelligence of the Medium, and no proof whatever of the agency of Spirits of the Dead; while the spiritualists hold it as a faith, not demanding further proof, that Spirits of the Dead are the sole agents in the production of all the phenomena. Thus the controversy resolves itself into a pure question of fact, only to be determined by a laborious and long continued series of experiments and an extensive collection of psychological facts, which should be the first duty of the Psychological Society, the formation of which is now in progress."

It has frequently struck me, especially in connexion with certain investigations that I have been making during the last few years, that Spiritualism is going through much the same phases as Positivism. It seemed at first impossible that the Positive Philosophy of Auguste Comte could culminate in a highly ornate Religion of Humanity, with its fall ritual, its ninefold sacramental system. It is even curious to notice that it was the death of Clotilde which brought about the change, by revealing to him the gap which Philosophy always does leave between the present and the future. So too Spiritualism is beginning to "organize" and exhibits some symptoms of formulating a Creed and Articles of Belief. The British National Association of Spiritualists, which has honoured me by placing my name on its Council, thus states its principles, under the mottoes:—

"He that answereth a matter before he heareth it, it is folly and shame unto him."—Proverbs xviii. 13.

"In Scripture we are perpetually reminded that the Laws of the Spiritual World are, in the highest sense, Laws of Nature."—Argyll.

"He who asserts that, outside of the domain of pure Mathematics, anything is impossible, lacks a knowledge of the first principles of Logic."—Arago.

declaration of principles and purposes.

"Spiritualism implies the recognition of an inner nature in man. It deals with facts concerning that inner nature, the existence of which has been the subject of speculation, dispute, and even of denial, amongst philosophers in all ages; and in particular, with certain manifestations of that inner nature which have been observed in persons of peculiar organizations, now called Mediums or Sensitives, and in ancient times Prophets, Priests, and Seers.

"Spiritualism claims to have established on a firm scientific basis the immortality of man, the permanence of his individuality, and the Open Communion, under suitable conditions, of the living with the so-called dead, and affords grounds for the belief in progressive spiritual states in new spheres of existence.

"Spiritualism furnishes the key to the better understanding of all religions, ancient and modern. It explains the philosophy of Inspiration, and supersedes the popular notion of the miraculous by the revelation of hitherto unrecognised laws.

"Spiritualism tends to abrogate exaggerated class distinctions; to reunite those who are now too often divided by seemingly conflicting material interests; to encourage the co-operation of men and women in many new spheres; and to uphold the freedom and rights of the individual, while maintaining as paramount the sanctity of family life.

"Finally, the general influence of Spiritualism on the individual is to inspire him with self-respect, with a love of justice and truth, with a reverence for Divine law, and with a sense of harmony between man, the universe, and God.

"The British National Association of Spiritualists is formed to unite Spiritualists of every variety of opinion, for their mutual aid and benefit; to promote the study of Pneumatology and Psychology; to aid students and inquirers in their researches, by placing at their disposal the means of systematic investigation into the now recognised facts and phenomena, called Spiritual or Psychic; to make known the positive results arrived at by careful scientific research; and to direct attention to the beneficial influence which those results are calculated to exercise upon social relationships and individual conduct.

It is intended to include spiritualists of every class, whether members of Local and Provincial Societies or not, and all inquirers into psychological and kindred phenomena.

"The Association, whilst cordially sympathizing with the teachings of Jesus Christ, will hold itself entirely aloof from all dogmatism or finalities, whether religious or philosophical, and will content itself with the establishment and elucidation of well-attested facts, as the only basis on which any true religion or philosophy can be built up."

This last clause has, I believe, been modified to suit certain members of my profession who were a little staggered by its apparent patronizing of Christianity. For myself (but then, I am unorthodox) I care little for these written or printed symbola. Having strained my conscience to join the Dialecticians, I allow my name, without compunction, to stand on the Council of the Association,—and shall be really glad if it does them any good. The fact is, I care little for formal creeds, but much for the fruit of those creeds. I stand by that good old principle—"By their fruits ye shall know them;" and that reminds me that to my shreds and patches of "experience" I am to append some pros and cons of this matter. They have cropped up incidentally as we have gone on: but I could with advantage collect them if my limits admitted of sermonizing.

As to the fruits of Spiritualism, I can only say that I have never witnessed any of these anti-Christianizing effects which some persons say arise from a belief in Spiritualism. They simply have not come within the sphere of my observation, nor do I see any tendency towards them in the tenets of Spiritualism—rather the reverse.

Then again, to pass from practice to faith, Spiritualism professes to be the reverse of exclusive. In addressing the Conference of 1874, and defending my position as a clerical inquirer, I was able to say:—"On the broad question of theology I can conceive no single subject which a clergyman is more bound to examine than that which purports to be a new revelation, or, at all events, a large extension of the old; and which, if its claims be substantiated, will quite modify our notions as to what we now call faith. It proposes, in fact, to supply in matters we have been accustomed to take on trust, something so like demonstration, that I feel not only at liberty, but actually bound, whether I like it or not, to look into the thing.

Whether your creed is right or wrong is not for me to tell you; but it is most important for me that I should assure myself. And while I recognise that my own duty clearly is to examine the principles you profess, I find this to be eminently their characteristic, that they readily assimilate with those of my own Church. I see nothing revolutionary in them. You have no propaganda. You do not call upon me, as far as I understand, to come out of the body I belong to and join yours, as so many other bodies do; but you ask me simply to take your doctrines into my own creed, and vitalize it by their means. That has always attracted me powerfully towards you. You are the broadest Churchmen I find anywhere."

I am not writing thus in any sense as the apologist of Spiritualism. I am not offering anything like an Apologia pro vitâ meâ in making the inquiries I have done, am doing, and hope to do. I have elected to take, and I elect to maintain, a neutral position in this matter. All I have done is to select from the Pros and Cons that present themselves to my mind. If the Pros seem to outweigh the Cons—or

vice versâ—be it so. I cannot help it. I have scarcely
decided for myself yet, and I am a veteran investigator.
Others may be more speedy in arriving at a conclusion.

Among the more obvious "Cons" are the oft-quoted facts
that some people have lost their heads and wasted a good
deal of their time on Spiritualism. But people lose their
heads by reading classics or mathematics, or overdoing any
one subject however excellent—even falling in love: and
the ingenuity displayed in wasting time is so manifold that
this is an objection that can scarcely be urged specially
against Spiritualism, though I own Dark Séances do cut
terribly into time.

Then again one is apt to be taken in by mediums or even
by spirits. Yes; but this only imposes the ordinary
obligation of keeping one's eyes open. I know spiritualists
who believe in every medium quâ medium, and others who
accept as unwritten gospel the idiotic utterances of a
departed buccaneer or defunct clown: but these people are
so purely exceptional as simply to prove a rule. Do not
accept as final in so-called spiritual what you would not
accept in avowedly mundane matters. Keep your eyes open
and your head cool, and you will not go far wrong. These
are the simple rules that I have elaborated during my
protracted study of the subject.

"We do not believe, we know," was, as I said, the proud
boast a spiritualist once made to me. And if the facts—any
of the facts—of Spiritualism stand as facts, there is no
doubt that it would form the strongest possible
counterpoise to the materialism of our age. It presses the
method of materialism into its service, and meets the
doubter on his own ground of demonstration—a low
ground, perhaps, but a tremendously decisive one, the very

one perhaps on which the Battle of Faith and Reason will have to be fought out.

If—let us not forget that pregnant monosyllable—if the assumptions of Spiritualism be true, and that we can only ascertain by personal investigation, I believe the circumstance would be efficacious in bringing back much of the old meaning of the word πιστις which was something more than the slipshod Faith standing as its modern equivalent. It would make it really the substance of things hoped for, the evidence of things not seen.

Even if the dangers of Spiritualism were much greater than they are—aye, as great as the diabolical people themselves make out—I should still think (in the cautious words of the Dialecticians) Spiritualism was worth looking into, if only on the bare chance, however remote, of lighting on some such Philosophy as that so beautifully sketched by Mr. S. C. Hall in some of the concluding stanzas of his poem "Philosophy," with which I may fitly conclude—

And those we call "the dead" (who are not dead—

Death was their herald to Celestial Life)—

May soothe the aching heart and weary head

In pain, in toil, in sorrow, and in strife.

That is a part of every natural creed—

Instinctive teaching of another state:

When manacles of earth are loosed and freed—

Which Science vainly strives to dissipate.

In tortuous paths, with prompters blind, we trust

One Guide—to lead us forth and set us free!

Give us, Lord God! all merciful and just!

The Faith that is but Confidence in Thee!

Printed in Great Britain
by Amazon